PAUL MULDOON

PAUL MULDOON

Tim Kendall

seren

Seren is the book imprint of
Poetry Wales Press Ltd
2 Wyndham Street, Bridgend, Wales
UK

© Tim Kendall, 1996

A CIP record for this publication is available
from the CIP Office at the British Libray

ISBN 1-85411-160-4
1-85411-161-2 pbk

All rights reserved. No part of this publication may be reproduced, stored in a retrieval system, or transmitted at any time or by any means electronic, mechanical, photocopying, recording or otherwise without the prior permission of the copyright holder

The publisher works with the financial support of the Arts Council of Wales

Cover photograph: Niall McDiarmid

Printed in Plantin by
WBC Book Manufacturers Ltd Bridgend

Contents

6	Acknowledgements
7	Preface
9	Fathers and Mothers: on Paul Muldoon's Life
25	Learning to Fly: *New Weather* and Early Poetry
44	Between Heaven and Earth: *Mules*
64	Singleminded Swervings: *Why Brownlee Left*
90	A Moral For Our Times: *Quoof*
119	Something Else Again: *Meeting the British*
149	Parallel to the Parallel Realm: *Madoc — A Mystery*
175	The Poetry of Architecture: *Shining Brow*
192	Muldoodles: *The Prince of the Quotidian* and *Six Honest Serving Men*
209	A Deep-Seated Hurt: *The Annals of Chile*
241	Bibliography
252	Index

Acknowledgements

Extracts from Paul Muldoon's work are reprinted by kind permission of the following publishers:

New Weather (1973) and *Shining Brow* (1993): Faber & Faber.
Mules (1977), *Why Brownlee Left* (1980), *Quoof* (1983) and *Meeting the British* (1987): Faber & Faber and Wake Forest University Press.
The O-O's Party, New Year's Eve (1980), *The Wishbone* (1984) and *Six Honest Serving Men* (1995): Gallery Press.
Madoc — A Mystery (1990) and *The Annals of Chile* (1994): Faber & Faber and Farrar, Straus and Giroux.
The Prince of the Quotidian (1994): Gallery Press and Wake Forest University Press.

Acknowledgements are also due to the editors of the following publications, where some of my work on Paul Muldoon first appeared: *Irish University Review*, the *London Magazine*, *Oxford Poetry*, *Verse*.

This book may never have been completed without the help and enthusiasm of several people; as Gerald Durrell once observed, this should be mentioned so that blame can be laid in the right quarter. Many of the more perceptive ideas and readings have been inspired by Craig Raine's suggestions. I have also benefited from discussions with John Redmond and Steve Burt. Bernard O'Donoghue provided a useful translation of the Irish in 'Yarrow'. Particular thanks to Fiona for all her advice and support; and to Paul Muldoon, who provided me with reviews and biographical information, corrected factual errors, but left me the freedom to make as many interpretational mistakes as I wanted.

Preface

The following study is intended as a detailed and accessible introduction to Paul Muldoon's poetry. While employing close readings, it will also convey the necessary contextual information: biographical material, relevant Irish history and mythology, and sources for the countless allusions. I hope such details encourage readers to return to Muldoon's poetry with greater understanding and appreciation. The book should also promote my belief that Muldoon's is a distinct and important poetic voice, one of the very few genuine originals of our age.

For the sake of simplicity I have not footnoted reviews of Muldoon's poetry; the bibliography lists all the texts cited. Muldoon's unreferenced quotations in chapter one have been drawn from 'Chez Moy', an unpublished autobiographical essay.

Undertaking a study of Muldoon's poetry brings peculiar difficulties. He has described his poetic technique as a means of reassuring readers that all's well, then leaving them "high and dry, in some corner at a terrible party, where [he has] nipped out through the bathroom window". No doubt this book stumbles into its share of terrible parties, but I hope that, more often than not, I've been able to pursue the poems out through the bathroom window and beyond.

Fathers and Mothers:
on Paul Muldoon's Life

Paul Muldoon was born on 20 June 1951, in Portadown, County Armagh. His parents Patrick and Brigid (née Regan) Muldoon had been living in Dungannon, County Tyrone, and the family moved soon afterwards to the nearby village of Eglish, where two more children, Maureen and Joseph, were born in 1953 and 1954 respectively. After Joseph's birth the family settled in Collegelands, County Armagh, where it would be based for the next thirty years.

Muldoon's parents both came from poor Catholic families. Patrick Muldoon's mother had died when he was seven, and his father remarried — in Muldoon's own phrase — "an unsympathetic woman". Forced to hire himself out as a farm labourer from a young age, Patrick received no secondary education, and throughout his life could read and write only with difficulty. Brigid's background was also financially unprepossessing, but as the youngest of her family she had the advantage of sibling support. Her education at St Joseph's Convent, Donaghmore, and St Mary's College, Belfast, where she trained as a teacher, was partly underwritten by older brothers and sisters. It was her success in gaining a post at the local primary school in Collegelands which took the family in 1954 to the area of North Armagh now designated, by one recent literary guide to Ireland, as "Muldoon Country".[1]

Muldoon has described his father as "close to the soil — it sounds romantic but it's what he was".[2] Following his wife wherever her teaching career took her, Patrick tried any kind of work that happened to be available: shepherd, navvy, farm-worker, shop-keeper, builder's labourer, and, as he is most familiarly presented in Muldoon's poetry, cauliflower- and mushroom-grower. Muldoon has noted that his parents were a toned-down version of the Morels in Lawrence's *Sons and Lovers*,[3] and 'The Mixed Marriage' from *Mules* (1977) captures this almost geometric dichotomy between them:

> My father was a servant-boy.
> When he left school at eight or nine
> He took up billhook and loy
> To win the ground he would never own.
>
> My mother was the school-mistress,
> The world of Castor and Pollux.

> There were twins in her own class.
> She could never tell which was which.
>
> She had read one volume of Proust,
> He knew the cure for farcy.

Much of Muldoon's poetry embodies, and attempts to reconcile, the split inheritance of bookishness and agricultural life. However, despite comparisons with *Sons and Lovers*, he seems to have chosen different sides from Paul Morel. Muldoon has described his father as "anything but a coarse, lumbering man — he's a very refined man".[4] Brigid, by comparison, is variously portrayed as narrow-minded, religiose and snobbish. There is still enough in Muldoon's work to indicate that his relationship with his mother was (and even two decades after her death, still is) far more complex than these passing negative references would suggest. Brigid died of cancer in 1974; written almost twenty years later, the oblique and agonizing elegy 'Yarrow' betrays an intense personal grief which can only now, it seems, begin to be salved.

The first four years of Muldoon's life, spent in Eglish, feature hardly at all in his poetry ('The Right Arm' from *Quoof* is a rare exception), but his short autobiographical essay 'A Tight Wee Place in Armagh' remembers them in some detail. One end of the house which the family rented in Eglish had been transformed into a shop by a previous owner. The shop sold Bird's Custard, Saxa Salt, bootlaces — "the kind of thing anybody could see nobody wanted, at least not badly";[5] Muldoon's father maintained it only in a desultory way, much preferring to chat with customers than to sell them anything. Most of Muldoon's memories from these years, however, focus on the back yard:

> My sister running very fast through the yard, tripping, falling onto a sharp stick that went halfway down her throat. My father keeping a few hens ... When one hen ate a crawful of hay he tied up her feet, hung her on a nail, opened her up with a razor-blade, removed the hay, sewed her up again with a needle and thread he borrowed from my mother, and sent her on her way.[6]

They kept pigs too, and Muldoon recalls his father spotting the pig-killer, James Blemmings, coming across the Oona Bridge a quarter of a mile down the valley. The children were kept inside, which seems only to have excited their curiosity about how the pig-killer "did it". 'Ned Skinner' from *Mules*, although fictionalized

Fathers and Mothers: on Paul Muldoon's Life 11

and displaced onto an uncle's farm, is clearly inspired by the incident:

> Ned Skinner wiped his knife
> And rinsed his hands
> In the barrel at the door-step.
>
> He winked, and gripped my arm.
> 'It doesn't hurt, not so's you'd notice,
> And God never slams one door
> But another's lying open.
> Them same pigs can see the wind.'

During these years Muldoon's mother would cycle the ten miles to the primary school in Collegelands where she taught. Finally in 1955 the family bought an acre of land in Collegelands and built a bungalow on it. Muldoon's "uncle-in-law" Dinny McCool was a water-diviner, and had already pointed out the best place to sink the well; Muldoon recalls that he always felt the house was somehow an "afterthought to the well". But when the mains water supply eventually reached the house, the well became defunct; it was boarded over and bricked up "like the door of a room where someone had claimed to have seen a ghost".[7]

The area around Collegelands is renowned for its fertility, producing good-quality pasture and a wide range of crops from which Muldoon's father benefited as a market-gardener — apples, potatoes, barley, strawberries, cauliflowers, mushrooms. The "college" of Collegelands is Trinity College, Dublin; many of the Muldoons' neighbours were families whose ancestors had been tenants of Trinity College for several generations, up until the founding of the Irish Free State in the 1920s. The result is, according to Muldoon, "a little enclave of Roman Catholics living within the predominantly Protestant parish of Loughgall, the village where the Orange Order was founded in 1795". In 'Armageddon, Armageddon' Protestant Loughgall is described as "An orchard full of No Surrenders"; possibly the religious geography of the area made the Catholic community suspicious, since Muldoon has commented that his family, being "blow-ins", were always "a little isolated". Certainly his mother's class-consciousness ("there's still something of the priest/ doctor/teacher triumvirate in rural communities"[8]) did not help matters. As newcomers the children "were somehow removed from the place", and the problem was exacerbated by their mother ordering them not to mix with their peers: "'Stay well away from

those louts and layabouts at the loanin' end'", she commands in
'Yarrow'. Such isolation was offset by the all-pervasiveness of the
Roman Catholic Church, which perhaps held even greater sway
amidst a slight siege mentality. Muldoon has complained that

> The Catholic church presided over almost every aspect of our
> lives, both literally — the building itself was two fields away —
> and metaphorically.

The experience was not a happy one. The Catholic Church is
presented as repressive in Muldoon's work, and in an untypically
self-revealing moment he has claimed there is "a very fine line
between organized religion and organized crime".[9]

Apart from the countryside around Collegelands, the most common backdrop for Muldoon's poetry is the nearby village of the
Moy. The word "Moy" would figure largely in any Muldoon
concordance, being granted at least one mention and usually more
in most of his collections. The extent of this attachment can be
gauged from the poem 'The Soap Pig', which reports that during
the late seventies, when Muldoon was living in Belfast, his flat came
to be known as *Chez Moy* — a real home from home. The Moy even
lends itself to Muldoon's poetic techniques: he grew up with the
half-rhyme Moy / magh (as in Armagh), which as Blake Morrison has
pointed out, sounds uncannily like one of his own inventions.[10]
Muldoon has also made clear a deeper engagement with the place
and its history:

> It's an area very rich in history and folklore, just as every
> square mile of Ireland is coming down with history and is
> burdened by it. The Moy itself was built by a man called
> James Caulfeild, who was at one stage Lord Lieutenant of
> Ireland, Earl of Charlemont, which is a little sister hamlet to
> the Moy. This story may be totally apocryphal, but Caulfeild
> is supposed to have designed it on the principle of an Italian
> town, Marengo.[11]

The merging of the familiar and the exotic in this account typifies
Muldoon's treatment of his childhood home. His father's mushroom farm, the village of the Moy and the "brawling townlands"
around it, become fixtures in his work against which to explore
anything from psilocybin-induced hallucinations to sexual encounters with a syphilitic Cathleen ni Houlihan.

The 1947 Education Act, enabling the rural farming classes to
pursue a secondary education, had ensured that Muldoon and his

brother and sister would experience none of the difficulties in finding a good education that their parents had suffered. Muldoon's mother in particular was highly ambitious for her children, who were at one stage packed off to elocution classes and then piano lessons; each "failed miserably", and the piano which had been bought at great expense was sold and replaced by a tape recorder. It was a worthwhile exchange: "we all sat round the fire talking into the tape-recorder and making our own amusement".[12] Surprisingly, there were few books in the house; comics were frowned on, improving publications like *Look and Learn* and *Classics Illustrated* were subscribed to, but the only book Muldoon remembers is a copy of *The Poems of Rupert Brooke*, which his mother cherished because she had received it as a prize from her teacher training college. 'Ma' from *Mules* notes that "Old photographs would have her bookish", before sardonically revealing the limitation of the pose: "She reads aloud, no doubt from Rupert Brooke". Nevertheless, despite the paucity of books, as a child Muldoon still seems to have read voraciously. 'Yarrow' is, among other things, a homage to the adventure stories he consumed: *King Solomon's Mines, The Sign of Four, The Lost World, Rob Roy, Treasure Island*, 'An Occurrence at Owl-Creek Bridge'. Film and television Westerns were another favourite: *Rawhide, Bonanza*, and slightly later, John Ford's *Cheyenne Autumn* (1964), which, in its more sophisticated treatment of American Indians, alerted Muldoon's own sympathies. It is important not to underestimate the influence of film on Muldoon's poetry. He describes the technique of his Troubles masterpiece 'The More a Man Has the More a Man Wants' as "cinematic",[13] and employs Hitchcockian strategies (such as the famous "MacGuffin") elsewhere in his work. Occasionally a poem's landscape seems to have come straight out of a Western: 'The Field Hospital' from *New Weather*, for example, is partly inspired by *The Good, the Bad and the Ugly*, Sergio Leone's spaghetti Western in which "the civil war scenes must be a most faithful reconstruction of what it would have been like".[14]

After attending the primary school at Collegelands where his mother taught, Muldoon progressed to St Patrick's College, Armagh, which was run by the Vincentian order. The dedication of *New Weather* to "my Fathers and Mothers" perhaps acknowledges Muldoon's indebtedness to the exceptional teachers he met there:

> One man, Sean O'Boyle, who was a scholar of the Irish language and music, taught me Irish and gave me, and

everyone round me, a sense of this marvellous heritage of song and culture in Gaelic. I was also blessed — it may sound corny, but I really do feel blessed — by a man called Jerry Hicks, a singer, who taught English. These were people whose knowledge exuded from them.[15]

Muldoon's intellectual and poetic development was profoundly shaped by such men. No doubt inspired by O'Boyle's teaching, his first published poems were in Irish, although he soon gave it up because he lacked "a real control of the language".[16] Another teacher, Gerard Quinn, introduced him to Robert Frost's work, which has remained arguably the largest influence on Muldoon's poetry. The poem 'Gold' from *Meeting the British* (1987) remembers Quinn's enthusiasm for Frost; and when questioned about Frost as late as 1985, Muldoon still prefaced his reply with the acknowledgement that he was "to some extent reflecting the ideas of my friend Gerard Quinn".[17] Muldoon was first encouraged to write poetry by another English teacher, John McCarter, who was willing to accept a poem in lieu of the weekly essay. McCarter had been involved in the Dublin literary scene, and gave Muldoon "the sense that there were writers alive in Dublin".[18] He also introduced his pupil to *The Faber Book of Modern Verse*, which Muldoon claims almost to have learnt by heart; and to the poetry of T.S. Eliot, whom Muldoon for a time thought "was God".[19]

Believing there might be writers alive in Dublin may have been encouraging for a young poet, but a more extraordinary poetic renaissance was underway closer to home, in Belfast. Seamus Heaney published *Death of a Naturalist* in 1966; Derek Mahon's *Night-Crossing* appeared in 1968; and the following year Michael Longley's *No Continuing City* was published. Partly through his teachers and partly because of the considerable publicity it began to attract, Muldoon had become aware of the so-called Belfast 'Group' which had been operating under the auspices of Philip Hobsbaum since 1962; and he read each collection as it came out. Admiration was tempered with emulation: "These people were publishing poems about walking through fields and I thought, 'I can do that' — it was a very familiar activity to me".[20] In April 1968 his English teacher Jerry Hicks introduced Muldoon to Longley and Heaney after a poetry reading they gave at Armagh Museum. Hicks is said to have presented Muldoon to Heaney as a poet who would one day surpass him, adding in a whisper, "Rara avis". The story sounds apocryphal — or sounds, at least, like it ought to be — as does the rumour that Heaney carried Muldoon's poetry around the literary circles of Belfast, enthusing to his friends "This is *it*". Destined to become twenty-first-century thesis fodder, the relationship between Heaney and Muldoon has already begun to be mythologized.

However, Muldoon certainly did find his poetic elders welcoming. He had by now written dozens of poems, two of which — 'Thrush' and 'Behold the Lamb' — he sent to Heaney for his opinion. These poems both appear in *New Weather*, but neither is particularly successful. It is a tribute to Heaney's critical skills that he immediately sensed Muldoon's potential, and accordingly published both poems in an issue of *Threshold*, a magazine he was guest-editing. Heaney also steered Muldoon's work to Karl Miller, then literary editor of *The Listener*, and to Charles Monteith at Faber & Faber. Written around this time and dedicated to Heaney, Muldoon's 'Unborn' offers some insight into the elder poet's rôle:

> Then the poem will live, will live
> Outside my life.
>
> I will wrap
> It in paper. Leave it on your step.

It was not only Heaney whom Muldoon found approachable and encouraging. Michael Longley, for example, detected enough promise in Muldoon's work to mention him, in a 1971 essay on Ulster poetry, as a "particularly interesting" writer who had already produced "poised and original" poetry.[21] Muldoon's early publication history is a record of extraordinary precocity and extraordinary luck. By the time he went up to Queen's University, Belfast, in 1969, he had already published poems in *The Honest Ulsterman*; before he left, in 1973, he had published a pamphlet with Ulsterman publications, a selection in the Faber & Faber *Poetry Introduction 2*, and, at the age of only twenty-one, his first Faber collection, *New Weather*, for which he had also received an Eric Gregory award.

Muldoon was as fortunate in his university as in his secondary school. With Philip Hobsbaum having taken a post in Glasgow, the Group had lost some of its momentum, but it was still operating when Muldoon arrived in 1969:

> There were weekly meetings for a time in Seamus Heaney's house, and later in a pub, where new poems were discussed. It was very important for me, since a writer must be a good critic of his own work. There was no sloppiness in the group, everyone was quite outspoken. It was a very healthy kind of

> society, and I use the word 'society' to describe the group. It's scarcely a group at all, even though it's become a critical convenience to see them as presenting a united front to the world: you only have to read them to be aware of the variety. They're not united by any kind of manifesto.[22]

Muldoon's friends from these years make a high-powered list: Seamus Heaney, who briefly tutored Muldoon at Queen's; the Longleys, of whom Edna has remained Muldoon's most persuasive advocate; the critic Michael Allen, to whom *Why Brownlee Left* is dedicated; and fellow students Ciaran Carson, Frank Ormsby and Medbh McGuckian. Remembering that Muldoon "was writing amazing poems when he was a mere boy", Carson recalls their friendship during these years in a way which suggests that the legendary meticulousness of the Group was not necessarily inescapable:

> On the odd occasion, he might show me a poem and I'd read it and say 'Aye', or, 'I think it works' and he might say, 'Aye, I think so myself', or whatever. And vice versa.[23]

How far the remarkable convergence of energies at Queen's helped Muldoon's poetic development is, ultimately, imponderable, but there is little doubt that he has benefited from the sense of belonging to a poetic community, however loosely-knit: his switch from the past tense to the present when discussing the Group ("It's scarcely a group at all") is not accidental.

When he was not writing poetry, or, by his own admission, playing snooker and drinking cider, Muldoon studied for a B.A. in English, with subsidiaries in Celtic and Scholastic Philosophy. He did not especially enjoy the course — which he has described as the "if it's Friday it must be Trollope" approach to English literature.[24] Nevertheless, references to Thomas Aquinas, Scotus Eriugena and the like, dotted through Muldoon's work, may constitute the remnants of his subsidiary topic; and the mammoth *Madoc — A Mystery* (1990) is, in passing, an idiosyncratic potted history of Western philosophical thought. Other events during Muldoon's time at Queen's did not go unnoticed:

> Though my student days coincided with a period of extreme political unrest in Northern Ireland, I myself never took any direct part in political activity. My family would have had Nationalist or Republican leanings, of course, but were firmly opposed to political violence. I've often considered how easily, though, I might have been caught up in the kinds

of activity in which a number of my neighbours found themselves involved. As it was, I preferred to try to come to terms with the political instability of Northern Ireland through poetry, often in an oblique, encoded way: in *New Weather,* for example, a poem like 'The Year of the Sloes, for Ishi' was written as a direct response to Bloody Sunday, 1972, a fact that may not be immediately apparent to many readers.

'The Year of the Sloes' is one of several poems which parallel the plight of the native Americans with that of Northern Irish Catholics. The passage is also suggestive of Muldoon's response to the violence in other ways: he states that his poetry is written only so that he himself can "come to terms with the political instability" — there are no grandiose claims for art as a midwife to society. The different course Muldoon imagines he could "easily" have taken signals more his interest in alternative lives than any real possibility that he might ever have resorted to political violence. Frost's 'The Road Not Taken', a poem greatly admired by Muldoon, should be considered the starting-point for this obsession:

> Two roads diverged in a wood, and I —
> I took the one less traveled by,
> And that has made all the difference.

Much of Muldoon's poetry can be seen as an attempt to take both roads, one literally and the other imaginatively: his 1990 volume *Madoc — A Mystery,* for example, imagines what would have happened if Coleridge and Southey really had emigrated to the United States to establish their planned Pantisocracy. However, Muldoon's belief that he could easily have become "caught up" in political violence — with the image of entrapment lending the scenario a modicum of credibility — still seems one of Muldoon's less convincing alternative lives.

It was at Queen's that Muldoon met his first wife, Anne-Marie Conway. The couple were married during the Ulster Workers' Council Strike in 1974, while, Muldoon notes, his mother was already dying of cancer. The marriage was not to be a happy one, for which Muldoon blames his own "incorrigible immaturity"; a sequence of poems in *Why Brownlee Left* (1980) tells of the subsequent break-up and divorce. By the time of his wedding Muldoon had found a job as a radio producer for the B.B.C. in Belfast. He would continue to work for the B.B.C., both as a radio and television producer, for the next thirteen years, making a wide range of programmes including magazines, documentaries, and dramatized features on the arts in Ireland. Muldoon has given several reasons for his decision to leave the B.B.C. in 1986: dissatisfaction with the way the Corporation was developing; the feeling that he had covered the arts in Ireland to the point of exhaustion; his father's death in 1985 and the subsequent sale of the family home in Collegelands; and most importantly, the "realization that if I continued to work in television I'd probably never write another poem".

During his time at the B.B.C., Muldoon's poetic reputation grew steadily on both sides of the Atlantic. For a first volume, *New Weather* had received an extraordinary number of reviews, and an ensemble of praise: Alisdair Maclean, in *The Listener*, was only slightly more enthusiastic than the norm when declaring that "There can have been few more impressive first collections". *Mules* (1977) and *Why Brownlee Left* (1980) were each published simultaneously by Faber & Faber in London and Dillon Johnson's Wake Forest University Press in the United States. Again the acclaim was almost uniform: Anne Stevenson, Peter Porter, Peter Scupham, Douglas Dunn and Seamus Heaney all gave *Mules* favourable reviews, with Heaney declaring his friend "one of the very best"; and *Why Brownlee Left*, which won the Geoffrey Faber Memorial Prize and was made quarterly Choice of the Poetry Book Society, was praised by Derek Mahon, Gavin Ewart, Andrew Motion, Fleur Adcock, Alan Jenkins and Peter Porter. The influential *Penguin Book of Contemporary British Poetry*, edited by Blake Morrison and Andrew Motion and published in 1982, confirmed Muldoon's elevated status among his older contemporaries (he is the youngest poet in the anthology) by giving him fifteen pages — tied with Douglas Dunn, and behind only Heaney. The list of Muldoon's admirers constitutes a fairly inclusive Who's Who of British and Irish poetry; and clearly — often all too clearly — Muldoon has since become the poetic father of a new generation including Simon Armitage, Ian Duhig and Don Paterson. However, suspicions have sporadically been voiced that Muldoon is a poet's poet, innovative and technically flawless, but aloof from the common reader. Only with *Quoof* (1983), another Poetry Book Society Choice which won more plaudits even than earlier volumes, did sales really pick up, although Muldoon was still far from achieving the big-league popularity of a Heaney or a Hughes.

After the break-up of his marriage, Muldoon began a relationship with the artist Mary Farl Powers; the elegy 'Incantata', published in *The Annals of Chile* (1994) after her death from cancer in 1992, is a powerful celebration of their life together. Aside from 'Incantata', the influence of Powers on Muldoon's poetry can only be guessed at, although her print *Pink Spotted Torso* is the starting-point for the helpfully-titled 'Mary Farl Powers *Pink Spotted Torso*' in *Quoof*. Much of Muldoon's pamphlet *The Wishbone*, published by Peter Fallon's Gallery Press in 1984 and dedicated to Powers, was written around the end of their relationship, which it charts in an extremely cryptic, almost private style. As Muldoon has rather coyly commented, "around that time I was trying to write a couple of poems that brought to its logical conclusion the idea of leaving".[25] Believing his poetry had taken a wrong turn, Muldoon salvaged just five of twelve poems for his next volume, *Meeting the British* (1987).

Muldoon's father died in 1985, and *Meeting the British* is dedicated to his memory. It seems feasible that Muldoon's profound, unproblematical love for his father made his death easier to mourn than his mother's had been eleven years earlier; certainly a comparison of the simple elegy 'The Fox' with the frantic and, at times, desperate evasions of 'Yarrow' would support such a conclusion. After his father's death Muldoon no longer felt "the same kind of tug" towards Northern Ireland;[26] but another reason for leaving the North soon presented itself. Several months later he met the American poet and novelist Jean Hanff Korelitz at an Arvon writing course. Between January and September 1986 they lived in Dingle, County Kerry, where, taking advantage of a small stipend from the Irish government-funded Aosdana scheme, Muldoon completed *Meeting the British*. He had also been busy in the meantime. In 1986 he edited *The Faber Book of Contemporary Irish Poetry*, an anthology which, setting out to represent "the most consistently impressive Irish poets after Yeats", outraged many of the prime movers on the Irish literary scene. In place of an introduction, Muldoon quotes verbatim — and without comment — an exchange between Louis MacNeice and F.R. Higgins, which MacNeice unsurprisingly wins. Having been told by Higgins that as an Irishman he cannot escape from his "blood-music that brings the racial character to mind", MacNeice (and tacitly Muldoon) replies:

> I have a feeling that you have sidetracked me into an Ireland versus England match. I am so little used to thinking of poetry in terms of race-consciousness that no doubt this was very good for me. However, I am still unconverted. I think one may have such a thing as one's racial blood-music, but

that, like one's unconscious, it may be left to take care of itself.

However, Muldoon's editorial disappearing act infuriated reviewers less than the anthology's exclusivity. Within the confines of its genre the book is a masterpiece, tactlessly candid. Just ten poets are represented: Kavanagh, MacNeice, Kinsella, Montague, Heaney, Longley, Mahon, Durcan, Paulin and McGuckian; reviews also made cases for Clarke, Devlin, Murphy, Simmons, Boland, Ní Dhomhnaill and others. Deploring such omissions, Derek Mahon in the *Irish Times* hoped the volume would "sink without trace", and wondered whether Muldoon had "lost his reason". Mahon was not alone in imagining a Northern conspiracy theory, but in fact the anthology is the result of nothing more sinister than considered value judgements. Whatever arguments are made in support of other writers, the most striking, if understandable, omission is Muldoon himself.

Muldoon's absence from the anthology was to some degree rectified later in 1986, when Faber & Faber issued his *Selected Poems*; the American edition, published the following year by Ecco Press in New York, also incorporated a selection from *Meeting the British*. If the publication of a *Selected Poems* was a stocktaking exercise, Muldoon did not need long to take stock. *Meeting the British* appeared in the spring of 1987. Reviewing it in the *Times Literary Supplement*, Mick Imlah heralded the volume as "perhaps the most eagerly awaited poetry book of 1987" — no small compliment to Muldoon's reputation, given that Seamus Heaney's *The Haw Lantern* was published in the same year. But amidst the usual fanfare, no less a critic than John Carey, in the *Sunday Times* (London), wrote one of the most hostile reviews Muldoon's poetry has ever received, declaring it "tricky, clever, tickled by its own knowingness", and comparing Heaney's "Derby winner" with Muldoon's "pantomime horse". Carey's review has remained the most powerful and convincing case for the prosecution, articulating unignorable anxieties about what he calls Muldoon's "arcane, allusive poetry, packed to the gunwales with higher education".

Having spent the academic year 1986-87 on fellowships at the Universities of Cambridge and East Anglia, Muldoon moved to the United States, where he married Jean Hanff Korelitz in August 1987. For the next three years he accepted various invitations to teach, at Columbia, Princeton, Berkeley and Massachusetts. But despite his switch from the B.B.C. to academia, and from Northern

Ireland to the United States, he had not abandoned all links with his first employers. In 1989 the B.B.C. broadcast *Monkeys*, a highly acclaimed account of the events leading up to the arrest and subsequent acquittal of the businessman John De Lorrean; although Muldoon's input was "finally very small", he had edited and adapted the transcripts of the F.B.I. and Drug Enforcement Agency tapes to produce a condensed, coherent narrative.[27] Muldoon returned to Princeton in 1990, to take up a lectureship. He has since conducted courses in Irish literature, in translation, and in modern British poetry, but is chiefly involved with an undergraduate creative writing program:

> I suppose what I try to instil — although I don't like the word *instil*, it's not as if I have any particular wisdom in these matters — what I try to suggest is that [students] become interested in language and the adventures that they might have with language if they allow themselves to be taken over by the possibilities of language and if they are *humble*, as it were, before language. Rather than using language to — quote, unquote — *express themselves*.[28]

Muldoon's career change seems to have produced the desired effect of allowing him to devote more time to literature. Within two years of leaving the B.B.C. he had published *The Faber Book of Contemporary Irish Poetry*, his *Selected Poems*, and *Meeting the British*. These were followed by *Monkeys* and, also in 1989, *The Essential Byron*, selected and introduced by Muldoon and issued by the Ecco Press of New York. Muldoon had never made a secret of his admiration for Byron's poetry, and certainly the Byron described in the introduction sounds more than a little like a kindred spirit:

> Byron's mature style is wonderfully discursive, ranging from Aristotle through hitting the sack to hitting the bottle of sack, while relishing the rhyme on "Aristotle" and "bottle" along the way.

The mixture of high and low culture, the weird but insistent logic of punning, and the sheer delight in outrageous rhymes confirm Byron as an important influence throughout Muldoon's poetry. Byron is actually the immediate inspiration for Muldoon's next volume, *Madoc — A Mystery* (1990); the 246-page title poem grew out of Muldoon's edition of Byron, who is often quoted and who actually appears in the poem on several occasions. Proclaimed a *"tour-de-force"* by Lucy McDiarmid in the *New York Times Book*

Review, and "a dazzling achievement" by Lachlan MacKinnon in the *Times Literary Supplement*, *Madoc* nevertheless resurrected doubts about Muldoon's accessibility: many reviews expressed exasperation, and *Bluff Your Way in Literature*, as ever attuned to the fashions of the coteries, declared that "the mad *Madoc — A Mystery* fully lives up to its subtitle, being simply incomprehensible".

Settled at Princeton, Muldoon remained productive. Having worked on *Madoc* daily for eighteen months, he began a more modest project. Following his children's book *The O-O's Party*, published by Gallery Press in 1980, Muldoon now returned to the genre with *The Last Thesaurus* — a poem about a small, linguistically gifted dinosaur (who, in an act of self-sacrifice, ends up being eaten by a Tyrannosaurus Rex). Then in 1992 came *The Astrakhan Cloak*, published by Gallery Press as a joint venture between Muldoon and Nuala Ní Dhomhnaill: Ní Dhomnaill's Irish language poems appear on the left-hand page, opposite Muldoon's parallel translations. In January of the same year Muldoon wrote a poem a day, and the resulting 'January journal' was issued by the Gallery Press as *The Prince of the Quotidian* in 1994; occasional in theme, and not originally intended for publication, the book is an idiosyncratic insight into Muldoon's (sometimes transitory) views on subjects as various as U2 and Field Day. However, his major undertaking during this period was the libretto *Shining Brow*, commissioned by Madison Opera, Wisconsin:

> Daron Hagen, the composer, and I were in the MacDowell Colony in Peterborough, New Hampshire. He got this phone call from Madison Opera, asking if he would write the opera ... He said to me — I'm not quite sure how serious he was — 'You want to write an opera?' and I said, 'Sure. Why not?' So, that's how it started. This was Madison Opera's first commission, and they specified that it be an opera about Frank Lloyd Wright. I think they might have even come up with the title, though I no longer recall ...[29]

The libretto took Muldoon a year to complete, and the opera received its premiere in Madison on 21 April 1993. Aware that libretti usually attract scant attention, Faber & Faber marketed *Shining Brow* as "a dramatic poem in its own right"; nevertheless, apart from a long and intelligent review by Paul Driver in *The London Review of Books*, and an unsympathetic *Irish Times* piece by Peter Sirr, it went largely unnoticed in Britain and Ireland.

In July 1992, Muldoon's daughter Dorothy was born — "One of the most joyous things that's happened to me in a long time, I think perhaps ever".[30] Published in 1994, *The Annals of Chile* includes poems about the gestation and birth — 'The Sonogram', 'Footling', 'The Birth' — which offset the predominantly elegiac tone of the collection. Publicity generated in Britain by *The Annals of Chile* suggested that Muldoon's reputation was entering a new sphere: Ruth Padel in *The Times* declared it "humbling and absorbing to watch an original intelligence, perfectly tuned to its time, swing into full maturity"; the *London Magazine* announced there were "few contemporary poets, if any, who can match his achievement"; and Giles Foden's grammar betrayed only the vestiges of circumspection, as he argued in *The Guardian* that "if [Muldoon] is not the greatest of contemporary poets working in English today, his influence is without doubt the greatest among the younger generation of British poets". *The Annals of Chile* was awarded the prestigious T.S. Eliot Memorial Prize in January 1995, for the best volume of poetry published in Britain during 1994. Later in 1995 Gallery published a verse play, *Six Honest Serving Men*. And future projects were already being mooted: another collaboration with Daron Hagen; a film script — "a smallish-scale, modest film";[31] a critical — judging by 'Yarrow' and 'Incantata', highly critical — poetic autobiography. Whether all or any of these possibilities will be fulfilled, as he approaches mid-career Muldoon has already displayed the Yeatsian gift of abandoning past achievements and remaking himself, finding new challenges. As he explains,

> what I want to avoid is self-parody — a risk that all writers are up against in one way or another. That doesn't mean though that I'm interested in doing something different for the sake of doing something different, but I'm certainly not interested in repeating myself — or repeating a poem, whatever it has had to say.[32]

Notes

1. Kavanagh, P. J. *Voices in Ireland* (London: John Murray, 1994), 34.
2. 'Reclaiming Poetry', interviewed by Alan Jenkins, *Sunday Times* (London), 14 December 1986.
3. 'Paul Muldoon', interviewed by John Haffenden, *Viewpoints* (London: Faber, 1981), 131.
4. *ibid.*, 131.
5. Muldoon, P. 'A Tight Wee Place in Armagh', *Fortnight* (Belfast), July/August 1984, 19.
6. *ibid.*, 19.
7. *ibid.*, 19.
8. *ibid.*, 23.
9. 'An Interview with Paul Muldoon', interviewed by Lynn Keller, *Contemporary Literature* (Madison), 35 (1), Spring 1994, 17.
10. 'Way down upon the old Susquehanna', interviewed by Blake Morrison, *The Independent on Sunday* (London), 28 October 1990.
11. Interviewed by John Haffenden, 130.
12. 'A Tight Wee Place in Armagh', 23.
13. 'A Conversation with Paul Muldoon', interviewed by Michael Donaghy, *Chicago Review*, 35 (1), 81.
14. Interviewed by John Haffenden, 134.
15. *ibid.*, 132.
16. *ibid.*, 132.
17. Interviewed by Michael Donaghy, 84.
18. Interviewed by John Haffenden, 132.
19. *ibid.*, 132.
20. Interviewed by Alan Jenkins.
21. Longley, M. 'Poetry', *Causeway*, ed. Longley, M. (Belfast: The Arts Council of Northern Ireland, 1971), 109.
22. Interviewed by John Haffenden, 132-3.
23. Ciaran Carson interviewed by Rand Brandes, *Irish Review* 8, Spring 1990, 79.
24. Interviewed by Alan Jenkins.
25. 'An Interview with Paul Muldoon', interviewed by Clair Wills, Nick Jenkins and John Lanchester, *Oxford Poetry* III (1), Winter 1986/7, 18.
26. 'Lunch with Paul Muldoon', interviewed by Kevin Smith, *Rhinoceros* 4, 1991, 77.
27. *ibid.*, 92.
28. *ibid.*, 79-80.
29. Interviewed by Lynn Keller, 3.
30. *Muldoon in America*, interviewed by Christopher Cook, B.B.C. Radio 3, 1994.
31. Interviewed by Kevin Smith, 92.
32. *ibid.*, 86.

Learning To Fly:
New Weather and Early Poetry

In interview with Michael Donaghy, Muldoon has argued that there should be "some other reason why a book is a book, not just because it's forty pages or sixty, or because it has three dozen poems in it ... there's got to be some other shape or rationale".[1] Consequently it makes sense to approach his work by collection; close critical explications of individual poems must always consider the larger structures of the volume, remembering Muldoon's interest in new images emerging from his setting up of poems "like mirrors at angles to each other".[2] However, it is not until his second collection, *Mules*, that Muldoon develops the craftsmanship and consistent sense of purpose necessary for such conscious arrangement. Poems prior to *Mules* can be yoked together as apprentice-work without sacrificing any discrete unity; they are the work of a young poet of tremendous promise, but who is still tentatively feeling his way towards his proper subject and distinctive voice.

Muldoon's first pamphlet, *Knowing My Place*, appeared in 1971, and the following year fourteen of his poems were printed in the *Faber Poetry Introduction 2*. No doubt reassured by reviews hailing Muldoon as the star of their anthology, Faber & Faber quickly promoted him to senior status. In 1973 they published *New Weather*, a full-length volume incorporating many poems from the earlier selections.[3] A bizarre mix-up meant that the book was printed throughout in italic, which according to the anonymous critic in the *Times Literary Supplement* gave it "the appearance of a monstrous refrain". But once production values had been attacked, reviews of *New Weather* were almost uniformly enthusiastic: Alan Brownjohn welcomed "a remarkably mature and accomplished talent"; Peter Porter "didn't meet a single infelicity in the book"; Brendan Kennelly believed that Muldoon could already produce "lyric poetry to equal the best". Rather more predictable was the reflex urge to compare Muldoon with Heaney. Both from Northern Ireland, both rural poets, both published by Faber & Faber — even at this stage many reviewers interlocked the poetic destinies of the two men. While acknowledging the similarities, the more perceptive critics of *New Weather* also highlighted crucial differences. Having noted that Muldoon's poetic landscape is far more emblematic than Heaney's, Edna Longley wondered caustically whether in Britain "Irish poets resemble each other like Chinamen"; and Alisdair

Maclean, writing in *The Listener*, found that "unlike Heaney's firm rock, there are shifting sands beneath these poems".

Ironically, Heaney's achievement explains the undue praise awarded to *New Weather*, which seemed from the same stock. Despite such a favourable batch of reviews, it is obvious in retrospect that Muldoon should have waited longer to publish his first volume, and curious that he allowed *New Weather* to be reissued in 1994. Few of these early poems constitute unequivocal successes. Rather, they are important more for what they prophesy than for themselves; they often provide clumsy examples of characteristic strains developed with far greater panache in mature work. Too much of *New Weather* is technically flawed. Muldoon has expressed disapproval of poets revising their work at a later date — preferring to "lose the entire limb rather than try to doctor it"[4] — so the extent to which he doctors his early poems only confirms their original sickness. 'Wind and Tree', for example, begins in the *Faber Introduction* as follows:

> In the way that most of the wind happens where there are trees
> Most of the world is centred about ourselves.

The opening is rhythmically inert, cluttered with monosyllables and stumbling breathlessly towards the more assured tone of the second line. Dissatisfied with the result, Muldoon's clever solution in *New Weather* is to create natural pauses by shortening the lines:

> In the way that the most of the wind
> Happens where there are trees,
>
> Most of the world is centred
> About ourselves.

Although betraying the arbitrariness of the poem's enjambements, this revised version is altogether more effective. A certain syntactic awkwardness remains, but the rhythm is less hurried. Muldoon bravely adds yet another monosyllable — "In the way that *the* most of the wind" (my italics) — to an already stuttering line, but in doing so he transforms "most" into a noun and enhances its stress. With a nod of gratitude to Robert Frost's 'The Most of It', the line becomes regularly anapaestic.

Not all the poems in *New Weather* have been patched up quite so successfully. Like 'Wind and Tree', 'The Indians on Alcatraz' suffers from Muldoon's early fondness for long lines and conspicuous subsequent efforts to correct their limp rhythms. The poem's ending, for example, is changed from the convoluted "each morning / Leaves me more grateful for the fact that they never attack after dark" to an alternative almost as clumsy: "Though only if he believes / As I believed of his fathers, / That they would not attack after dark". Other poems in *New Weather* also suggest a makeshift lineation, and hint at the existence of earlier, unpublished versions. The opening of 'Party Piece' might have been adapted from — and if so, should have remained — a prose poem: "The girl alone in the wood's / Corner had just then filled her / Glass with tomato and crushed / Ice". And the sonnet 'Kate Whiskey' exhibits none of Muldoon's later genius with the form as it pads out its lines in order to deliver rhyme-words. Other poems like 'Easter Island' and 'Skeffington's Daughter', having whittled down their lines often to just one stress, fail to maintain any kind of rhythmical impetus. Muldoon's revisions for *New Weather* prove that even at the age of twenty-one he had developed enough technical know-how to recognize, and sometimes to conceal, the failings of his teenage poems. But speaking in 1985, he argues that if a poem "doesn't work" then it should be forgotten and thrown out.[5] His failure to have been so scrupulous when putting together *New Weather* results in a highly uneven first collection.

The volume's title might promise originality, but it is almost inevitable at this stage in Muldoon's poetic development that parts of *New Weather* should be derivative. Having been introduced to T.S. Eliot's poetry while still at high school, Muldoon for a time "thought [Eliot] was God";[6] it is a tribute to the pace of his development that *New Weather* bears few traces of this influence. Certainly the punctuation of several poems in *Knowing My Place* and the *Faber Introduction* — or rather their lack of punctuation — owes something to Eliot's later style. But only once does *New Weather* display the vestiges of Muldoon's obsession. 'Blowing Eggs' contains the passage, "This is the breathless and the intent // Puncturing of the waste / And isolate egg"; in case the Eliot tone is missed, "waste" semaphores the indebtedness even more blatantly. Other voices — Plath in 'The Waking Father', Longley in 'Thinking of the Goldfish' and 'Leaving an Island' — occasionally intrude, but more important than any of these to *New Weather* is Robert Frost, who has remained consistently the major influence on Muldoon's poetry. Muldoon has acknowledged that

> the writer who excited me most at university was Robert Frost: an apparently simple, almost naive, tone of voice and

> use of language, underneath which all kinds of complex
> things are happening ... He's a good man to learn from in
> that he has no particular nervous tics, no characteristics but
> the strong, classic, lyric line. But the most important thing
> for me in Frost was his mischievous, sly, multi-layered quality
> under the surface.[7]

Besides providing a vicarious summary of his own poetic ambitions, Muldoon's comments emphasise a conscious effort in his early work not to seem derivative: Frost is a useful mentor because, at least according to this account, his presence is largely invisible.

Muldoon's faith is borne out by reviews of *New Weather* which remain too blinded by the obvious parallels with Heaney even to notice the influence of Frost. Only Roger Conover, in *Eire-Ireland*, senses the common ground between "the Master and the master poet" — that is, between Frost and Muldoon. In fact, Frost is almost inescapable throughout *New Weather*. Not only does the revised opening line of 'Wind and Tree' — "In the way that the most of the wind" — trumpet the Frostian source of Muldoon's improved craftsmanship, but the volume's diction and even its poetic landscape are ghosted by Frost. Pools, rivers, plains, woods, fences and hedges, meadows, mountains — individually, none of these backdrops are peculiarly Frostian, but taken together, as they are in *New Weather*, Frost's influence is obvious. Heaney has praised Patrick Kavanagh for making "the rural outback ... a cultural resource for us all".[8] Frost plays much the same rôle in Muldoon's development, his very example conferring authority and authenticity on the chosen landscape of *New Weather*.

Occasionally, Frost's influence is even more direct. Despite its prominent evocation of 'The Most of It', for example, 'Wind and Tree' is more heavily indebted to another Frost poem, the lesser-known 'Tree at My Window'. Taking as its starting-point an old Irish saying that two-thirds of the wind happens where there are trees,[9] Muldoon's theme is the emotional pain which results from destructive relationships:

> Often where the wind has gathered
> The trees together and together
>
> One tree will take
> Another in her arms and hold.
>
> Their branches that are grinding
> Madly together and together,

> It is no real fire.
> They are breaking each other.
>
> Often I think I should be like
> The single tree, going nowhere,
>
> Since my own arm could not and would not
> Break the other. Yet by my broken bones
>
> I tell new weather.

'Wind and Tree' is the earliest published example of an insistent association in Muldoon's poetry of sex and pain: the madly grinding branches are only "breaking each other", without the passion of "real fire". Still, the tranquillity of the single life is rejected in favour of the "broken bones" caused by an old relationship and sensing the onset of a new one. The imagery and diction bear a more than passing resemblance to 'Tree at My Window'. Considering the bond with his "window tree", Frost's speaker recalls that "I have seen you taken and tossed", and concludes, "That day she put our heads together, / Fate had her imagination about her, / Your head so much concerned with outer, / Mine with inner, weather".[10] From subject matter to the rhyme "together / weather", the origin of Muldoon's inspiration is unmistakable.

Frost is the pervasive presence in Muldoon's early work, but several poems predict the allusive style of later poetry by actively evoking, and conducting variations on, other literary sources. 'Poem for Lawrence' from the *Faber Introduction*, for example, takes issue with a quotation from Lawrence's 'Lizard': "If men were as much men as lizards are lizards they'd be worth looking at". The title of 'The Inheritors' — Muldoon's earliest poem about mushrooms — acknowledges Golding's novel of the same name; and an unpublished poem takes as its epigraph a passage from Golding's *Free Fall* (recognizing a fellow parabolist, Muldoon is a great admirer of Golding's fiction). In *New Weather* the most important example of Muldoon's literary appropriations is 'Good Friday, 1971. Driving Westward', a poem which ostentatiously echoes John Donne's powerful religious meditation, 'Good Friday, 1613. Riding Westward'. Muldoon's 'Good Friday' foreshadows later, better poems such as 'Immram' and 'The More a Man Has the More a Man Wants' in the way it exploits its source. Like Donne's, Muldoon's poem has forty-two lines; but as the respective titles announce, Muldoon updates Donne for a more secular age. Donne claims that if he looked toward the east he should "see a sun, by rising set, / And by that setting endless day beget".[11] Muldoon's sun possesses no such metaphysical significance, and the "endless day" is supposedly begotten by driving fast enough to keep up with its westward journey — "It was good going along with the sun". However, the two poems are also associated on a more fundamental level. Muldoon's 'Good Friday' is ostensibly about a drive with a girl picked up "out of love". At one point the speaker loses control of the car "and she thought we hit something big / But I had seen nothing".

> We had just dropped in from nowhere for lunch
>
> In Gaoth Dobhair, I happy and she convinced
> Of the death of more than lamb or herring.
> She stood up there and then, face full of drink,
> And announced that she and I were to blame
> For something killed along the way we came.
> Children were warned that it was rude to stare,
> Left with their parents for a breath of air.

Mention of the "herring" is awkward, as Muldoon introduces the Christian symbols of lamb and fish too conspicuously. This heavy-handedness gives away the parabolic intent: Muldoon's poem is about the pointlessness and even the self-importance of religious guilt. Donne's 'Good Friday' contemplates the horrors of Christ's death, and pleads that Christ should "think me worth thine anger, punish me". The crucifixion is downgraded in Muldoon's revision to nothing more significant than driving over a stick in the road. Despite the girl's histrionic confession, Muldoon's speaker refuses to be burdened by any feelings of guilt or responsibility.

In Muldoon's 'Good Friday', as the car heads through Donegal, "The sky went out of its way for the hills / And life was changing down for the sharp bends". These lines typify one of Muldoon's most consistent trademarks. Throughout *New Weather* and subsequent work he renovates cliché: 'Blowing Eggs' describes a nest "pulling itself together / In the hedge's intestine"; the fish in 'Thinking of the Goldfish' "looked like a change of heart"; 'Vespers' concludes with the image of frost having "designs" on a window; the birds in 'Elizabeth' begin as "an isolated shower". Muldoon has commented that clichés are clichés for the good reason that "there's a lot in them";[12] often only one remove from proverb and folklore, cliché naturally lends itself as a poetic resource to Muldoon's parabolic style. His use of cliché also owes something to Louis MacNeice, whose early 'Homage to Clichés' begins a poetic career exploiting their possibilities; and MacNeice has remained an important example and a kindred spirit.[13] Most instances of cliché in *New Weather* are pure mischief, but occasionally such linguistic retrieval uncovers something more sinister. 'Skeffington's Daughter', for example, uses enjambement to literalize the metaphorical in the lines "Not one to lose / Her head". And 'February' plants the cliché of "wearing her heart on her sleeve" amidst other possible mutilations and dismemberments. Perhaps most sophisticated is 'The Field Hospital', a parable about poetic rather than religious responsibility, which employs two clichés simultaneously to reinforce the ambivalences and divisions within the poem. It opens "Taking, giving back their lives": "Taking" suggests killing (to take a life), but the line also evokes a common phrase for compromise (give and take). These two buried clichés pull the poem in opposite directions. Set during the American Civil War but clearly analogous to the conflict in Northern Ireland, the poem claims a humanitarian autonomy which transcends rivalries and allegiances, answering neither to "grey South // Nor blue North". Yet the morality of the field hospital is not allowed to go unchallenged:

> Would this girl brought to our tents
> From whose flesh we have removed
> Shot that George, on his day off,
>
> Will use to weight fishing lines,
> Who died screaming for ether,
> Yet protest our innocence?
> George lit the lanterns, in danced
>
> Those gigantic, yellow moths
> That brushed right over her wounds,
> Pinning themselves to our sleeves
> Like medals given the brave.

Although the contorted syntax again betrays Muldoon's technical immaturity, the poem remains balanced between a scrupulous *sang-froid* and an impartiality bordering on callousness. Not until the last stanza does 'The Field Hospital' settle the conflict stemming from the two clichés. Yellow is the colour of cowardice, and the dying girl considers the medical team culpably negligent; but in fact the "gigantic, yellow moths" connect her wounds with their deserved commendation. A tacit manifesto for the poet's rôle in a divided society, 'The Field Hospital' argues that the greatest courage of all, and the greatest responsibility, lies in remaining dispassionate.

Besides cliché, another of Muldoon's common resources in *New Weather* and beyond is what William Empson has termed the "self-inwoven simile",[14] a figure also frequently found in the work of Northern Irish poets like Heaney, Mahon and Longley. Such similes come easily, sometimes almost instinctively, to Muldoon. Even when, in interview, he illustrates the type of story found in the *National Enquirer*, his examples include reports of "men giving birth to themselves".[15] There is already a handful of "self-inwoven" images — some obvious, some hidden — in *New Weather*: the fish in 'Thinking of the Goldfish' has its head "in the clouds of its own breath"; the snail in 'Hedgehog' is "held up by a / Rubber cushion of itself"; in 'The Year of the Sloes, for Ishi' a star cuts "a slit / In the wall of itself"; in 'Elizabeth' the woman becomes her "own captive"; and more subtly, 'Seanchas' opens with the lines, "Coming here, we were like that mountain whose base / We kept side-stepping". It has been persuasively argued that the sudden popularity of reflexive similes among Northern Irish poets might mirror a society divided against itself.[16] However, in *New Weather* the figure is associated, on an immediate level at least, not with national but with individual identity. 'Vampire', for example, tells of a woman attempting to live a hermetic life; suitably, its dominant figure is the self-inwoven simile. The poem begins with an evocation of "the birds in winter / Drinking the images of themselves / Reflected in a sheet of ice". The woman gradually spends "the daylight / Hours in bed", believing herself "Native soil enough for herself". In this respect the poem evokes the Victorian notion of the palace of art; and more specifically 'The Lady of Shalott', as shared concerns with mirrors and reflections might indicate. Like Tennyson's Lady, the woman in 'Vampire' cannot sustain absolute isolation from the external world: each night she slips outside for her milk bottle, its top having been "repeatedly / Punctured by a thirsting bird". This ending gives the poem a "self-inwoven" enclosure, by echoing the opening metaphor of the birds "Drinking the images of themselves"; while depicting the solipsistic inadequacy of the woman's chosen lifestyle, the poem reflects a similar hermeticism in its structure.

The woman in 'Vampire' reassures herself with empty tautologies: "I am alive / Because I am alive". Although hardly the strongest poem in *New Weather*, 'Vampire' epitomises the volume's obsession with personal identity and with factors challenging its security. Even the subject of 'Hedgehog' "keep[s] itself to itself", despite reassurances that "we will love you"; it is a "god / Under this crown of thorns", who will never again "trust in the world". The volume's dedication to "my Fathers and Mothers" is just as prickly; the poet keeps to himself by creating a polycentric pedigree which, while seeming generously inclusive, actually has the effect of diluting any debts which undermine the poet's individuality. In *New Weather* the main threat to the self is love. 'Wind and Tree', for example, finds refuge in the single life, but still remains inexplicably drawn towards a new relationship and its inevitable concomitant suffering. In 'The Radio Horse' the approaching woman is described in hostile terms as "another spy / Infiltrating my lines". And when the speaker of 'Thinking of the Goldfish' leaves a house, hand in hand with an unidentified second person, he remains glad that he will always "Own the light above my head, / If simply borrow from the side" — grammatically bungled, but with the implication that he is trapped like a goldfish in its bowl, no longer able to own anything outright. A similar concern with individuality and its erosion by a relationship marks the poem 'Identities'. An unnamed woman, fleeing from a country's authorities, asks the protagonist to return to the capital on her behalf:

> To search out an old friend who would steal
> Papers for herself and me. Then to be married,
> We could leave from that very harbour.
>
> I have been wandering since, back up the streams
> That had once flowed simply one into the other,
> One taking the other's name.

The ending does not entirely clarify whether the woman's proposal will be accepted or declined. The journey back inland suggests acquiescence, but also promises escape into a landscape of separation, prior to the streams' merging. Even aside from the dangers of returning to the capital, marriage is presented as a theft of identity: at their point of conjunction the streams flow "one into the other", not into each other; and just as 'The Field Hospital' plays on the word "taking" to balance judgement on the hospital workers, so in this context "taking" has connotations more of stealing than of sharing.

This preoccupation in *New Weather* with unity and division — as reflected in the simultaneous two- and one-ness of the volume's major trope, the self-inwoven simile — is pursued through several poems portraying the beginning or the end of a relationship. 'The

Kissing Seat', for example, describes the imminent break-up of lovers; they are "caught and fixed" in the kissing seat, one watching the sunset and one the moonrise, failing to agree on which star is the Pole, headed in opposite directions. 'Vespers', presumably conveying the start of a relationship, pleads for the warmth of a shared bed with the arch "I'll do nothing you won't"; Muldoon again exploits cliché, as the frost's "designs" on the window hint at sexual designs contradicting such claims of innocence. A stronger poem, 'Clonfeacle', seems to evoke a first kiss; the landscape is charged with erotic connotations which prompt the second person's "Coming round to my way // Of thinking". 'Clonfeacle' is related to the Gaelic *dinnseanchas* genre, a form which attempts to resurrect the music of Irish place-names, and the history embodied in them, through an etymological understanding of their origins: "each name a perfect equation with its roots", as a character in Brian Friel's *Translations* has it.[17] Accordingly, the poem opens with the legend of how it was "not far away / In this meadowland / That Patrick lost a tooth" — Clonfeacle literally means "the meadow of the tooth". This place-name legend is overtaken in importance by a sexual translation:

> The river would preach
>
> As well as Patrick did.
> A tongue of water passing
> Between teeth of stones.
> Making itself clear,
>
> Living by what it says,
> Converting meadowland to marsh.

The sexual connotations of the "tongue of water' and of "Converting meadowland to marsh" are immediately realized as the woman comes round to the same way of thinking, turning towards the speaker and "holding / [her] tongue between [her] teeth". The sermons of Patrick and the river end "on the air", forgotten in favour of more attractive concerns.

'Clonfeacle' is one of several poems in *New Weather* which combine myth with locale to convey the volume's preoccupation with love and individuality. Another example is the following poem, 'February' — titled 'Derryscollop' in *Knowing My Place*. 'February' is crucial in any record of Muldoon's development. Although pre-dating most of the other poems in *New Weather*, its blend of parable and brutality predicts the course Muldoon would take for his second volume, *Mules*:

> He heard that in Derryscollop there is a tree
> For every day of the year,
> And the extra tree is believed to grow
> One year in every four.
>
> He had never yet taken time to grieve
> For this one without breasts
> Or that one wearing her heart on her sleeve
> Or another with her belly slashed.
>
> He had never yet taken time to love
> The blind pink fledgeling fallen out of the nest
> Of one sleeping with open mouth
> And her head at a list.
>
> What was he watching and waiting for,
> Walking Scollop every day?
> For one intending to leave at the end of the year,
> Who would break the laws of time and stay.

The poem introduces what has since become recognized as one of Muldoon's most distinctive signatures — the half-rhyme. However, although interspersing full and half-rhymes in its *abab* scheme, occasionally 'February' fails to muster any kind of rhyme at all — for example "tree / grow", or marginally closer, "love / mouth". But disturbing half-rhymes such as "breasts / slashed" bear all the hallmarks of Muldoon's mature style. 'February' has transformed the influence of Frost into something enabling; Muldoon has aimed to recreate Frost's "apparently simple, almost naive, tone of voice and use of language", with its ability to present complex notions in "a simple, immediate way".[18] Nevertheless, the poem never labours under Frost's influence, because Muldoon has fleetingly found his proper voice and unpalatable subject-matter.

The poem's refusal to mourn bears obvious similarities to the emotional scrupulousness of 'The Field Hospital'. However, 'February' at first disconcerts much more because it evokes, but never explains or even confirms, apparent mutilation: the "one without breasts" may be merely flat-chested, and the "one wearing her heart on her sleeve" may be unable to hide her feelings, but both are given nasty connotations of dismemberment by the next example of "another with her belly slashed". Nor is the slashed belly accounted for; it might have been caused by a violent assault or by something as (relatively) innocuous as an appendectomy. The poem's third stanza comes closest to a definitive explanation, perhaps hinting that the slash is the product of a Caesarean section: this would account for the oblique extended reference to the "blind pink fledgeling fallen out of the nest / Of one sleeping with open mouth/ And her head at a list". By concealing the Caesarean under brutality, and displacing emotions onto a third person ("He heard that in Derryscollop"), the poet safeguards 'February' against biographical readings. But even if the identities of the "blind pink fledgeling" and the woman "with her belly slashed" remain unspecified, the concealed allusion overturns what could be mistaken for viciousness in the middle stanzas. Masquerading as sinister indifference to violence, 'February' conveys an obscure grief.

The middle stanzas of 'February' distract attention from the fact that the poem is also, like 'Clonfeacle', a poem of place. Muldoon's early work is filled with signposts; 'Good Friday' alone mentions Ballygawley, Omagh, Strabane, Letterkenny, Donegal and Gaoth Dobhair. Poems prior to *New Weather* suggest that the locale is actually the first source of Muldoon's poetic inspiration. The aptly-named pamphlet *Knowing My Place*, for example, consists of eleven poems, eight of which mention a place-name in their title, while the other three are also strongly associated with particular places; unfortunately this coherence becomes lost in the jumbled organization of *New Weather*. The pamphlet's opening poem 'Rodgers at Loughgall' (addressing the Ulster poet W.R. Rodgers, who had died in 1969, just before it was written) begins "You were before / My time, but Loughgall // Is my place". But for Muldoon, knowing his place involves knowing where he does not belong; his poetry always senses an intangible threat in urban life. 'Belfast' is an early example, as it describes walking through the city streets "With my head ducked for fear / Of their propaganda hissing from the sky". Aside from this unpleasant foray, Muldoon's early poetry is usually set in a rural environment authorized by Frost but still remaining recognizable as his home ground of North Armagh. It is difficult to overstate the importance of Muldoon's childhood locale to his poetry; literary guides are fully justified in designating North Armagh as "Muldoon Country".[19] Discussing the consistency and effect of these native surroundings in his work, Muldoon has remarked in interview that

> any landscape or locale is going to be re-mapped by a writer

— Hardy's Wessex, Faulkner's Yoknapatawpha, Joyce's Dublin, Yeats Country — I'm not setting myself against any of them, but these are places which are recognizable in their fixtures yet are changed by the creative process.[20]

While modestly downplaying his own talents amidst such élite company, Muldoon rightly emphasises that the imaginative world of his mature poetry is no less distinctive.

As a first volume, *New Weather* establishes some of these "fixtures" which come to form the backdrop for later work. 'Macha', for example, relates something of the legend of the giant who founded Armagh (she built *Ard Macha* — Macha's Height — which has become anglicized as Armagh). A goddess of war and personification of slaughter, Macha is exploited by Muldoon as a fitting avatar for his home county: she is "at war / With men, / Leading them against // Each other". 'Dancers at the Moy' also merges history and myth as it recounts a local economic disaster. Having heard that Greeks were arriving at the Moy's fair to buy horses for a war of independence, the people in the area roundabout brought all their horses to be sold. Unbeknown to the Irish, peace had been declared a week previously, leaving the Moy overrun with starving horses:

> The black and gold river
> Ended as a trickle of brown
> Where those horses tore
> At briars and whins,
>
> Ate the flesh of each other
> Like people in famine.
> The flat Blackwater
> Hobbled on its stones
> With a wild stagger
> And sag in its backbone,
>
> The local people gathered
> Up the white skeletons.
> Horses buried for years
> Under the foundations
> Give their earthen floors
> The ease of trampolines.

Like its subject, the poem's rhythm and syntax also hobble until the effortlessness of its final four lines. But the bridge from history to myth is superbly managed. Muldoon's reference to the horses eating "the flesh of each other" alludes to similarly unnatural reports in *Macbeth* when Duncan is murdered.[21] The poem goes on to draw comparison with something presented as less unusual, and therefore less worthy of note, in Irish history: human cannibalism during famine. The conclusion switches to folklore, as 'Dancers at the Moy' highlights the layers of suffering and catastrophe — whether mythical or historical — which underlie and still influence Muldoon's home landscape.

As poems such as 'Macha' and 'Dancers at the Moy' indicate, Muldoon's rural background is typically transmuted through the poetic resources of folklore, parable and myth. Muldoon has praised the "super-real" paintings of Dermot Seymour,[22] but in his own poetry, parable creates a similar effect. Edna Longley has convincingly highlighted the accuracy with which Muldoon's poetry fulfils the criteria of parable as established by Louis MacNeice: allegorical or emblematic elements, dream logic, Everyman protagonists, a concern with questions of identity, interest in narrative, and the creation of a special world.[23] Although Longley focuses chiefly on Muldoon's later work, this list provides an uncannily thorough resume of the strategies and themes of *New Weather*. The volume's landscape glows with emblematic significance: the hedgehog becomes a shy god ('Hedgehog'), there is a tree for every day of the year ('February'), birds assume Hitchcockian potential ('Elizabeth'), streams both prompt and mimic lovers ('Clonfeacle' and 'Identities'). Beginning with a traditional piece of rural wisdom, 'Cuckoo Corn' presents a similar world:

> The seed that goes into the ground
> After the first cuckoo
> Is said to grow short and light
> As the beard of a boy.

This lore is immediately contradicted; although the seed is planted late, the corn still grows "long / And heavy as the hair of any girl". However, the internal logic of this super-real, emblematic landscape quickly intercedes. The speaker's lover — "whose hair floated as if underwater / In a wind that would have cleaned corn" — is strangled by the flapping belt of the corn thresher. Human action is dictated by the necessities of parable, not by individual choice; the death is presented as an inevitable act of self-sacrifice. Although only miniatures by comparison, such early poems as 'Cuckoo Corn' prepare for Muldoon's later, more fully-orchestrated creation of alternative worlds — in volumes such as *Madoc* with their own peculiar laws, whether physical or moral.

Signs of this future development are most apparent in 'The Electric Orchard'. The poem offers proof of Muldoon's improved craftsmanship as early as its second line: in the *Poetry Introduction*, the electric people "had experience of falling off"; what sounds like bad translationese is replaced in *New Weather* by the more natural and colloquial "They knew all about falling off". But the chief interest of the poem rests in Muldoon's anthropological invention — his parabolist's fascination with special worlds. Having harnessed electricity, the "early electric people" have a penchant for climbing, and even for falling ("It was accepted as an occupational hazard"). Many of their discoveries are attributed to this way of life: the law of gravity, for example, is grasped by "thinking of the faller fallen". However, when they start "running out of things to do and see", they introduce legislation

> Whereby they nailed a plaque to every last electric pole.
> They would prosecute any trespassers.
> The high up, singing and live fruit liable to shock or kill
> Were forbidden. Deciding that their neighbours
> And their neighbours' innocent children ought to be stopped
> For their own good, they threw a fence
> Of barbed wire round the electric poles. None could describe
> Electrocution, falling, the age of innocence.

After all the detailing of this peculiar electric civilization, the final stanza confirms that Muldoon's attention has also been directed closer to home. The symbolic landscape of the electric people, like so many landscapes in *New Weather*, lends itself naturally to parable; in this case, a parable about the evils of moral prohibition. "Fruit", "falling", "the age of innocence" — such references introduce the Biblical myth of Eden, and tacitly argue in favour of the *felix culpa*, the fortunate fall. Justifiably, Muldoon has condemned the last line of the poem as ponderous;[24] but its association of falling with innocence targets the moral cant of those who decide what is best for others, legislating accordingly against free will and restricting human potential.

Although the poetic voice in *New Weather* is not always assured or accomplished, it is striking that many of the volume's weaker poems — 'Thrush', 'Thinking of the Goldfish', 'Behold the Lamb' — at least appear to convey direct personal experience. For a poet whose mature work often plays on obliquity and the untrustworthiness of the first person voice, these poems are false starts. As 'The Electric Orchard' would suggest, nearly all the strongest poems in *New*

Weather exploit parable, folklore and myth. 'Lives of the Saints', for example, focuses on St Brendan as he prepares to set sail, on a voyage during which he is said to have discovered America. (The 'Navigatio Sanctii Brendani' is an early Irish myth probably based on the 'Immram Mael Duin', which Muldoon himself updates in 'Immram' from *Why Brownlee Left*.) The contemporary Chronicles are agreed in recording that "the boat was stone". Muldoon's attitude to such legends is ambivalent. While reducing the Chronicles to nothing more than the tabloid journalism of their day, and indulging in a knowing wryness ("Those saints have the last laugh"), the poem is too sophisticated to discredit the legendary account of Brendan's departure, and almost joins with the assembled crowd in wishing the saint "Good Luck, Good Luck" as he sails away. By comparison 'The Cure for Warts' at first appears much more dismissive of folklore:

> Had I been the seventh son of a seventh son
> Living at the dead centre of a wood
> Or at the dead end of a lane,
> I might have cured by my touch alone
> That pair of warts nippling your throat,
>
> Who had no faith in a snail rubbed on your skin
> And spiked on a thorn like a king's head,
> In my spittle on shrunken stone,
> In bathing yourself at the break of dawn
> In dew or the black cock's or the bull's blood,
>
> In other such secrets told by way of a sign
> Of the existence of one or other god,
> So I doubt if any woman's son
> Could have cured by his touch alone
> That pair of warts nibbling your throat.

This might seem a clear-cut rejection of folk remedies; however, the deliberately ambiguous syntax prevents any such definite reading. The sceptic of the second stanza could be the poetic voice, but is more logically the hypothetical "seventh son of a seventh son" who, by placing faith only in the power of his own touch, and rejecting traditional wisdom, is therefore destined to fail. The poem's attitude towards folk cures may balance between belief and scepticism, but Muldoon's savouring of their more outlandish techniques reveals a natural partiality.

The longest and last poem in *New Weather*, 'The Year of the Sloes,

Learning to Fly: *New Weather* and Early Poetry

for Ishi', draws together the volume's preoccupations with folklore and parable in an extended pastiche of North American Indian iconography. The dedicatee, Ishi, was the last surviving member of a Californian tribe which had been discovered as late as 1910; together with 'The Indians on Alcatraz', 'The Year of the Sloes' highlights a sympathy for, and curiosity at, native American culture which has persisted throughout Muldoon's work. The poem is divided into twelve stanzas, each representing one lunar month: "the Moon / Of Frost in the Teepees", "the Moon / Of the Dark Red Calf", "the Moon / Of the Snowblind" and so on. As in 'The Cure for Warts', there is an obvious poetic delight in such lore merely for its own sake; but this time a darker story also begins to emerge from the arcana. In the eighth moon — "the Moon / Of the Black Cherries" — the native ominously discovers "two wagons / Lying side by side", while people in "blue shirts" are "Felling trees for a square". By the eleventh moon, a greedy and destructive first person voice has encroached on both the poem and the land: "I had just taken a bite out of the / Moon and pushed the plate / Of the world away". (This switch in narrative perspective from innocent native to aggressive coloniser confirms Muldoon's debt to Golding's *The Inheritors*.) Concluding the colonization process, the first person finds a motive for genocide during the twelfth moon:

> In the Moon
> Of the Trees Popping, two snails
> Glittered over a dead Indian.
> I realized that if his brothers
> Could be persuaded to lie still,
> One beside the other
> Right across the Great Plains,
> Then perhaps something of this original
> Beauty would be retained.

There is no direct textual evidence to support Muldoon's assertion that 'The Year of the Sloes' was written as a response to Bloody Sunday. But the poem does gain allegorical power as a result of its shift from celebrating American Indian iconography to toying with the natives' extermination. Genocide may still be only an idea, couched in euphemism and politesse ("if his brothers / Could be persuaded to lie still"), but it is the more horrific for being aesthetically motivated; even the description of the snails' paths over the dead Indian conveys a terrible beauty. Nothing in the volume — not even the seeming mutilation described in 'February' — prepares for this dispassionate gaze. 'The Year of the Sloes' is a Janus-faced conclusion, embodying the mythical preoccupations of *New Weather*, while introducing a concern with the horrors of colonization which becomes so insistent in later work that, finally, in *Shining Brow* Muldoon spoofs his own obsession.

Notes

1. 'A Conversation with Paul Muldoon', interviewed by Michael Donaghy, *Chicago Review* 35 (1), Autumn 1985, 81-2.
2. 'Paul Muldoon', interviewed by John Haffenden, *Viewpoints* (London: Faber, 1981), 136.
3. The texts examined in this chapter are *Knowing My Place* (Belfast: Ulsterman Publications, 1971); *Poetry Introduction 2* (London: Faber, 1972), 73-84; and *New Weather* (London: Faber, 1973).
4. Interviewed by Michael Donaghy, 82.
5. *ibid.*, 82.
6. Interviewed by John Haffenden, 132.
7. *ibid.*, 133-4.
8. Seamus Heaney interviewed by Caroline Walsh, *Irish Times*, 6 December 1975, 5.
9. Muldoon has stated that the inspiration for 'Wind and Tree' came from a partially-remembered Irish proverb: "Two-thirds of sickness happens at night; two-thirds of wind where there are trees". Proving his own point, Muldoon claims to have forgotten the third part of the proverb, but suspects it runs something like: "We forget one-third of everything we are ever told". Introducing the poem 'Wind and Tree', *Muldoon in America*, B.B.C. Radio 3, 1994.
10. Frost, R. *The Poetry of Robert Frost*, ed. Latham, E.C. (London: Jonathan Cape, 1971), 251-2.
11. Donne, J. *Poetical Works*, ed. Grierson H. (Oxford: Oxford University Press, 1929), 306.
12. Interviewed by Michael Donaghy, 83.
13. 'Homage to Clichés' is in MacNeice, L. *Collected Poems*, ed. Dodds, E. R. (London: Faber, 1966), 59-60. For Muldoon's relationship to MacNeice, see Edna Longley's '"Varieties of Parable": Louis MacNeice and Paul Muldoon' in *Poetry in the Wars* (Newcastle-upon-Tyne: Bloodaxe, 1986), 211-243.
14. Empson, W. *Seven Types of Ambiguity* (London: Chatto, 1930), 1947 edn, 160-1.
15. Introducing the poem 'Cauliflowers', *Muldoon in America*.
16. Ricks, C. *The Force of Poetry* (Oxford and New York: Oxford University Press, 1984), 51-5.
17. Friel, B. *Selected Plays* (London: Faber, 1984), 422.

18. Interviewed by John Haffenden, 133.
19. Kavanagh, P.J. *Voices in Ireland* (London: John Murray, 1994), 34.
20. Interviewed by John Haffenden, 130-1.
21. Cf. *Macbeth* II, iv. 14-20.
22. Introducing the poem 'Cows', *Muldoon in America*.
23. MacNeice, L. *Varieties of Parable* (Cambridge: Cambridge University Press, 1965), 76. Quoted by Edna Longley, *Poetry in the Wars*, 214.
24. Interviewed by John Haffenden, 135.

Between Heaven and Earth: *Mules*

When *Mules* appeared in 1977, reviewers agreed that the promise of *New Weather* had begun to be fulfilled. Seamus Heaney, on Radio Telefís Eireann, echoed the general consensus when hailing "a strange, rich second collection" and concluding that Muldoon was already "one of the very best". Critics who compared *Mules* with *New Weather* admired the greater technical accomplishments of the later volume. Seán Lucy in *The Tablet* welcomed *Mules* as proof of the poet's "continuing and growing poetic power"; while Peter Scupham, writing in the *Times Literary Supplement*, noted that "the diction has become less pushy than it was in *New Weather*". Muldoon himself endorses the view that *Mules* constitutes his major poetic breakthrough, both in craft and scope. There is no clean break between volumes; the list of renovated clichés in *Mules*, for example, is even more extensive. But the technical frailties which in *New Weather* often marred poems like 'The Field Hospital' have, by now, all but disappeared. The extent of Muldoon's development between collections is suggested by the very few poems in *Mules* ('The Rucksack' and, possibly, 'Cider') which would not have seemed out of place amidst the occasional gaucheries of the earlier volume.

Besides the assurance of its poetic voice, the most striking feature of *Mules* is its broaching, often for the first time, of many subjects destined to become perennial Muldoon fodder: the inescapability of home, the yoking of sex and violence, hermaphroditism, the tyranny of names, the rival pulls of heaven and earth. 'Lunch with Pancho Villa', the volume's opening poem, introduces another of Muldoon's common preoccupations — poetic responsibility in time of civil violence. Pancho Villa may sound like a stereotypical Mexican revolutionary, but his lifestyle is rather more mundane. A "celebrated pamphleteer", he lives in a "quiet suburban street", and helps himself over lunch to an "untroubled Muscatel" which symbolises his leisurely lifestyle. Despite these cosy surroundings, he urges the young poet to respond to contemporary events:

> 'Look, son. Just look around you.
> People are getting themselves killed
> Left, right and centre
> While you do what? Write rondeaux?
> There's more to living in this country
> Than stars and horses, pigs and trees,

Between Heaven and Earth: *Mules*

> Not that you'd guess it from your poems.
> Do you never listen to the news?
> You want to get down to something true,
> Something a little nearer home.'

Even in its use of direct speech, the poem extends the narrow technical range of *New Weather*. But what Pancho Villa actually tells the poet shifts significantly during this passage. The advice "Just look around you" is later equated with listening to the news: the visual and direct becomes aural and second-hand. Muldoon has commented that one of his main poetic duties is to write about "what is immediately in front of me, or immediately over my shoulder".[1] Despite Pancho Villa's urgency, he sees no sign of people "getting themselves killed / Left, right and centre"; the much-maligned "stars and horses, pigs and trees" are indeed "a little nearer home" than the violence reported on the radio.

Muldoon seemingly rejects Pancho Villa's advice by filling *Mules* with poems mentioning stars ('Largesse', 'Duffy's Circus', 'Armageddon, Armageddon'), horses ('The Centaurs', 'The Big House', 'Keen', 'Vaquero', 'Mules', 'Armageddon, Armageddon'), pigs ('Cass and Me', 'Ned Skinner') and trees ('Bang', 'How to Play Championship Tennis'). These cross-references help grant *Mules* a unity absent from *New Weather*; they award even the most peripheral allusion a larger significance, as Muldoon eschews a poetry of commitment in favour of something nearer home. Yet 'Lunch with Pancho Villa' is not an outright *non serviam*. The speaker ultimately owns up to the poem's flimsy artifice: the suburban revolutionary's surroundings were "All made up as I went along / As things that people live among"; the two-dimensional house implicitly opens onto the poet's own "back yard". However, although both the overblown rhetoric and the genteel middle-class setting have been loaded heavily against him, Pancho's argument is never dismissed, and it forces the young poet to question his own position:

> What shall I say to this callow youth
> Who learned to write last winter —
> One of those correspondence courses —
> And who's coming to lunch today?
> He'll be rambling on, no doubt,
> About pigs and trees, stars and horses.

Reference to the correspondence course is clearly a sneer, but the necessary solitude of such courses has granted the "callow youth" all the benefits of an uncorrupted, unburdened innocence, which the more worldly speaker now wonders whether he should attempt to destroy.

While resisting Pancho Villa's demands for a dutiful journalese, Muldoon acknowledges that there is indeed more to living in Northern Ireland than stars and horses, pigs and trees; civil strife is a largely dormant presence, but a presence nevertheless. His self-appointed duty to write about his immediate environment does entail a responsibility to tackle the pervasive sectarianism of which bloodshed is, sporadically, a product. But this sectarianism is approached with a suggestive obliquity unlikely to satisfy the likes of Pancho Villa, as 'The Merman' powerfully illustrates:

> He was ploughing his single furrow
> Through the green, heavy sward
> Of water. I was sowing winter wheat
> At the shoreline, when our farms met.
>
> Not a furrow, quite, I argued.
> Nothing would come of his long acre
> But breaker growing out of breaker,
> The wind-scythe, the rain-harrow.
>
> Had he no wish to own such land
> As he might plough round in a day?
> What of friendship, love? Such qualities?
>
> He remembered these same fields of corn or hay
> When swathes ran high along the ground,
> Hearing the cries of one in difficulties.

'The Merman' is one of eighteen sonnets in *Mules*, the volume which first heralds Muldoon's obsession with the form; the poem's idiosyncratic rhyme scheme (*abcc bdda efg feg*), and use of pararhyme, prepare for more outrageous liberties with the sonnet in *Quoof* and later volumes. Like the best of *New Weather*, 'The Merman' also displays all the qualities found and admired by Muldoon in Frost's poetry: "an apparently simple, almost naive, tone of voice and use of language, underneath which all kinds of complex things are happening".[2] This naive tone befits the neighbours' failure of communication. Lacking any sense of empathy, the farmer appropriates the merman's domain to fit his own limited vision: the sea is viewed as a farm, the merman "ploughing his single furrow" but inevitably, and stupidly, wasting his time with the "wind-scythe" and "rain-harrow". The merman is seen as different from humankind, unable to share the farmer's values, and his apparently irrelevant response seems only to stress his ignorance of friendship and of love. The reader, however, is forced to transcend the farmer's presumptions. The "cries of one in difficulties" have less to do with drowning than sexual pleasure — or pain, the two often being inseparable in Muldoon's work. The merman, like the farmer, can understand only within the narrow confines of his own preoccupations; he displays incomprehension and mistrust of any lifestyle alien to his own. On one level 'The Merman' is, then, a powerful parable for a sectarian society; but as MacNeice argues, "the [parabolist's] mythopoeic faculty transcends both his personal background and his so-called message".[3] While several parables in *New Weather* — 'The Electric Orchard', for example, or 'Good Friday, 1971. Driving Westward' — seem to fulfil little purpose other than to convey their moral, the weird fantasy of 'The Merman' awards the poem a life which incorporates, but extends far beyond, its parabolic intent.

'The Merman' typifies a volume in which Muldoon achieves — to quote the title poem — "the best of both worlds"; like the callow youth, *Mules* "rambl[es] on" about stars and horses, pigs and trees, while simultaneously recognizing the latent violence even in this rural environment. As Seamus Heaney has noted, this oblique approach also has the advantage of avoiding political statement:

> [Muldoon's] swerves away from any form of poker-faced solidarity with the political programs of the Northern Catholic minority (from which he hails) have kept him so much on his poetic toes that he has practically achieved the poetic equivalent of walking on air.[4]

The extent of Muldoon's swerving in *Mules* is illustrated by comparison with Heaney's *North*, published two years previously and written from a political — even tribal — stance. Muldoon's dislike of Heaney's bog poems is hardly a secret, despite his not having condemned them in print; their absence from his selection of Heaney's work for the *Faber Book of Contemporary Irish Poetry* is conspicuous. Muldoon views the bog poems as a simplistic fusion of two wholly distinct cultures. By comparison 'The Centaurs' from *Mules* highlights crucial differences in the historical procedures of the two poets:

> I can think of William of Orange,

> Prince of gasworks-wall and gable end,
> A plodding, snow-white charger
> On the green, grassy slopes of the Boyne,
> The milk-cart swimming against the current
>
> Of our own backstreet. Hernan Cortes
> Is mustering his cavalcade on the pavement,
> Lifting his shield like the lid of a garbage-can.
> His eyes are fixed on a river of Aztec silver,
> He whinnies and paws the earth
>
> For our amazement. And Saul of Tarsus,
> The stone he picked up once has grown into a hoof.
> He slings the saddle-bags over his haunches,
> Lengthening his reins, loosening his girth,
> To thunder down the long road to Damascus.

While Heaney draws a direct correspondence between the blood sacrifices of Iron Age Jutland and modern victims of civil violence (a parallel which, to be fairer than many critics of *North,* Heaney partially resists), Muldoon's connections in 'The Centaurs' are more ludic. The poem brings together three historical figures: William of Orange, "Prince of gasworks-wall and gable-end"; Hernan Cortes, conqueror of Mexico; and Saul of Tarsus, prior to seeing the light on the "long road to Damascus". Each man represents a colonizing Empire — British, Spanish and Roman respectively; symbolising a successful harnessing of superior force, each has been metamorphosed into a centaur. Jacqueline McCurry has pointed out that there is a "logical connection" between them: June 30, St Paul's commemoration, coincides with the eve of the Battle of the Boyne; and June 30 is called *noche triste* ("sad night") in Mexico, commemorating the year 1520, when Cortes's actions incited the Aztecs to revolt and Montezuma, their chief, was killed.[5] Muldoon relishes not only this quirk of the calendar, but also the aesthetic possibilities provided by the men's transformations: despite the title's warning, the realization that William of Orange is the "plodding, snow-white charger" still comes as a surprise; similarly Cortes "whinnies and paws the earth"; and Saul "slings the saddle-bags over his haunches". These parallels confirm that the historical enterprise of 'The Centaurs' is altogether different from that of Heaney's bog poems. Reference to the graffitoed gable ends of contemporary Northern Ireland might promise what Muldoon in *Quoof* mockingly calls "a moral for our times", but the poem ultimately offers only a whimsical correlation between its colonizing figures. 'The Centaurs' tacitly argues that such historical juxtapositions are more valid, and more suggestive, precisely because, unlike those of Heaney, they have not been manipulated out of prejudiced motives.

The obliquity with which sectarian issues are handled in 'The Merman' and 'The Centaurs' characterizes a volume which never directly confronts, but never forgets, violence in the North. Both poems express such concerns through the volume's 'mule' motif: as the sterile offspring of a male donkey and female horse, the mule is representative of the many hybrids which populate the volume. Some are announced by poem titles — not only 'The Centaurs' and 'The Merman', but 'The Bearded Woman, by Ribera', or 'Mules' itself. Others include the giant formed in 'Cass and Me' by a boy sitting on a man's shoulders; the woman in 'Blemish' born with one brown and one blue eye; and Jeanne Duval, Baudelaire's lover, who is mentioned in 'Armageddon, Armageddon' for no better reason, apparently, than that she is often described as a "mulatto". Any single explanation of the hybrids' significance, beyond Muldoon's enjoyment of the fantastic and grotesque possibilities they offer, must risk over-simplification. Nevertheless, Muldoon himself suggests that he was trying to explore

> those lives that couldn't quite reproduce themselves, and that were sterile in themselves ... lives caught between heaven and earth.[6]

Whereas Yeats could construct a complex metaphysical system around William Blake's dictum "Without contraries is no progression", the contraries of the hybrids' parentage result only in sterility. Because the hybrid motif represents mule-like lives, consigned to barrenness by the conflicting pulls of their pedigrees, the volume can be read as an extended parable for life in the hybrid state of Northern Ireland. Certainly the hybrids, divided against themselves like the self-inwoven similes of *New Weather*, contribute to the inexplicably threatening atmosphere of *Mules*; they are born out of a violent or unnatural union which, in later work such as 'The Frog' from *Quoof*, comes to symbolise events in Ireland's history. And although the predominance of stars and horses, pigs and trees might be expected to augur a pleasant pastoral, instead the volume overbrims with death, violence and outlandish transmutations; Peter Porter's comment in *The Observer* that he had not read "a book of poems for several years with quite such a friendly tone" seems almost comically imperceptive.

However, *Mules* cannot be simply reduced to a parable for life in the North. As 'The Merman' and 'The Centaurs' indicate, the volume's grotesque transformations take on an autonomous imaginative life of their own. Any suggestion that the book's atmosphere and hybrid motif simply parallel the situation in the North crudely ignores the "mischievous, sly, multi-layered quality"[7] developed in *Mules* from Robert Frost's precedent. One aspect of this mischief is captured by the title of 'The Mixed Marriage', which, as Muldoon has acknowledged,[8] deliberately evokes the expectation of a marriage mixed by religion, only to grant the poet a completely different kind of hybrid status: as the son of a bookish mother and an illiterate, farming father. Teasing the reader, Muldoon hints at the connection between the mule motif and life in Northern Ireland even while stressing that, on its own, such an interpretation is damagingly reductive.

In the overall structure of *Mules* the hybrids perform a function similar to that of the stars and horses, pigs and trees: whatever their immediate context, their evocation of earlier poems endows them with added significance. The hybrid motif establishes parallels not just with the particularities of life in the North, but also with humankind's dual nature; the volume's recurrent images of earth and stars emphasise the dichotomy between mortal and immortal, or beastly and divine. Given centrality by Muldoon's observation that *Mules* explores those "lives caught between heaven and earth", 'Blemish' economically captures these rival inheritances:

> Were it indeed an accident of birth
> That she looks on the gentle earth
> And the seemingly gentle sky
> Through one brown, and one blue eye.

'Blemish' is even grammatically a hybrid, resting somewhere between a question and a detached subordinate clause. Despite Seamus Heaney's observation that a character in *One Hundred Years of Solitude* shares the same eye-colouration blemish,[9] the woman's identity at first seems equally indeterminate. The poem echoes a Yeatsian theme which is announced, for example, in 'Tom at Cruachan': "The stallion Eternity / Mounted the mare of Time, / 'Gat the foal of the world".[10] Yet 'Blemish' seems more to recall the violent incarnation of 'Leda and the Swan'. The woman's blemish might be "an accident of birth", but the poem takes no chances: the possibility of fusion between the human and divine explains the otherwise mysterious reference to what is only a "*seemingly* gentle sky" (my italics), beyond which the gods, presumably, lurk until the next sudden engendering.

No poem in *Mules* juxtaposes divine and earthly elements more immediately than 'Largesse', as Muldoon rewrites with exultant humour (or "monstrous and disgusting hyperbole", according to Peter Scupham in the *Times Literary Supplement*) the age-old theological debate about how many angels can fit on a pinhead: "Numberless cherubim and seraphim / Alleluia on my prick!" More often the volume depicts conflict between the opposing pulls of earth and heaven. The title poem, 'Mules', begins with a pertinent question — "Should they not have the best of both worlds" — which would grant the benefits of two homes and two inheritances (with obvious relevance to life in the North) and not displacement from each. Muldoon has described the contraries of the mule's pedigree in interview:

> the mare came to stand for me as some sort of basic earth force — a pagan force, if we can use that word — an animal that was worshipped by the Celts. On the other hand, the donkey is significant in Christian mythology. [11]

However, 'Mules' undercuts these reductive emblems. The mare represents "some sort of basic earth force", but the "star burned in [her] brow" gives the lie to her "feet of clay", and saliently hints at even her mixed ancestry; and the donkey supposedly "significant in Christian mythology", far from offsetting this earth force, seems overladen by the "cross" he is literally forced to bear. Even the parents are therefore hybrid, but their mating to produce a mule — its sterility announced by the adjective "sexless" — still encourages onlookers to polarize its origins:

> It was as though they had shuddered
> To think, of their gaunt, sexless foal
> Dropped tonight in the cowshed.
>
> We might yet claim that it sprang from earth
> Were it not for the afterbirth
> Trailed like some fine, silk parachute,
> That we would know from what heights it fell.

On the purely parabolic level, 'Mules' is a poem about inheriting two formative but irreconcilable traditions. However, introducing 'Mules' on a Faber Poetry Cassette, Muldoon claims as its inspiration a newsreel from the Korean war (a civil war) which showed mules, laden with ammunition and wearing parachutes, floating down over a battlefield.[12] And the verb "shuddered" may again evoke the "shudder in the loins" which, in 'Leda and the Swan', provides the seed of human tragedy.[13] Despite opposing references to divine and to autochthonous origins, Muldoon's mule has fallen from an intermediate height, its hybrid nature unaltered by what might be called a sectarian impulse to assign origin exclusively to one or other realm.

One of the reasons why the opposing strains of the hybrids' pedigrees resist reconciliation is explained by the volume's almost reflexive union of sex and violence — with parabolic connotations also relating to the origin of the state of Northern Ireland. Throughout *Mules* sex is nasty, sinister or grotesque: even the farmers in the title poem, having loosed their mare and jackass in the one field, "tense for the punch below their belts". The list of further instances is extensive: 'Blemish' is shadowed by sexual threat and earlier rape; 'The Merman' confuses drowning with what could either be cries of agony or of sexual pleasure — it is impossible to distinguish; 'Cheesecake' (American slang for women photographed for their sex appeal) describes a mother discovering her son's collection of pornography, and finding that "Among those bodies her own body posed"; in 'How to Play Championship Tennis' the school caretaker entices a boy with the offer of a tennis book, before grabbing his "pecker"; and 'The Ducking School' hints at sexual abuse, as a terrified girl, summoned to play hide-and-seek with her grandfather, hides in a wardrobe "Among stinking, mildewed foxes". Even by comparison with these, the sonnet 'At Martha's Deli' is an horrific example:

> So Will had finally broken off with Faith!
> There she stood, gnawing a shish-kebab.
> It seemed they no longer soaked in one bath-tub
> And made that kind of little wave.
>
> Now she came over, wiping her hands on her dress
> And asking if I might not be her friend.
> I led her down through the bracken
> And listened again to what the doctors told her
>
> Of how she might live only a year,
> To where earlier on I had come upon the vixen
> That must have thought this her finest kill.
>
> The taste of blood on a greased knife

Between Heaven and Earth: *Mules*

> Whereby she would happily drink herself to death.
> She kissed me hard. I might have been her own Will.

There is something Shakespearean about the play on the name "Will" but the poem contains several of Muldoon's distinctive signatures: in particular the connection between sex and violence, and the sonnet's unique rhyme-scheme and use of pararhyme. Grammatical confusion signalled poor craftsmanship in *New Weather*, but now it is deliberately intended to disorientate: "earlier on" presumably means before Faith is led through the bracken, but in which case, it is puzzling that the vixen "must have thought this her finest kill". Events are as muddled as time-scales: the poem never divulges whether Faith is murdered by the speaker, or kills herself, or whether what is being enacted is a violent sexual fantasy.

Not all the poems in *Mules* which fuse — and confuse — sex and violence are quite so unpalatable; 'Duffy's Circus', for example, introduces a poignant innocence. The circus of the poem's title "had shaken out its tent / In the big field near the Moy". Despite his father's admonition that under such circumstances "God may as well have left Ireland / And gone up a tree", the young boy is taken to the circus, where he loses his father "in the rush", and slips out the back:

> Now I heard
> For the first time that long-drawn-out cry.
>
> It came from somewhere beyond the corral.
> A dwarf on stilts. Another dwarf.
> I sidled past some trucks. From under a freighter
> I watched a man sawing a woman in half.

The poem upholds a tenet fundamental to Muldoon's poetry: that life is more bizarre and freakish than anything even a circus can offer. As Muldoon acknowledges, he subscribes to Huxley's argument in *The Doors of Perception* — "I think the world is hallucinogenic".[14] The circus acts and the dwarves on stilts appear mundane beside the scene viewed by the boy from under a freighter. 'Duffy's Circus' employs a technique similar to that of 'The Merman', where the reader is required to correct a skewed or naive understanding; and in each case it is an ambiguous cry which causes the initial puzzlement. But this ending is more complex, because Muldoon conveys three possibilities concurrently: the boy witnesses, literally, a man sawing a woman in half; the well-known magical illusion of a man sawing a woman in half; and, of course, a couple having sex.

Mules even manages to invest those tired old circus animals of poetry — "stars and horses, pigs and trees" — with grotesque or sinister associations. Horses are ubiquitous in Muldoon's work, winning at least a mention and usually more detailed treatment in each of his volumes to date; one possible reason is the Moy's renown for its annual horse fairs, of which 'Dancers at the Moy' from *New Weather* commemorates a disastrous example. Besides representing "something a little nearer home", the horses' presence in *Mules* seems to evoke — or more precisely, to debunk — the Cartesian ideal of symbiotic union between horse and rider, brute strength and intellect: the metamorphosis of the colonizers in 'The Centaurs' constitutes a *reductio ad absurdum* of this ideal. Other poems spoof any such notion by carrying over the link between horses and death first established by Muldoon in 'Dancers at the Moy'. 'The Big House', for example, presents a gothic whodunit as the "girl under the stairs" relates how the squire met his curious demise:

> The squire's sure-footed little piebald mare
> Had found her own way home, as always.
> He swayed some. Then fell headlong on the cobbles.
> There was not so much as the smell of whiskey on him.

Similarly the first sign of catastrophe in 'Keen' occurs when

> your horse came back to me
> With long reins trailing,
> Your blood on its brow
> And your polished saddle
>
> Empty.

The horrible 'Vaquero' tells of a man lashed upright in his saddle but dead a week, a feast for buzzards as his corpse is brought into town by his "dilapidated, riddled / Jennet". In 'Armageddon, Armageddon' a man is killed when "torn between his own two ponies", "going their different ways". Trees can be ominous too. 'Bang' reports a close thing as the poet tells how "For that moment we had been the others / These things happen to": a tree "would give its neighbour the elbow", resulting in

> Our slow coming to in a renovated clearing,
> The far-fetched beginning to reassemble.
> Which of us had that leg belonged to?

Mules is mainly set in rural surroundings, but the fact that even horses and trees have been transformed into unlikely instruments of doom stresses the inscrutable, at times surreal, danger barely hidden by the landscape.

Not that violence in *Mules* is restricted to the area around the Moy. 'The Country Club', for example, arrives by way of Frost at a Chandleresque tone which clearly foreshadows the more developed 'Immram' from *Why Brownlee Left*. Scrupulously acknowledging his debts, Muldoon creates a character called Lee Pinkerton who, as Edna Longley has noted,[15] is compounded of Robert Lee Frost and Philip Marlowe's detective agency. Even without the presence of Frost and Chandler, the poem conspicuously operates at two removes from the Moy of the poet's childhood: cicadas, highways, bougainvillaea and a Chevrolet all contribute to an American setting, and the feel of a forties' period piece is conveyed by the description of Ella Stafford "wearing one of those little black dresses / And a kiss-curl something like Veronica Lake's". Amidst this *film noir* atmosphere, linguistic confusion quickly leads to violence. Quoting Frost, the protagonist declares that "all the fun's in how you say a thing", but his unsuccessful flirtation with Ella, who seems "high as a kite", shows how such fun can have dangerous consequences:

> She was right side of thirty, husband out of town,
> It seemed I might have fallen on my feet.
>
> Neither of them was so far gone, as it turned out.
> She slept the whole way to their villa
> On the Heights. She kissed me wetly on the chin
> And staggered in through the bougainvillaea.

Lee Pinkerton later reports that Stafford "Took a shot at his wife" for "seeing a lot of some other fella", and confesses that he "can't make head nor tail of it". The poem's misunderstandings are variations on the passage appropriated from Frost's 'The Mountain', about a brook which seems "cold in summer, warm in winter" although in reality it is never so far gone: "it's warm / Compared with cold, and cold compared with warm".[16] The relativity and ambiguity of language may allow for fun in how you say a thing, but when loose talk leads to violence, it demands responsibility too. On the level of its parabolic application, 'The Country Club' comes as close as 'Lunch with Pancho Villa' to offering a manifesto for the poet's responsibility in a society divided against itself.

'The Country Club' is a rare foray outside the confines of the poet's childhood environment. Although set in the French capital, 'Paris', from earlier in the volume, emphasises the inescapability of home. The poem describes a couple dogged by a pervasive past. A "table for two" will scarcely seat them because they are crowded by old identities — "A convent girl, a crashing bore, the couple // Who aren't quite all they seem". And the novelty of the pair's cosmopolitanism is confirmed by reference to the "country faces at the window / That were once our own". Even here, reminiscences of home soon take over:

> Chicken Marengo! It's a far cry from the Moy.
> 'There's no such person as Saint Christopher,
> Father Talbot gave it out at Mass.
> Same as there's no such place as Limbo.'
>
> The world's less simple for being travelled,
> Though. In each fresh, neutral place
> Where our differences might have been settled
> There were men sitting down to talk of peace
> Who began with the shape of the table.

Paris is itself a limbo — a "fresh, neutral place" — though conflict has still infiltrated. The couple's differences, as well as their past identities, remain unresolved, and the rival factions cannot even agree on "the shape of the table"; negotiation fails because each side, ironically, argues for its own Platonic ur-table. The couple's complexities relate to their travelling: "The world's less simple for being travelled, / Though". Yet the Moy may not be so distant after all: local legend claims it was architecturally "designed on the principle of the Italian town, Marengo".[17] There is an effective renovation of cliché. Though Chicken Marengo is "a far cry from the Moy" due to its distancing exoticism, it represents another pull towards home — the "cry from the Moy" carries even to Paris.

Throughout *Mules* the area around the Moy is a place of adventure, of danger, often of magic. 'Our Lady of Ardboe', for example, points out the whin-field in which a farmer's daughter in 1953 or '54 "Saw the cattle kneel, and herself knelt". The poem's speaker resists the temptation to dismiss this vision of the Virgin Mary, but expresses equal allegiance to more native traditions:

> Our simple wish for there being more to life
> Than a job, a car, a house, a wife —
> The fixity of running water.

> For I like to think, as I step these acres,
> That a holy well is no more shallow
> Nor plummetless than the pools of Shiloh,
> The fairy thorn no less true than the Cross.

To hope that the fairy thorn is "no less true" than the Cross is not necessarily to express great faith in the validity of either. But certainly the poet, as he steps the acres of his re-mapped homeland, finds much more than the fixities of quotidian life. Mention of "a job, a car, a house, a wife" only emphasises how infrequently *Mules* addresses such ordinary considerations. Muldoon might not be sure whether the fairy thorn or the Cross are "true", but he seems to wish they were.

Domestic life in Muldoon's early work is interesting only insofar as it infringes traditional norms. The volume's most powerful family image is provided by 'The Bearded Woman, by Ribera', about a painting which, like the vision which concludes 'Duffy's Circus', even outstrips the excesses of traditional entertainment. The poet is transfixed by the "so unlikely Madonna" of the title: although he has "seen one in a foreground, / Swigging a quart of whiskey", she was still "nothing like this lady". Together with her child ("Who could not be less childlike") and the "Willowy, and clean-shaven" figure lingering in the painting's shadows, they might constitute "the Holy Family / Gone wrong". 'Cheesecake' is another example of a family gone wrong: the mother finds photographs amidst her son's possessions, and her inspection reveals that "Among those bodies her own body posed". Elsewhere in the volume, order is quickly re-imposed on domestic disruption. After the gothic half-revelations of 'The Big House' and the mysterious death of the squire, what the girl under the stairs remembers most is

> how calmly everyone took the thing.
> The mistress insisted that life would go on quietly
> As it always had done. Breakfast was served
> At nine exactly. I can still hear Mrs de Groot
> Telling how she had once bid seven hearts.

Mules is intrigued by those intrusions of sex, death, and visionary experience into the family sphere which challenge (but still, in 'The Big House', fail to disrupt) the dull etiquettes of everyday existence; as Muldoon admits in a review from 1981, he is prejudiced against "ordinary domestic life, the tedium of which ... is precisely what most of us spend most of our days trying to avoid or postpone".[18]

In *Mules* the domestic life conceals unsavoury secrets behind a veneer of decency and respectability, and these secrets are kept hidden by censorious relatives. So even though the father in 'Duffy's Circus' finally relents by taking his son to the circus, he first condemns its immorality and provides a theological lecture on how "There was no such thing as the five-legged calf" because "The God of Creation / Was the God of Love". Losing his father "in the rush" could be accidental or deliberate, but the young boy then "slips out the back"; it is only when the father has been evaded that the hallucinogenic potential of pure perception — "I watched a man sawing a woman in half" — can be realized. Similarly in the first-love poem 'Boon', the youngsters ascend a mountain and view "the extravagant wilderness / Of the brawling townlands round the Moy"; implicitly, they find a freedom and adventure here which would be stifled down in the village. In other poems a figure from outside the family circle introduces new insights and opportunities. 'Ned Skinner', for example, recalls the day Ned came round to dress a litter of pigs. The boy is kept indoors by his aunt, but afterwards Ned invades their sanitized lives:

> Ned Skinner wiped his knife
> And rinsed his hands
> In the barrel at the door-step.
>
> He winked, and gripped my arm.
> 'It doesn't hurt, not so's you'd notice,
> And God never slams one door
> But another's lying open.
> Them same pigs can see the wind.'
> My uncle had given him five shillings.
>
> Ned Skinner came back
> While my uncle was in the fields.
> 'Sarah,' he was calling, 'Sarah.
> You weren't so shy in our young day.
> You remember yon time in Archer's loft?'
> His faced blazed at the scullery window.
> 'Remember? When the hay was won.'
>
> Aunt Sarah had the door on the snib.
> 'That's no kind of talk
> To be coming over. Now go you home.'
> We heard the whiskey-jug
> Tinkle, his boots diminish in the yard.
> Aunt Sarah put on a fresh apron.

The boy's emotions are significantly absent from this account. He lends an authenticity to events by acting as a passive recorder, his ear finely tuned to the rural dialect: "When the hay was won"; "Now go you home". Despite this apparent objectivity, the poem's sympathies are never in doubt. Aunt Sarah keeps the door "on the snib", with the gesture (and even, somehow, the word) conveying an unpleasant snobbery. Ned Skinner is not allowed to sully the house's inner sanctum, getting no further than the door-step and the scullery window; yet he possesses a mischievous vivacity far more attractive than the aunt's stuffiness.

The community's talent for repression breaks down with mockingly apocalyptic consequences in 'Armageddon, Armageddon', the sonnet sequence which ends the volume. With its obvious play on his home county of Armagh, the poem's title reflects Muldoon's interest in "the way in which a small place, a parish, can come to stand for the world",[19] echoing in turn Patrick Kavanagh's famous dictum that "The parochial mentality ... is never in any doubt about the social and artistic validity of his parish".[20] As the hint of melodrama in the title suggests, 'Armageddon, Armageddon' simultaneously endorses and spoofs such arguments. The universality of the parish is a theme running throughout *Mules*, often too consciously to be wholly serious. Muldoon peoples the volume with "Jonsonian, emblematic" characters — Mercy, Will, Faith, Hunter, Archer — to gesture towards wider significance, while in fact imposing two-dimensionality. The penultimate sonnet (VI) of 'Armageddon, Armageddon', for example, introduces a new character called Grace:

> My brother had mislaid his voice
> Since it happened. His eyes had grown simple,
> His hand alone would describe
> Our father's return from the betting-shop
> To be torn between his own two ponies,
> Their going their different ways.
>
> He had guarded our mother bent-double
> Over the kitchen sink, her face in the basin.
> She had broken another of her best dishes,
> We would bury her when we were able.
>
> Some violence had been done to Grace,
> She had left for our next-of-kin.
> My brother gave us half of his last mangold
> And the warning of bayonets fixed in the bushes.

The mention of Grace might be expected to throw up questions about her relation to the speaker, the nature of the violence she had suffered, and the identities of its perpetrator and of the "next-of-kin". Yet the symbolism of her name — together with the ludicrous pervasiveness of the violence — disqualifies any such investigation; there is no suspension of disbelief. Seán Lucy quotes the poem to show Muldoon "com[ing] to grips with the terrors of the Northern Irish situation". Actually, as the concluding zeugma confirms, Muldoon adopts a tone almost akin to *Cold Comfort Farm* to satirize the inflated importance of parochial conflicts.

Through the sequence Armagh manages, in mock-heroic fashion, to subsume legend, literature, history, and finally the whole cosmos:

> We could always go closer if you wanted,
> To where Macha had challenged the charioteer
> And Swift the Houyhnhnm,
> The open field where her twins were whelped.
> Then, the scene of the Armagh Rail Disaster.
> Why not brave the Planetarium?

Macha, the legendary foundress of Armagh, was the eponymous heroine of a poem in *New Weather*, but Muldoon now demands a slightly more detailed knowledge. At a royal gathering Macha's husband had claimed that his wife, although pregnant, could outrun the king's horses. Macha warned that "A long-lasting evil will come out of this on the whole of Ulster", but the king still ordered the boast to be fulfilled. Immediately after the race Macha gave birth to twins, and with a final curse on Ulster, died. Muldoon shifts from legendary to fictional horses with mention of Swift's Houyhnhnms from *Gulliver's Travels*, and perhaps hints at the pedigree of the many talking horses which appear later in his work. With an equally analogic connection the wider consequences of Macha's death (and curse) lead to the Armagh Rail Disaster.

Reference to the Planetarium in Armagh City helps explain the star imagery of the sequence: in sonnet I the stars appear as olive stones; and IV contracts the stars — or extends the parish — still further, with "constellations" punched into train tickets by the inspector. Sonnet V presents a post-apocalyptic scene apparently orchestrated by the zodiac:

> Why should those women be carrying water
> If all the wells were poisoned, as they said,
> And the fish littering the river?

> Had the sheep been divided from the goats,
> Were Twin and Twin at each other's throats?
>
> I knew these fields. How long were they fallow?
> Those had been Archer's sixty yellow acres,
> These Hunter's forty green and grey.
> Had Hunter and Archer got it into their heads
> That they would take the stars in their strides?

The zodiac's disruption of community life creates a "super-real" effect similar to that encountered in the landscape of *New Weather*. The dichotomy in *Mules* between earthly and heavenly now disintegrates; given that the water is allegedly poisoned, the women are carrying it for no more logical reason than that they represent Aquarius. "Twin and Twin at each other's throats" harks back to Macha's twins, as well as suggesting sectarianism and civil war, but the twins also symbolise Gemini; similarly the fish represent Pisces. An astrological influence has shaped all the bizarre events: a previously-mentioned bull (Taurus), sheep (Aries) and goats (Capricorn) might all have escaped from the local Planetarium and run amok. The fate of the neighbouring farmers, Hunter (Orion) and Archer (Sagittarius), foreshadows that of many characters in *Why Brownlee Left* whose various destinies are determined by their names: they have abandoned their fields and returned to their proper sphere, the galaxies.

As the parish expands into macrocosmic significance, it seems more difficult to escape. Sonnet II presents the poet's home as debilitating, by drawing parallels with the legend of Oisin. When Oisin returns to the mainland after his magical adventures in the Western Isles, he dismounts to become "one again with the mountains, / The bogs and the little fields":

> There and then he began to stoop,
> His hair, and all his teeth, fell out,
> A mildewed belt, a rusted buckle.
> The clays were heavy, black or yellow,
> Those were the colours of his boots.
> And I know something of how he felt.

Although the poet compares himself with Oisin, the final line's wry understatement protects the sonnet from the mock-heroism employed elsewhere. In fact sonnet II typifies a sequence which soon declines into enervation and entrapment. 'Armageddon, Armageddon' begins in "purity of light" at Lawrence Durrell's "Snow-White

Villa" but it progresses to "darknesses" which "weigh down further the burgeoning trees". A similar movement towards restriction occurs in this second sonnet, as Oisin renounces the enchanted islands to return to his enfeebling homeland.

After the spoof apocalypses of sonnets V and VI, the sequence ends more placidly with "A summer night at Keenaghan". But now the stars, previously symbols of heavenly inspiration, have vanished completely, to leave only an unmitigated darkness: the night is "So dark my light had lingered near its lamp / For fear of it". When a beetle "light[s]" on the speaker's thumb, the semantically unrelated "light" serves to emphasise the gloom. The beetle naturally resists a religious dimension:

> My hand might well have been some flat stone
> The way it made for the underside.
> I had to turn my wrist against its wont
> To have it walk in the paths of uprightness.

Yet like the 'Mustard Seed Mission' at which "all was darkness", the paths of uprightness provide no light. 'Armageddon, Armageddon' moves from purity of light at Durrell's Snow-White Villa back to a pitch black night in Keenaghan where even the stars fail to materialise. *Mules* contains several heavenly agents: our Lady of Ardboe, Father Talbot in 'Paris', even the Bearded Woman or the "numberless cherubim and seraphim" of 'Largesse'. But whereas Hunter and Archer take the stars in their strides, the sequence 'Armageddon, Armageddon', and the volume as a whole, are given an unilluminated, mulishly earth-bound conclusion.

Notes

1. 'Paul Muldoon', interviewed by John Haffenden, *Viewpoints* (London: Faber, 1981), 130.
2. *ibid.*, 133.
3. MacNeice, L. *Varieties of Parable* (Cambridge: Cambridge University Press, 1965), 18. Quoted by Edna Longley in '"Varieties of Parable": Louis MacNeice and Paul Muldoon', *Poetry in the Wars* (Newcastle-upon-Tyne: Bloodaxe, 1986), 217.
4. Heaney. S. 'The Pre-Natal Mountain: Vision and Irony in Recent Irish Poetry', *The Place of Writing* (Atlanta: The Scholar's Press, 1989), 52.

5. McCurry, J. '"S'Crap": Colonialism Indicted in the Poetry of Paul Muldoon', *Eire-Ireland* XXVII (3), Fall 1992, 93.
6. Interviewed by John Haffenden, 131
7. *ibid.*, 134.
8. *ibid.*, 131.
9. Heaney, S. *Place and Displacement: Recent Poetry of Northern Ireland* (Grasmere: Trustees of Dove Cottage, 1985), 16.
10. Yeats, W.B. *The Poems*, ed. Finneran, R. (London: MacMillan, 1984), 269.
11. Interviewed by John Haffenden, 131.
12. Introducing 'Mules' on *Ted Hughes and Paul Muldoon*, (London: Faber Poetry Cassette, 1982).
13. Yeats, W.B. *The Poems*, 214.
14. 'A Conversation with Paul Muldoon', interviewed by Lynn Keller, *Contemporary Literature* (Madison) 35 (1), Spring 1994, 21.
15. Longley, E. *Poetry in the Wars*, 225.
16. Frost, R. *The Poetry of Robert Frost*, ed. Latham, E. (London: Jonathan Cape, 1971), 40-44.
17. Interviewed by John Haffenden, 130.
18. Muldoon, P. 'Ordinary People', *Times Literary Supplement*, 1 May 1981, 496.
19. *ibid.*, 130-1.
20. Kavanagh, P. *Collected Pruse* (London: Martin Brian and O'Keeffe, 1973), 282.

Singleminded Swervings:
Why Brownlee Left

Consisting of twenty-seven short lyrics and the 300-line 'Immram', Muldoon's third collection, *Why Brownlee Left*, was published in 1980. 'The Year of the Sloes, for Ishi' and 'Armageddon, Armageddon' had both provided substantial finales to Muldoon's previous volumes; but because 'Immram' surpassed even these in scale and ambition, many critics ignored the unity of *Why Brownlee Left* by reviewing the collection almost as two discrete halves. The merits of 'Immram' were undisputed: Gavin Ewart acclaimed a "masterpiece"; Andrew Motion called it "much the best poem Muldoon has written"; and Peter Porter found a "joyful *tour-de-force*" which combined "the smoothness of Praed, the story-telling power of Kipling and the wit and good humour of Gay". The lyrics were given less attention, and more muted praise. Having lauded 'Immram', Peter Porter complimented the shorter poems merely for duplicating earlier successes: "Muldoon's other poems maintain the unusual combination of tones established in *Mules* — sharpness and warmth together". And while Derek Mahon and Alan Jenkins wrote detailed, enthusiastic pieces for the *London Review of Books* and the *Times Literary Supplement* respectively, Andrew Motion complained that many of the lyrics had been "suffocated" by an "excessive refinement".

Why Brownlee Left conforms to the interlocking structure of a typical Muldoon collection: a series of short, often sonnet-length lyrics prepares for, refracts, and even commentates directly on the long concluding poem. Reviewers were partially justified in finding a neat division. 'Whim', the opening poem, ends in Belfast's Botanic Gardens, and the last lyric before 'Immram', 'The One Desire', returns to the same location. Similarly in 'Immram' itself, "Foster's pool-hall" (or "pool-room") is both starting-point and final destination. However, these two trajectories do cross. So while describing a recently divorced couple dividing up their possessions, 'Making the Move' also manages to smuggle in sources for 'Immram':

> I edge along the book-shelf,
>
> Past bad Lord Byron, Raymond Chandler,
> *Howard Hughes: The Hidden Years* ...

Taken together with allusions elsewhere in *Why Brownlee Left* to Irish myth ('Whim', 'Bran') and *Tristram Shandy* ('October 1950'), the list almost constitutes a reader's guide to the longer poem. There are thematic correlations too. Concerns with pedigree, with the fusion of sex and violence, with escape and evasion, and with alternative lives, are integral both to the lyrics and to 'Immram'. Introducing *Why Brownlee Left* for the *Poetry Book Society Bulletin*, Muldoon recounts a story which embodies several of the volume's motifs. His father and a friend had, in the 1930s, determined to emigrate to Australia; they were to meet at a crossroads in Tyrone, and make their way together to Belfast and the boat. When the friend did not show up, Muldoon's father waited for a while, then went back home:

> It's an image that's troubled me for ages, since it underlines the arbitrary nature of so many of the decisions we take, the disturbingly random quality of so many of our actions. I would speculate on my father's having led an entirely different life, in which, clearly, I would have played no part. And suddenly my poems were peopled by renegades, some of them bent on their idea of the future, some on their idea of the past. All bent, though. All errantly going about their errands.
>
> I seem to remember my father telling me that he determined once to emigrate to Australia. Now he tells me it was a hen's yarn. Either he, or I, must have made it up.[1]

The self-negating conclusion is a characteristic sleight-of-hand, to be repeated by Muldoon three years later when introducing *Quoof* for the same publication. Whatever its inspiration, the story is carefully crafted to reflect the poet's preoccupation with alternative lives. Frost's 'The Road Not Taken' is the ur-poem for this account as for so much of Muldoon's later work: significantly, the father is left waiting at a crossroads. However, *Why Brownlee Left* explores beyond this juncture, as Muldoon speculates on the "entirely different life", the road not taken.

Both 'Immram' and 'Immrama', the singular and plural of the Irish for "voyage", take the errant father down one of these roads. In 'Immram' he is a drugs "mule" (and as such, bridges the hybrids of *Mules* and the hallucinogens of *Quoof*). After accidentally ruining a "fifty or sixty thousand dollar" consignment, he goes into hiding:

> He would flee, to La Paz, then to Buenos Aires,
> From alias to alias.

> I imagined him sitting outside a hacienda
> Somewhere in the Argentine.
> He would peer for hours
> Into the vastness of the pampas.
> Or he might be pointing out the constellations
> Of the Southern hemisphere
> To the open-mouthed child at his elbow.
> He sleeps with a loaded pistol under his pillow.

This passage encapsulates Muldoon's most important technical advance since *Mules* — an experimentation with tenses, first augured by 'Blemish' and 'At Martha's Deli', but fully developed in *Why Brownlee Left*. Edna Longley has observed that "The indicative mood has a low count in Muldoon's poetry, as compared with subjunctive, conditional, optative, interrogative and imperative forms of the verb".[2] These tenses frequently operate in the gap between the real and the hypothetical, the roads taken and not taken. So after the father is imagined "sitting outside a hacienda / Somewhere in the Argentine", it is unclear whether the following lines are conditional (were he in the Argentine, he would ...) or past habitual (when he was in the Argentine, he would ...). Later the father "might be pointing out the constellations", but with a sudden switch of mood and tone the possibility becomes concrete: "He sleeps with a loaded pistol under his pillow". Distinctions between the actual and the imagined are not so much blurred as eradicated.

Something similar occurs in 'Immrama'. Written before 'Immram' and more closely related to the "hen's yarn", Muldoon has described 'Immrama' as a poem about "never having been born":[3]

> I, too, have trailed my father's spirit
> From the mud-walled cabin behind the mountain
> Where he was born and bred,
> TB and scarlatina,
> The farm where he was first hired out,
> To Wigan, to Crewe junction,
> A building site from which he disappeared
> And took passage, almost, for Argentina.
>
> The mountain is coming down with hazel,
> The building-site a slum,
> While he has gone no further than Brazil.
>
> That's him on the verandah, drinking rum
> With a man who might be a Nazi,

His children asleep under their mosquito-nets.

'Immrama' is disrespectful of traditional sonnet conventions, with lines varying from six to twelve syllables, and rhymes such as spirit / out, mountain / junction and Nazi / nets. However, Muldoon does exploit the sonnet's turn. The octet's "almost" — "And took passage, almost, for Argentina" — is presented as a refining afterthought, but it marks the point where the father's real and fantastic lives diverge. In the concluding sestet it is his renegade history, the road not taken, which becomes authentic. Brazil is a fitting destination for the part-actual, part-imaginary voyage. It is named after Hy Brasil, the legendary Atlantic island (mentioned in 'Cider' from *Mules*) supposed to be situated west or south-west of Ireland, and previously thought to exist by so many people that explorers were convinced they had discovered it when they first came to South America. But the fact that the father ends up in Brazil also lends new connotations to the crucial "almost", which had been subtly positioned in the middle of the line: it is not that he "almost" takes passage, but that he does take passage for Brazil — "almost" Argentina. Through a syntactical trick, the hypothetical journey is rendered real.

Muldoon's exotic speculations do not always evade the routine of the real so successfully. The father's alternative life in 'Immrama' is untypical of a volume which presents the renegade history as precarious, liable to break down and drag the protagonist back to his proper destiny. In 'The Bishop', for example, the road not taken offers a reprieve which is almost lifelong but still, ultimately, impermanent. The title provides a fixed designation for the poem's protagonist, even after he ignores his calling in the Church: the bishop packs "a shirt and safety razor" on the night before his ordination, and starts out for "the middle of nowhere". As in 'Immram', tenses soon become confused: "He would court / A childhood sweetheart" could be a conditional, a past habitual, or an expression of intent. Just as importantly, the phrase allows immediate modulation into the authority of an indicative: "He came into his uncle's fortune". The man becomes a farmer and raises a family, refusing the fate decreed for him in the poem's title. This respite, however, proves temporary:

> His favourite grand-daughter
> Would look out, one morning in January,
> To find him in his armchair, in the yard.

> It had snowed all night. There was a drift
> As far as his chin, like an alb.
> 'Come in, my child. Come in, and bolt
> The door behind you, for there's an awful draught.'

Reference to the "alb" suggests the bishop's destiny has finally engulfed him, overhauling the comforts of his escapist life and returning him to his proper dimension. The sudden disorientation of inner and outer worlds befits a man who, having mistakenly believed he could evade the spiritual life by refusing ordination, has inverted a pre-ordained fate.

Despite the failure of the bishop's alternative destiny, the title of *Why Brownlee Left* gestures towards achieved departures. In interview Muldoon even elevates the renegades' evasions into an archetypal aspect of the human condition:

> One of the ways in which we are most ourselves is that we imagine ourselves to be going somewhere else. It's important to most societies to have the notion of something out there to which we belong, that our home is somewhere else ... there's another dimension, something around us and beyond us, which is our inheritance.[4]

Muldoon's argument that "home is somewhere else", perhaps even in "another dimension", effectively disowns the "place" his earliest published poetry claims to know. Yet this quest is in fact nomadically intransitive, imagining a non-existent home which provides a cover for the characters' genuine motivation: the desire to abscond from their programmed lives. The title poem of *Why Brownlee Left* apparently portrays an accomplished disappearing act, as a small farmer abandons his land and sets out for the freedom of a new "inheritance", leaving no clue as to his whereabouts:

> Why Brownlee left, and where he went,
> Is a mystery even now.
> For if a man should have been content
> It was him; two acres of barley,
> One of potatoes, four bullocks,
> A milker, a slated farmhouse.
> He was last seen going out to plough
> On a March morning, bright and early.
>
> By noon Brownlee was famous;
> They had found all abandoned, with
> The last rig unbroken, his pair of black

> Horses, like man and wife,
> Shifting their weight from foot to
> Foot, and gazing into the distance.

Technically, the poem is more flawed than critics have acknowledged. Discussing the third line, Bernard O'Donoghue argues that Muldoon is borrowing a technique from the Gaelic *deibidhe* tradition, whereby a monosyllable rhymes with a disyllable whose accent falls on the unrhymed syllable: went / content.[5] Even if true, such an influence would not excuse a rushed and stumbling line; Muldoon himself comments that writers who try to carry over Gaelic forms and rhythms produce poetry which is "very stilted, not quite appropriate to English".[6] Despite its technical blemish, however, 'Why Brownlee Left' embodies a pivotal ambiguity in the deserter's fate. The poem judges Brownlee's happiness according to purely external expectations of a small farmer's needs; Brownlee's occupation overwhelms his individuality to such an extent that the man's private life is never once considered. Rather than resting "content" with his farmerly creature comforts, Brownlee disappears because he fits too snugly into community expectations: as Muldoon has commented, "the name itself, Brownlee, suggests a brown meadow, a ploughed field, and so ... his end is in his name; he's fulfilled his purpose even before he begins".[7] In his review of *Why Brownlee Left* Derek Mahon confidently explains that Irish bachelor farmers have sometimes been known to walk out of their house and take ship to America, leaving everything behind. Yet as Muldoon's reference to the brown meadow implies, it is not so obvious that Brownlee has succeeded in escaping his unsatisfactory lifestyle. In fact the poem offers two alternative fates: that Brownlee heroically evades his destiny, and abandons his farm to set out for an inheritance other than that decreed by his name; or, crucially, that he has become so much a part of his environment that he is indistinguishable from the ploughed field which is his namesake.

Brownlee is the presiding spirit of a volume which focuses on evasion. However, the doubts surrounding his fate signal the problematic nature of these bolts for freedom throughout *Why Brownlee Left*, the most fatalistic of all Muldoon's volumes. Departure entails freedom of choice, a luxury the characters rarely enjoy. While the protagonist of Frost's 'The Road Not Taken' considers both paths before regretfully opting for one, in *Why Brownlee Left* the decision is usually predestined. A sequence of seven poems charting the decline and end of a relationship (or relationships) — from

'History' to 'The Princess and the Pea' — captures this paralysis, as departure proves at the same time necessary and impossible. 'History' opens the sequence with an attempt at remedial nostalgia:

> Where and when exactly did we first have sex?
> Do you remember? Was it Fitzroy Avenue,
> Or Cromwell Road, or Notting Hill?
> Your place or mine? Marseilles or Aix?
> Or as long ago as that Thursday evening
> When you and I climbed through the bay window
> On the ground floor of Aquinas Hall
> And into the room where MacNeice wrote 'Snow',
> Or the room where they say he wrote 'Snow'.

The poem implies the irretrievability of the past — a past which, as Edna Longley has pointed out, constitutes public as well as private history: Fitzroy Avenue and Notting Hill evoke Ulster's British connection, Marseilles and Aix represent foreign entanglements, and Cromwell Road and Aquinas Hall acknowledge religious oppositions; according to Longley, "Aquinas Hall, later a hostel for Catholic women students, was the palace of the Anglican bishops of Down, Connor and Dromore when MacNeice's father held that office".[8] The larger significance of 'History' within the sequence, however, rests in its retrospective inquisitions, its appeal to happier beginnings in order to rescue or at least salve a dying relationship. The following poem, 'Palm Sunday', again announces a foreign presence in Ulster; the yews in Irish graveyards "Are bent on Fitzwilliams, and de Courcys". But like 'History', the poem teeters between departure and the rival pull of home. Its speaker seeks a world devoid of political or religious symbolism,

> where everything stands
> For itself, and carries
> Just as much weight as me on you.
> My scrawny door-mat. My deep, red carpet.

Ironically, the concluding metaphors undercut a world where everything is meant to stand for itself. And for all its sexual innuendo, the comparison of a lover with a "scrawny door-mat" is a dubious attempt at reconciliation. The next poem, 'The Avenue', opens with an admission of defeat — "Now that we've come to the end" (the word "avenue" is from the French *avenir*, "to come to") — before the speaker finds nostalgic refuge in a shared past by piecing together the Miltonic journey, from the first moment of "taking each other's hand / As if the whole world lay before us". Despite the expulsion from Eden ("a party that lasted all night"), and intimations of mortality in the "song-thrush taking a bludgeon / To a snail", the poem delays the break-up by looking back to more idyllic times.

The titles of the following poems — 'Something of a Departure', 'Holy Thursday', 'Making the Move' — predict the inevitable parting, but in each case departure is again deferred. In 'Something of a Departure', even though the lover is "altogether as slim / As the chance of our meeting again", the only "departure" is from the heterosexual norm: the speaker asks to rest for one last time near "the plum-coloured beauty spot / Just below your right buttock", so that his lover can "take it like a man". The sonnet 'Holy Thursday' depicts a couple, who know "that it's over", lingering in a restaurant "Long after the shutters are up". The minutiae of the waiter's behaviour as he tidies up and rearranges the cutlery are carefully detailed:

> The waiter swabs his plate with bread
> And drains what's left of his wine,
> Then rearranges, one by one,
> The knife, the fork, the spoon, the napkin,
> The table itself, the chair he's simply borrowed,
> And smiles, and bows to his own absence.

This concluding sestet shows Muldoon's mastery of the sonnet's resources. The octet had rhymed, or half-rhymed, *abab cdcd*; only the final line of the sestet has no rhyme at all, reflecting both a lack of union and of closure. A buried allusion in the poem also confirms the relationship's imminent break-up. The biblical imagery employed previously in the sequence — 'Palm Sunday', the myth of Eden in 'The Avenue' — should alert the reader to the Christian significance of the date Holy Thursday: the waiter's bread and wine evoke the Last Supper. However, the couple are in no hurry to finish their last meal together; their close observation of the waiter acts as both a distraction and a delaying tactic. The waiter "bows to his own absence" as though he is two people. The implicit comparison is with the lovers, still pretending to be a couple.

In 'Making the Move' leavetaking seems imminent. Finding a mythical analogy (which foreshadows the voyage literature evoked in 'Immram'), the speaker recalls that "When Ulysses braved the wine-dark sea / He left his bow with Penelope, // Who would bend for no one but himself". Penelope's inflexibility towards her suitors perhaps tacitly contrasts with the present-day persona's own spouse.

The departure of this modern Ulysses is caused not by the pull of Homeric adventure, but the "gulf / Between myself and my good wife", into which mutual possessions clatter:

> A primus stove, a sleeping bag,
> The bow I bought through a catalogue
>
> When I was thirteen or fourteen
> That would bend, and break, for anyone,
>
> Its boyish length of maple upon maple
> Unseasoned and unsupple.
>
> Were I embarking on that wine-dark sea
> I would bring my bow along with me.

Claiming the unheroic bow as a personal possession because it pre-dates his marriage, the speaker confirms that, unlike his mythical predecessor, he does not expect to return. Yet his final couplet, while underlining that this departure is more prosaic than a Homeric journey over a "wine-dark sea", cunningly adopts a conditional tense to suggest that far from merely deferring his journey, he may not in fact be leaving at all.

The following poem, 'The Princess and the Pea', provides a nasty coda: now the option of departure has disappeared. The poem plays on the tale of a young princess whose high birth was proven by her bruising after she slept on a pile of expensive quilts, underneath which a tiny pea had been placed. Muldoon's less palatable tale is of her elder sister,

> Who is stretched on the open grave
> Of all the men she has known.
> Far down, something niggles. The stir
> Of someone still alive.
> Then a cry, far down. It is your own.

This is a bitterly ironic end to a sequence obsessed with departure: the speaker is trapped, unable to escape from a dead relationship. Such poems chart a loss of free will; whatever their autobiographical significance — and despite the reference to "Elizabeth" in 'Something of a Departure', several of the poems in the sequence relate specifically to Muldoon's recent divorce — the horrific, suffocating image which concludes 'The Princess and the Pea' betrays an acute anguish.

Singleminded Swervings: *Why Brownlee Left*

Although the poems from 'History' to 'The Princess and the Pea' form a sequence sharing thematic preoccupations and providing a loose narrative of emotional entrapment, they are not so much more closely related than other poems in *Why Brownlee Left*. It is no coincidence that the poem after 'The Princess and the Pea' is called 'Grief'; the volume has been carefully arranged to link lyric to lyric. For example the opening poem, 'Whim', ends in Belfast's Botanic Gardens, with a couple stuck fast during sex. 'October 1950' follows by ruminating on "My father's cock / Between my mother's thighs", and ends "in the dark". Taking up the final image, 'The Geography Lesson' imagines bananas turning from green to gold as they are transported in "unremembering darkness". The analogic connection between neighbouring poems in the volume predicts the interrelated monologues of '7, Middagh Street' from *Meeting the British;* their purpose in *Why Brownlee Left*, however, is to convey a sense of enclosure, a journey which begins and ends in the Botanic Gardens or, in 'Immram', Foster's pool-hall. These circular voyages — enacted in miniature by 'The Bishop' — frustrate the renegades who set out believing that, in Muldoon's phrase, "home is somewhere else". For all its talk of departure, *Why Brownlee Left* focuses on the inescapability of home and of a destiny over which individuals have no control. Even names wield a Platonic power which preempts and determines character: as the earthly counterpart to Hunter and Archer, who in *Mules* "take the stars in their strides", Brownlee is perhaps more likely to have merged into his ploughed field than to have escaped it; the gravedigger of 'Come into My Parlour' is called Coulter; and by writing 'Immram', a poetic voyage based on the adventures of his legendary ancestor in the eighth-century 'Immram Mael Duin', even Muldoon himself kowtows to a nominal fate.

After relating the "hen's yarn" of his father's near emigration to Australia, Muldoon suggests that the story is troubling because it illustrates "the disturbingly random quality of so many of our actions". When chance is injected into the predominantly fatalistic model of *Why Brownlee Left*, this random element restricts rather than liberates. 'October 1950' — the approximate date of the poet's conception — finds neither comfort nor understanding in "a chance remark":

> Whatever it is, it all comes down to this;
> My father's cock
> Between my mother's thighs.
> Might he have forgotten to wind the clock?

> Cookers and eaters, Fuck the Pope,
> Wow and flutter, a one-legged howl,
> My sly quadroon, the way home from the pub —
> Anything wild or wonderful —
>
> Whatever it is, it goes back to this night,
> To a chance remark
> In a room at the top of the stairs;
> To an open field, as like as not,
> Under the little stars.
> Whatever it is, it leaves me in the dark.

The first stanza is a curious mixture of Larkin and Sterne, as vulgarity gives way to a graceful allusion to *Tristram Shandy*. The particularities of conception cannot be recovered, but they are seen to determine the course of the poet's life. "Anything wild or wonderful" — whether it be local argot, an obsession with mules (a "quadroon" being the offspring of a "mulatto" and a white), or a cannibalistic sectarianism ("Cookers and eaters") based on the orchards of North Armagh — can be accounted for by this missing key. The poet is left "in the dark" because he is incapable of retrieving his source; but more than a cliché, the phrase also makes a metaphysical point about his subsequent lack of free will and direction.

Nor is there free will in the powerful 'Anseo', which, consisting of three fourteen-line sonnet-stanzas, returns to a fatalistic world where the sins of the fathers are unthinkingly duplicated by rebellious sons. The poem tells of the primary school at Collegelands, where the Master would call the roll and the pupils reply "*Anseo*" (Irish for "here" or "present"). The truant Joseph Mary Plunkett Ward, named after the 1916 revolutionary Joseph Mary Plunkett — and so perhaps nominally pre-destined to support armed struggle — is punished for his frequent absences:

> I remember the first time he came back
> The Master had sent him out
> Along the hedges
> To weigh up for himself and cut
> A stick with which he would be beaten.
> After a while, nothing was spoken;
> He would arrive as a matter of course
> With an ash-plant, a salley-rod.
> Or, finally, the hazel-wand
> He had whittled down to a whip-lash,
> Its twist of red and yellow lacquers
> Sanded and polished,

> And altogether so delicately wrought
> That he had engraved his initials on it.

The passage, of course, fleshes out a buried cliché: the boy is making a rod for his own back. As an indictment of a specific Republican mind-set, with its aestheticisation of suffering and glorification of martyrdom, 'Anseo' is unanswerable. The poem also implies that punishment corrupts, and that terrorism copies and even exaggerates the very activities it rebels against. Joseph Ward grows up to fight "for Ireland", and rises through the ranks to "Quartermaster, Commandant"; these provide echoes of "Master" and "Collegelands", amplified by Joe Ward's reading of the roll each morning to his "volunteers", who "would call back *Anseo* / And raise their hands / As their names occurred". One question the poem does not decide is where — or whether — to apportion blame. The word "volunteers" is a euphemism, but it also suggests freedom of choice. However, Muldoon has commented that in 'Anseo' "the society from which the child emerges is an oppressive, cruel one, and it's a Catholic society";[9] in fact the "volunteers" are victims as much as perpetrators. Joe Ward circles back to, even becomes, the punitive Master at Collegelands; he is a renegade whose rebellion, shaped by his name and childhood history, is deeply conformist.

Unlike some Protestant thought, Catholicism stresses the existence of free will; it is ironic then that in 'Anseo' the Catholic society is responsible for determining the course of Joe Ward's life. The Catholicism of the poet's childhood is portrayed no more favourably in 'Cuba' (titled 'Cuba 1962' in the interim pamphlet *Names and Addresses*). Although less surreal than 'Armageddon, Armageddon', 'Cuba' also examines the impact of world apocalypse on the parish: Muldoon has laconically recalled that during the Cuban missile crisis the queue for the confessional in his local church was longer than ever.[10] The poem only masquerades as autobiography — Muldoon's sister is called Maureen, not May, and she is his only, and younger, sister, not his "eldest" — but the original version of 'Cuba' does employ the poet's childhood memory of the Cuban crisis, in an exchange between May and the priest:

> 'How long is it since your last confession?'
> 'I'm not right sure. A month maybe.'
> 'A queue a mile long to the chapel
> And you can't remember so small a thing?'[11]

It is clear why this passage is dropped from *Why Brownlee Left*. The priest bullies May so much that he personally, rather than what he represents, appears repugnant. In the final version May is lectured by suspicious-minded authority-figures who reinforce repressive moral and religious rules. Disgusted by the "white muslin evening dress" she had worn to a dance, May's father concludes that she must need confession, and suggests she "make [her] peace with God". And the priest, although more benign than his earlier manifestation, makes similar presumptions when May confesses that "a boy touched me once":

> 'Tell me, child. Was this touch immodest?
> Did he touch your breast, for example?'
> 'He brushed against me, Father. Very gently.'

Whether political, biological or religious, the poem's fathers manipulate May, imposing their narrow prejudices on her; 'Cuba' is a parable of innocence destroyed, rather than preserved, by their sanctimonious codes.

Despite the presence of censorious relatives, in *Mules* the poet's childhood environment had been filled with wonder and adventure. *Why Brownlee Left* is more claustrophobic: in both 'Cuba' and 'Anseo' childhood is victimized, and only Will Hunter, mentioned in 'The Weepies', is carried over from the bizarre cast list of *Mules*. However, even in this pre-ordained universe the Moy has not completely lost its surrealism. 'Grief', for example, re-introduces the association between horses and death: the poet imagines a hearse-pulling horse on Charlemont Street collapsing and almost instantaneously disappearing under "a frenzy of maggots", which "make short work of so much blood and guts". Religious faith is ludicrously irrelevant, as the "immediate family, and their family friends" look on, and leaf through their Bibles. Yet 'Grief' lacks the panache, the relishing of horror, which typified *Mules*. Bleaker and more despairing, it ushers something close to misanthropy into Muldoon's work. The following poem, 'Come into My Parlour', arrives at Collegelands graveyard (unlike the hearse in 'Grief'), to view the unmarked family plots which are pre-destined resting places for villagers living thereabouts: fate is a grave. The poem also depicts a desolate, dehumanized landscape where only the detritus of civilization lingers:

> The wreckage of bath-tubs and bedsteads,
> Of couches and mangles,
> That was scattered for miles around.

Singleminded Swervings: *Why Brownlee Left*

Collegelands graveyard is the place where "a neighbour had met his future". Implicitly, it is also where humankind meets its future: a rusting residue of manufactured products, scattered over a landscape of buried corpses. The severity of this vision culminates in 'The One Desire', which records the ambition behind the palm-house in Belfast's Botanic Gardens: to outdo the modern by the more modern, beating iron and bending glass "to our will", so heaven might be brought closer and we "converse with the angels". As in 'Come into My Parlour', all that remains is a wreckage which is testimony to the folly of human endeavour: rusting girders, and a missing pane a tree has "broken through". 'The One Desire' is a revealing misfit in Muldoon's work, as clumsily constructed as the palm house it describes (a "missing pane / Through which" a tree has "broken through") and unusually blunt in its contempt. The poem's conclusion — "We have excelled ourselves again" — offers only sardonic world-weariness.

What 'October 1950' describes as "wild or wonderful" — sectarian abuse, local demotic, "the way home from the pub" — hardly matches the weird circus of earlier work. The lyrics in *Why Brownlee Left* are more mundane, at times (as in 'The One Desire') mean-spirited: human potential has diminished, with the truly "wild or wonderful" almost entirely absent. 'Whim' is one of few poems to evoke the bizarreries of *Mules*, as a couple saunter through the Botanic Gardens:

> by and by one thing led to another.
> To cut not a very long story short,
> Once he got stuck into her he got stuck
> Full stop.
> They lay there quietly until dusk
> When an attendant found them out.
> He called an ambulance, and gently but firmly
> They were manhandled on to a stretcher
> Like the last of an endangered species.

'Whim' is, in its way, "wild or wonderful", but its dominant tone — "To cut not a very long story short", "Once he got stuck into her" — is merely cynical. The shift in Muldoon's perceptions from *Mules* to *Why Brownlee Left* is easily gauged by comparing this brutish sex with the kaleidoscopic vision which ends 'Duffy's Circus'. There is a sour, mock-heroic joke at the couple's fate: the man had promised "the flavour of the original", after seeing the woman reading Standish O'Grady's translation of *Cu Chulainn and the Birds of Appetite* ("More like *How Cu Chulainn Got His End*"); and he does indeed provide a working demonstration of the real thing, without recourse to any translation. Other close encounters, again via Irish mythology, are conveyed by 'Bran':

> While he looks into the eyes of women
> Who have let themselves go,
> While they sigh and they moan
> For pure joy,
>
> He weeps for the boy on that small farm
> Who takes an oatmeal Labrador
> In his arms,
> Who knows all there is of rapture.

Mules recreates childhood; 'Bran' mourns its irretrievability. The detached gaze at the faintly ridiculous ecstasy of lovers prompts only a misty-eyed nostalgia for the "pure joy" of the protagonist's boyhood. The poem's title reflects more than just the labrador's colour; 'Immram Bran' — an eighth-century Irish legend — at one point relates the transformation of a woman into a dog. This time, however, the women fall short, failing to inspire the same "rapture" as the oatmeal labrador.

Despite the sourness of much of *Why Brownlee Left*, it would still be wrong to conclude that the volume represents an imaginative falling off after the freakshows of *Mules*. Muldoon now employs more humdrum images to tackle similar themes, but through an economy of description he endows those images with shocking connotations. This technique is nowhere more effective than in the volume's depiction of sectarianism and civil war. The tiny 'Ireland', for example, captures the macrocosm through an apparently inconsequential detail:

> The Volkswagen parked in the gap,
> But gently ticking over.
> You wonder if it's lovers
> And not men hurrying back
> Across two fields and a river.

In his review of *Why Brownlee Left*, Andrew Motion condemns 'Ireland' as a poem where "what is meant to be glancingly evocative merely sounds rather coyly 'significant'". But there is nothing at all coy about the poem's significance: it presents a society either where lovers in a parked car are more unusual, and therefore more worthy of mention, than terrorists returning to their getaway vehicle; or where people have become so sensitized to civil violence that they suspect it even in the inconsequentialities of everyday life. 'Truce' also contrasts war and love-making. Describing the famous Christmas ceasefire during the first world war, the poem undoubtedly keeps its eye on festive ceasefires closer to home, in contemporary Northern Ireland. The men share food and drink, sing and play cards, before their inevitable return to respective trenches:

> They draw on their last cigarettes
>
> As Friday-night lovers, when it's over
> Might get up from their mattresses
> To congratulate each other
> And exchange names and addresses.

Under the flourish of this final metaphor, there is a despairing prognosis for such truces: despite its intimacies and mutual delights, the ceasefire is ultimately no more committed or long-term than a one-night stand.

'The Boundary Commission' manages to combine the economies apparent in 'Truce' and 'Ireland' with the super-real landscapes of earlier work. MacNeice's *Varieties of Parable* had provided almost a précis of Muldoon's initial strategies and preoccupations; and Mac-Neice's emphasis on the parabolist's fascination with borders, whether geographical or ontological, is borne out by 'The Merman' and 'Boon'. Similarly 'The Boundary Commission' begins by recalling the village where the border ran down the middle of the street, "*With the butcher and the baker in different states*". The elements mimic this arbitrary division:

> Today he remarked how a shower of rain
>
> Had stopped so cleanly across Golightly's lane
> It might have been a wall of glass
> That had toppled over. He stood there, for ages,
> To wonder which side, if any, he should be on.

Because it is in this super-real landscape that rain-showers stop so neatly, the poem emphasises that borders are unnatural, decreed by boundary commissions and bearing little relation to social and geographical realities. However, while the poem's title suggests that the borders under discussion are lines on a map, sectarian divisions are just as relevant. The unidentified protagonist who wonders "which side, if any, he should be on" is bothered by geographies of allegiance as well as of land.

Muldoon himself avoids taking sides, refusing to grant sectarianism even the limited respectability which would result from showing preference — as Heaney perhaps does in *North* — to one faction over the other. *Why Brownlee Left* calls down a plague on both houses. While 'Cuba' and 'Anseo' attack a particular form of parochial Catholicism (inherent in Muldoon's own family background), 'Early Warning' helps redress the balance by criticizing the complacency of a neighbouring brand of Protestantism. The poet tells how his father would spray their crab-apple tree — always bowed down more by children than apples — to protect it against apple-scab disease. Meanwhile their Protestant neighbour would ignore radio warnings of apple-scab in the air, sling up a hammock between "two sturdy Grenadiers", and "work through the latest Marvel comic". In passing, 'Early Warning' sketches several Catholic stereotypes: "they have lots of children, they are notoriously given to factions"[12], and so on. Yet its most pointed criticisms target the Protestant Billy Wetherall, fooled (perhaps by his name) into believing himself a man for all seasons. The poem constitutes an allegorical history lesson which recalls the factors leading up to the outbreak of the Troubles. A grenadier is an old kind of apple tree, but the military connotations are obvious: supported by grenadiers (in both senses), Billy believes himself in control, untouchable. His confidence is stupidly misplaced, because unlike the rain-shower in 'The Boundary Commission', apple-scab — symbolizing civil unrest — will affect both sides equally.

Discussing those poems from *Why Brownlee Left* which portray life in Northern Ireland, Peter Porter argues that "It's no wonder Brownlee, and so many like him, left". The same poems show why it is so difficult — perhaps, in Brownlee's case, impossible — to leave. Despite Muldoon's reference in interview to a "home" "somewhere else", most of the characters in *Why Brownlee Left* find that home is actually where they start from: the volume's quests are circular. 'I Remember Sir Alfred' suggests that the only way to evade the restrictions of home is through incessant "singleminded swervings". The poem opens with a tiny parable:

> The gardens of Buckingham Palace
> Were strewn once with Irish loam
> So those English moles that knew their place
> Would have no sense of home.

This is founded on the curious absence of moles in Ireland, but it also implies that, at least for moles, home is a problematic construct which relies more on convenience than sentiment. The exiles of the following stanzas make no such contingencies, and share no geographical doubts. The Sir Alfred of the poem's title is Sir Alfred McAlpine, the construction engineer, who upholds Euclid's principle that "The shortest distance between two points / Is a straight line". This belief provides Sir Alfred with romantic reassurance of his origins: he fixes his theodolite on "love, or fidelity", which only exist "beyond the horizon" — that is, in his idealized homeland. Muldoon dismisses such undeviating simplicity. Knowing his place means taking into account "Charles Stewart Parnell, the I.R.A., / Redheaded women, the way back to the digs". The real world, of politics, violence, betrayal, sexual passion, even "the way back to the digs" (like "the way home from the pub" in 'October 1950'), remains far too intractably complex to fit Sir Alfred's pat reductionism. A sentimental attachment to home is resisted as resolutely as the place itself:

> Now Sir Alfred has dislodged a hare
> That goes by leaps and bounds,
> Across the grazing,
> Here and there,
> This way and that, by singleminded swervings.

As Muldoon explains elsewhere through the mouthpiece of MacNeice, attachment to origins should be left to take care of itself.[13] The hare's "swervings" are "singleminded" not through any search for an alternative "inheritance", but because it has just one objective: escape.

Even in 'Immram', set against a backdrop of downtown L.A. drug-trafficking and filtered through a Chandleresque medium, Ireland proves difficult to evade. One of the characters, James Earl Caulfield III, is named after the Lord Lieutenant of Ireland who founded the Moy. Brendan O'Leary, another lieutenant in 'Immram' but this time belonging to local police force, also has Irish ancestry, as his name suggests: he combines the Irish Saint Brendan, whose legendary voyage to the New World is portrayed in 'Lives of the Saints', and the sixties' drugs guru Timothy O'Leary.[14] As the lieutenant goes on to explain,

> 'My father, God rest him, he held this theory
> That the Irish, the American Irish,

> Were really the thirteenth tribe,
> The Israelites of Europe.
> All along, my father believed in fairies
> But he might as well have been Jewish.'
> His laugh was a silent hiccup.
> I guessed that Lieutenant Brendan O'Leary's
> Grandmother's pea was green,
> And that was why she had to leave old Skibbereen.

Lieutenant O'Leary mocks the wilder fantasies of his father, but his own subtle shift from "the Irish" to "the American Irish" — its emphasis significantly weighted against the more accurate label of Irish-Americans — raises the exiles to a more authentic level than their trans-Atlantic siblings. Yet despite allusions to the thirteenth tribe of Israel, Ireland is no promised land. Green may be the national colour, but since green urine is a classic symptom of venereal disease, the more likely truth behind O'Leary's grandmother's departure is that she was forced out of Skibbereen through the moral indignation of others. In such circumstances the grandmother would be no more successful than Brownlee: her alternative life represents compulsion, not freedom.

The clearest association of 'Immram' with Ireland comes from its rewriting of the eighth-century Irish legend 'Immram Mael Duin': in the acknowledgements at the end of *Why Brownlee Left*, Muldoon notes his indebtedness to "Whitley Stokes's translation of 'Immram Mael Duin' (*Revue Celtique* IX-X)". Several reviewers remained sceptical: Patricia Craig, for example, found the only similarity in the names Mael Duin and Muldoon, and concluded that the source "may have acted as a starting-point, no more"; more recently, Richard Brown reports having been assured by Muldoon himself that the acknowledgement was "a joke".[15] The only possible joke, however, is Muldoon's pernickety reference to a clumsy transliteration which was published in a Parisian journal in 1888-9; the 'Immram Mael Duin' legend is more easily, and more enjoyably, available elsewhere. Despite the suspicions of critics, 'Immram' does employ what T.S. Eliot calls — while discussing *Ulysses* and its relation to the *Odyssey* — the "mythical method"; that is, it manipulates "a continuous parallel between contemporaneity and antiquity".[16] In 'Immram Mael Duin' the legendary protagonist sails from island to island in a quest to avenge his father's death. The urban setting of 'Immram' is filled to overflowing with watery reminders of this source, from its opening at "Foster's *pool*-hall" (my italics) to the "steady stream" of "pilgrim[s]" returning there at the end. Locations in the poem include the "Atlantic Club", a "Deep Water Baptist Mission", and an "Ocean Boulevard". Among the characters are a man like a "Barbary pirate" and a lifeguard with "dorsals" who preaches "The Way of the One Wave". The protagonist is variously found "clinging to an ice-pack / On which the Titanic might have foundered", or doing "a breast-stroke through the carpet" before surfacing alongside "the raft of a banquet-table". 'Shall We Gather at the River' plays in the background. A Cadillac sweeps "out of the distant past / Like a wayward bay mist"; and wonderfully, two cars collide head-on "Like a couple of turtles on their wedding-night". This constant undertow of imagery combines with references to "immram" (voyaging) literature from other cultures: evoking *The Tempest*, drug-trafficking cabals are portrayed as the accretion of ever more influential layers, so that "over every Caliban / There's an Ariel, and behind him, Prospero"; and the protagonist, describing his father, remembers

> a scar on his left forearm
> From that time he got himself caught in the works
> Of a saw-mill near Ithaca, New York.

This nods to the *Odyssey*, from mention of Ithaca down to the identifying scar. Tennyson's 'The Voyage of Maeldune' (a poem which Muldoon considers "dreadful")[17] is also recalled, provoking mention in 'Immram' of "a nervous couple" ahead of the protagonist at a hotel booking desk "Who registered as Mr and Mrs Alfred Tennyson"; Muldoon accordingly acknowledges his belated place in the tradition.

There are parallels between individual episodes of 'Immram Mael Duin' and 'Immram' as well, even though, as Muldoon notes, the Irish is twisted "out of all recognition".[18] The mythical Mael Duin learns in early adulthood that he had been fostered as a baby, after his father was killed by "marauders from Leix". Eager for revenge, he sets out on a voyage to find the killers; but the moment he tracks them down, a supernatural gust of wind takes his ship far out to sea. The main body of the legend charts the crew's experiences on various magical islands, until finally, having been taught by a Christian hermit to renounce vengeance, they are allowed to return home; on the way they again encounter the murderers, and become their guests. This plot is obviously far removed from a tale of Los Angeles drug-trafficking. But even apart from the extensive water imagery, Muldoon borrows and transforms numerous details from the original. At one of the magical islands in 'Immram Mael Duin', for example, the crew watch a man lifting sheep over a brazen palisade; the sheep change to white or black according to which side they are on. Earlier in the legend the crew encounter a white cat; with the same colour switch this becomes, in Muldoon's modern-day 'Immram', a "black cat" — that is to say, a black man. Although contorted almost to undetectability, Muldoon's playful treatment of his source is also evident in the opening stanza:

> I was fairly and squarely behind the eight
> That morning in Foster's pool-hall
> When it came to me out of the blue
> In the shape of a sixteen-ounce billiard cue
> That lent what he said some little weight.
> 'Your old man was an ass-hole.
> That makes an ass-hole out of you.'
> My grand-father hailed from New York State.
> My grand-mother was part Cree.
> This must be some new strain in my pedigree.

"Foster's pool-hall" is an updated version of Mael Duin's "foster-age"; like its source (and like much else in *Why Brownlee Left*) 'Immram' is concerned with "pedigree", particularly on the paternal side. While the legendary hero learns the truth about his parents from a fellow warrior jealous of his athletic prowess, the protagonist of 'Immram' faces an equally shocking revelation from a "billiard player" who, it soon transpires, exhibits twentieth-century vestiges of warriordom: he is "Dressed to kill, or inflict a wound".

Muldoon's use of his source in 'Immram' goes back to his interest in the "mischievous, sly, multi-layered" quality of Frost's poetry.[19] While charting the surreal adventures of a credulous billiard-player who determines to find out more about his father, 'Immram' surreptitiously plays a whimsical variation on an archetypal myth of self-discovery. At the same time, Muldoon rings quirky and individualistic changes on the pre-ordained source, thereby introducing limited free will into his fatalistic model. However, the characters in 'Immram' possess no individual volition. As Muldoon has commented in interview,

> The quest is the powerful and important centre of ['Immram']. Both the protagonist and his father are led through a maze. The protagonist is a cipher, the world envelops him, everything happens to him; he directs very little, and I'm very sceptical about how much we direct anything that happens to us.[20]

The protagonist of 'Immram' shares with other characters in *Why Brownlee Left* an absolute subservience before destiny. Whereas Mael Duin actively sets out to avenge his father's death, the present-day "cipher" struggles just to stay alive and atone for his father's actions; like 'Cuba' and 'Anseo', 'Immram' shows the sins of the fathers visited on sons and daughters alike. At least Mael Duin's journey is granted metaphysical significance, by means of the Christian hermit who instructs him to renounce vengeance. Muldoon's protagonist, by contrast, must placate a decaying Howard Hughes character who holds the son responsible for the father's bungling as a drugs mule, and who finally grants an arbitrary absolution: "'I forgive you,' he croaked. 'And I forget'". Similarly, while the hermit is brought ale, salmon and bread each day by an otter, the Hughes-figure is more banal, sending out his bodyguards for "Baskin-Robbins banana-nut ice-cream". Although the voyage of the legendary Mael Duin is governed by supernatural winds, the hero does at times exhibit individual volition; he refuses to eat or drink, for example, until told the identity of his father. This abstention constitutes an assertion of will which has no place in the world of *Why Brownlee Left*, and accordingly it is rewritten with a ruthless twist:

> My mother had just been fed by force,
> A pint of lukewarm water through a rubber hose.
> I hadn't seen her in six months or a year,
> Not since my father had disappeared.
> Now she'd taken an overdose
> Of alcohol and barbiturates,
> And this, I learned, was her third.
> I was told then by a male nurse
> That if I came back at the end of the week
> She might be able to bring herself to speak.

The mother's repeated attempts at suicide seek to impose control over her destiny. Not only do these attempts fail, but they only generate further paralysis: the inability even to speak.

It is entirely appropriate to the fatalistic logic of *Why Brownlee Left* that 'Immram' should be — in Muldoon's own term — "a version" of an earlier work.[21] Despite contemporary settings and idioms, many episodes in 'Immram' are compelled and shaped by the poem's source; and the fates of characters have already, in a sense, been mapped. By contrast, Muldoon's partial fidelity to his source is actually liberating, as are his technical debts, announced in

'Making the Move', to "bad Lord Byron" and Raymond Chandler. The ten-line stanza of 'Immram' — and in particular the often bathetic tone of the final couplet — has its roots in the eight-line Byronic stanza (*abababcc*); when Muldoon praises Byron for "relishing the rhyme on 'Aristotle' and 'bottle'",[22] he tacitly announces the poetic sanction for his own green / Skibbereen and other outlandish rhymes. 'Immram' also shares narratorial tricks with Byron. The narrative thread is frequently abandoned in favour of lengthy digressions, and doubts over the trustworthiness of Muldoon's protagonist are aroused rather than allayed by his assurances: "I am telling this exactly as it happened". The plot of 'Immram' — insofar as it can be said to have a plot — is as flimsy as that of *Don Juan*. But this lackadaisical attitude to plot has as much in common with the other major influence on 'Immram', Raymond Chandler: as Muldoon admiringly recalls, "Chandler said that when he was stuck, he'd have another body fall out of the cupboard".[23] Muldoon commemorates his discovery of Chandler's work in the title poem of his 1975 pamphlet *Spirit of Dawn*, the romantic overtones of which are deliberately misleading. The poem's epigraph, from Chandler's *Farewell, My Lovely*, quotes Philip Marlowe's observation of "a piece of black shiny metal on a stand": "'An interesting bit,' [Marriott] said negligently ... 'Asta Dial's *Spirit of Dawn*.' 'I thought it was Klopstein's *Two Warts on a Fanny*,' I said." Having grown up with more conventional reading matter, Muldoon registers his surprise at such material:

> It comes as something of a shock
> After *Classics Illustrated* and G.K. Chesterton
> To learn, in the space of one afternoon,
> That shoulder-holsters might be worn by the dicks
> Who would bring Art down to the level of Sex.[24]

It is clear even from this opening stanza why the title poem, alone in *Spirit of Dawn*, does not find its way into *Mules*; it is a lighthearted, occasional piece, dangerously close to doggerel. The poem's significance rests in its celebration of Chandler as a kindred spirit, who (in this account) frees Muldoon from the narrow decencies of his upbringing.

Paradoxically, the Chandler pastiche of 'Immram' allows free rein to Muldoon's own creativity. At times the poem delights in pure ventriloquism — "The age of chivalry how are you?", "I shimmied about the cavernous lobby" — but more often the idiom serves almost as a pretext for exploring the dark fixations of Muldoon's poetic world. 'Spirit of Dawn' hails Chandler's fusion of art, sex and violence, and although the protagonist of 'Immram' inhabits the same terrain as Philip Marlowe, he pushes these obsessions to new extremes. After he is "hit by a hypodermic syringe", his hallucinations go beyond anything that might be found in Chandler's fiction:

> There was one who can only have been asleep
> Among row upon row of sheeted cadavers
> In what might have been the Morgue
> Of all the cities in America,
> Who beckoned me towards her slab
> And silently drew back the covers
> On the vermilion omega
> Where she had been repeatedly stabbed,
> Whom I would carry over the threshold of pain
> That she might come and come and come again.

This represents an horrific addition to Muldoon's persistent yoking of sex and violence. Repeated orgasms are also spoof resurrections; stab wounds and female genitalia seem confused by the blurring, highbrow diction of a "vermilion omega"; and ecstasy is achieved only via "the threshold of pain". This passage epitomises the poem's complete absence of human warmth. The other reference to sex describes "Susan, or Susannah" "lay[ing] herself open" to a "select band of admirers" before "two men and a dog" begin "mowing her meadow". Elsewhere the protagonist is attacked with a billiard cue, almost crushed between two cars, and drugged and thrown into "a steaming pile of trash", before he is finally granted absolution by the reclusive figure who, from the "nineteenth floor" of the Park Hotel, controls all these wild and wonderful events:

> He was huddled on an old orthopaedic mattress,
> The makings of a skeleton,
> Naked but for a pair of draw-string shorts.
> His hair was waistlength, as was his beard.
> He was covered in bedsores.
> He raised one talon.
> 'I forgive you,' he croaked. 'And I forget.'

The old hermit of 'Immram Mael Duin' is also naked and hairy. However, Muldoon's creation is based largely on Howard Hughes in the last years of his life (information chiefly drawn from *Howard Hughes: The Hidden Years*, as 'Making the Move' implies), even down to Hughes's penchant for banana-nut ice-cream. He is a fitting god for the world of 'Immram' — arbitrary, banal, grotesque, and, in common with much of *Why Brownlee Left*, determined to visit the sins of the fathers (incompetence as a drugs mule) upon unsuspecting sons.

'Immram' is unrepeatable: as Muldoon has admitted, "that isn't my language; it's so far removed from my rhythms of speech".[25] However, the distance frees Muldoon to take greater risks, both in technique and — as the Morgue stanza incontrovertibly proves — in subject matter too. One of the technical preoccupations pushed to new extremes in 'Immram', for example, is renovation of cliché. Reflecting the influence of its croaking deity, the currency in 'Immram' is cocaine:

> Everyone taking a cut, dividing and conquering
> With lactose and dextrose,
> Everyone getting up everyone else's nose.

This passage intricately reworks several clichés: "taking a cut" refers as much to cutting drugs as to finance; "dividing and conquering" puns on "conk"; and "Everyone getting up everyone else's nose" alludes to cocaine snorting. Such details come easily throughout 'Immram'; the poem allows Muldoon to play on "slam"/ "salami"/ "Salome", to rhyme "Harlem" with "alarm", and to announce that Suzanne would never "pass out of fashion / So long as there's an 'if' in California". 'Immram' is, finally, a virtuoso performance, sharing thematic concerns with the lyrics in *Why Brownlee Left*, while offering a form large enough to accommodate the outrages of Muldoon's imagination.

Notes

1. Muldoon, P. 'Paul Muldoon writes ...', *The Poetry Book Society Bulletin* 106, Autumn 1980, 1.
2. Longley, E. 'Varieties of Parable: Louis MacNeice and Paul Muldoon', *Poetry in the Wars* (Newcastle-upon-Tyne: Bloodaxe, 1986), 223.
3. 'Paul Muldoon', interviewed by John Haffenden, *Viewpoints* (London: Faber, 1981), 140.
4. *ibid.*, 141.
5. O'Donoghue, B. *Seamus Heaney and the Language of Poetry* (London: Harvester Wheatsheaf, 1994), 33.

6. 'A Conversation with Paul Muldoon', interviewed by Michael Donaghy, *Chicago Review* 35 (1), Autumn 1985, 78.
7. Interviewed by John Haffenden, 140.
8. Longley, E. 'The Room Where MacNeice Wrote "Snow"', *The Living Stream: Literature &Revisionism in Ireland* (Newcastle-upon-Tyne: Bloodaxe, 1994), 259-260.
9. Interviewed by John Haffenden, 138.
10. *Ted Hughes and Paul Muldoon* (London: Faber Poetry Cassette, 1982).
11. Muldoon, P. *Names and Addresses* (Belfast: Ulsterman Publications, 1978), 3.
12. Interviewed by John Haffenden, p. 138.
13. Muldoon's introduction to the *Faber Book of Contemporary Irish Poetry* consists of an exchange between Louis MacNeice and F.R. Higgins. Higgins tells MacNeice that "you, as an Irishman, cannot escape from your blood, nor from our blood-music that brings our racial character to mind". MacNeice (and tacitly Muldoon) replies, "I am so little used to thinking of poetry in terms of race-consciousness that no doubt this was very good for me. However, I am still unconverted. I think one may have such a thing as one's racial blood-music, but that, like one's unconscious, it may be left to take care of itself." *The Faber Book of Contemporary Irish Poetry* (London: Faber, 1986), 18.
14. This connection is also made by Edna Longley in 'Varieties of Parable: Louis MacNeice and Paul Muldoon', *Poetry in the Wars,* 238. Longley's essay is, besides much else, an essential guide to allusion in 'Immram'.
15. Brown, R. 'Bog Poems and Book Poems: Doubleness, Self-Translation and Pun in Seamus Heaney and Paul Muldoon', *The Chosen Ground: Essays on the Contemporary Poetry of Northern Ireland*, ed. Corcoran, N. (Bridgend: Seren, 1992), 167.
16. Eliot, T.S. 'Ulysses, Order, and Myth' (1923), *Selected Prose of T.S. Eliot*, ed. Kermode F. (London: Faber, 1975), 177-178.
17. Interviewed by John Haffenden, 139.
18. *ibid.*, 139.
19. *ibid.*, 134.
20. *ibid.*, 140.
21. *ibid.*, 139.
22. Muldoon, P. 'Introduction', *The Essential Byron* (New York: Ecco Press, 1989), 5.
23. Interviewed by Michael Donaghy, 80.
24. Muldoon, P. *Spirit of Dawn* (Belfast: Ulsterman Publications, 1975), 5.
25. Interviewed by Michael Donaghy, 79.

A Moral For Our Times: *Quoof*

Since 1969 Northern Irish poets have expended disproportionate energy explaining why they have not been writing exclusively about the Troubles. The title of Seamus Heaney's collection of essays *The Government of the Tongue* (1988), for example, questions whether poetry should become subservient to civil life, act as a positive agent for social change, or be left to choose its own agenda. In the volume's introductory essay, 'The Interesting Case of Nero, Chekhov's Cognac, and a Knocker', Heaney re-examines a dilemma he and the singer David Hammond had faced in 1972, as they drove to a recording studio in Belfast to make a tape of poems and songs: the plan was abandoned when several bombs exploded in the city and "the very notion of beginning to sing at that moment when others were beginning to suffer seemed like an offence against their suffering".[1] In retrospect Heaney wonders whether "the joyful affirmation of poetry and music" can ever "constitute an affront to life", and implies that he and Hammond perhaps should have continued with their recording. But most surprising about Heaney's essay is the moral he draws from this account:

> Both Art and Life have had a hand in the formation of any poet, and both are to be loved, honoured and obeyed. Yet both are often perceived to be in conflict and that conflict is constantly and sympathetically suffered by the poet. He or she begins to feel that a choice between the two, a once-and-for-all option, would simplify things. Deep down, of course, there is the sure awareness that no such simple solution or dissolution is possible, but the waking mind desires constantly some clarified allegiance, without complication or ambivalence ... Perhaps Art and Life sound a little distant, so let us put it more melodramatically and call them Song and Suffering.

This sounds grandiose, even if Heaney does seem to recognize the speciousness of his argument: "no such simple solution or dissolution is possible"; "let us put it more melodramatically". The adjustment from one set of capitalized entities to another — from Art and Life to Song and Suffering — introduces a still more curious dichotomy, as if "Song" can never incorporate Heaney's bleak substitute for "Life": "Suffering". These simplifications point to something slightly fallacious in *The Government of the Tongue*: the conflicts and tensions which Heaney finds in the work of other writers provide the impetus for essays whose very writing blurs those abstract distinctions of Art and Life, Song and Suffering, around which the book revolves.

That a poet (and critic) of Heaney's extraordinary genius should be tempted by such reductions indicates the difficulties facing Northern Irish poets. As Paul Muldoon has complained, "the trouble with this place is that if you don't engage in it, you're an ostrich (whatever 'engage in it' means). If you do engage in it ... you're on the make, almost, cashing in".[2] Although Muldoon has always been considered more ostrich than opportunist, his early volumes evade both categories through their oblique, often parabolic approach to civil violence. *Quoof*, however, manages to meet the Troubles full-on, without "cashing in". Distinctions between Song and Suffering become meaningless; a poet writing about "what is immediately in front of me, or immediately over my shoulder" in Belfast during the hunger-strikes must incorporate assassinations, dirty protests, gun-running, car bombs, terrorist reprisals into his work. Heaney's sacrifice of his art in earshot of bomb-blasts might appear decent and responsible, but 'A Trifle' from *Quoof* makes this seem nothing more than the self-regard of a dilettante:

> I had been meaning to work through lunch
> the day before yesterday.
> Our office block is the tallest in Belfast;
> when the Tannoy sounds
>
> another bomb alert
> we take four or five minutes to run down
> the thirty-odd flights of steps
> to street level.
>
> I had been trying to get past
> a woman who held, at arm's length, a tray,
> and on the tray the remains of her dessert —
>
> a plate of blue-pink trifle
> or jelly sponge,
> with a dollop of whipped cream on top.

When a bomb explodes in Belfast, Heaney worries whether he ought to abandon his recording; some years later he writes an essay about his decision, and the anecdote leads into a lofty discussion of Art and Life. As its title suggests, 'A Trifle' is less self-important. Muldoon presents himself as an aesthete, contemplating a trifle (with its obvious double meaning) even while his office block is hurriedly evacuated. Yet this is merely *"another* bomb alert" (my italics) — implicitly a commonplace in inner-city Belfast, inconvenient for those trying to work through lunch or to finish their trifle. It takes "four or five minutes" to run down "the thirty-odd flights of steps"; the approximations suggest a routine mindless and monotonous, enlivened this time only by the wonderful absurdity of the "blue-pink" and vaguely mammary dessert. Muldoon's trifling, unrhymed sonnet captures the extent of the real "Suffering" in Belfast, where a bomb alert is itself no more than another trifle: paradoxically, only a dilettante would labour the event. The poem suggests that those who go about their everyday lives amidst the ever-present threat of violence cannot afford the indulgence of Heaney's artful scruples.

It is a characteristic irony that Muldoon's responsible stance should be conveyed by a poem called 'A Trifle', the weightiest of light verses. Reviewing *Quoof*, Peter Porter labelled Muldoon the "slickest stylist" of a group of Ulster poets who "have more urgent matters to write about than most" but still "opt for style before message"; however, the impact of 'A Trifle', like much of *Quoof*, is to render such distinctions obsolete. In a determinedly imperceptive review for the *Irish Press*, Roy McFadden mistook Muldoon's panache for primness and caution, and detected the poet "shelter[ing] behind the laconic phrase and unathletic sentence". Other critics in Britain, Ireland and the U.S.A. lauded the volume. Like *Why Brownlee Left*, *Quoof* was made the Choice of the Poetry Book Society; and John Kerrigan's influential review in the *London Review of Books* implicitly declared Muldoon the most gifted exemplar of a new narrative school of poetry. *Quoof* is in fact Muldoon's inescapable book. Whatever the more modest successes of earlier work, those technical accomplishments are now pushed to new limits; the volume outstrips anything Muldoon had even attempted before. What Neil Corcoran has termed "the disease of Northern Ireland" contaminates even the trifles of *Quoof*: the volume's dominant images are of entrapment and mutilation. Such images are intricately linked to an obsession with mushrooms and hallucinogens: 'The More a Man Has the More a Man Wants' mentions a vital etymology — "hash, hashish, *lo perfido assassin*". And the opening poem, 'Gathering Mushrooms', punningly refers to "the pair of us / tripping through Barnett's fair demesne", before this idyllic jaunt culminates in a vision which submerges human values under the harrowingly bestial world of H-blocks and dirty protests. 'Gathering

A Moral For Our Times: *Quoof*

Mushrooms' augurs a volume whose "trips" pass wide-eyed through the nightmare phantasmagoria of contemporary Ulster.

Where earlier volumes had offered parables about mermen and boundary commissions, *Quoof* provides the nitty-gritty of events and details in Irish history: Malone House is blown "sky-high"; the poet's Uncle Pat recalls the B-Specials' casual intimidation of Catholics; a mink discovers the grave of Robert Nairac, an "undercover liaison officer" tortured and killed by the I.R.A.; a hunger-striker is hooked up to a kidney machine in Belfast's Royal Victoria Hospital; U.D.R. patrols and snatch-squads of Paratroopers hunt for terrorists armed with Kalashnikovs and unstable gelignite. These references provide recognizable features in an otherwise incomprehensible world of brutality, obscured motives and confused allegiances. But *Quoof* is still more often concerned with unofficial accounts, stories which never make the bulletins and authorized versions. 'The Frog', for example, specifically recalls the Act of Union signed in Trinity College in 1800; however, the poem's secret history alludes to an explanation by Gerald of Wales (c. 1146-1223) that frogs are alien to Ireland and therefore a harbinger of "the coming of the English, and the imminent conquest and defeat of [the Irish] people".[3] In Muldoon's poem, the frog

> Comes to mind as another small upheaval
> amongst the rubble.
> His eye matches exactly the bubble
> in my spirit-level.
> I set aside hammer and chisel
> and take him on the trowel.
>
> The entire population of Ireland
> springs from a pair left to stand
> overnight in a pond
> in the gardens of Trinity College,
> two bottles of wine left there to chill
> after the Act of Union.
>
> There is, surely, in this story
> a moral. A moral for our times.
> What if I put him to my head
> and squeezed it out of him,
> like the juice of freshly squeezed limes,
> or a lemon sorbet.

This is a tiny masterpiece, offering a powerful but skewed alternative history. That Muldoon has read Gerald of Wales — the most entertainingly wayward of historians — is beyond question: the next volume, *Meeting the British*, mentions him in 'Brock' and, as Giraldus Cambrensis, in 'My Grandfather's Wake'. It is in keeping with Gerald's speculations about frogs that the "entire population of Ireland" should originate in — or, appropriately, "spring from" — a Trinity College pond during negotiations for union between Britain and Ireland. The frog's (and the poem's) present-day existence as "another small upheaval / amongst the rubble" emphasises the continued colonizing presence even while "the rubble" hints at some of the more disastrous by-products of the Act. The frog is an unnatural portent, the product of a coition as freakish as the political union taking place inside the college, having been born not out of other frogs but, helped by light-footed syntax, from "two bottles of wine left there to chill / after the Act of Union". Apparently rebuilding after a bomb-blast, the speaker connects the frog to its weird origins even in the first stanza when he notes that the frog's eye "matches exactly the bubble / in my spirit-level", stressing liquidity with just a dash of alcohol: spirit-level. But although the frog's presence indicts the English in the destruction, the speaker ultimately overstates his case. Given *Quoof*'s interest in hallucinogens and in native Americans, it is no coincidence that certain species of toad can be squeezed to produce a bubble of venom behind their eyes, which when dried and smoked — once common among several native tribes — causes hallucinations. Squeezing a frog, of course, will kill it. The wine of the second stanza has now been replaced, as the speaker, keen to draw an Aesop-like "moral for our times", interprets the history of colonization as violent and hallucinatory. The frog's presence indicts the British; perhaps the speaker wonders whether killing the frog will remove them.

Quoof is preoccupied with questions of taste: the lime juice or lemon sorbet of a crushed frog, or the trifle and whipped cream enjoyed even during bomb alerts. In '*from* Last Poems' a womb is removed and "lies in its own glar / like the last beetroot in the pickle jar", provoking the speaker to imagine having it "without relish, my own lightly broiled / heart on the side"; people in 'Trance' take turns drinking "mind-expanding urine"; 'Yggdrasill' juxtaposes the "glib cairn" left by a pony with the opening of "a can of apricots". These examples constitute acts of violence on the taste-buds and, by mock association, on good taste in general. *Quoof* consistently sets out to assault received notions of decorum and decency with the unpalatable truth: Muldoon employs modern-day realities to crush all

A Moral For Our Times: *Quoof*

forms of sentimentality and idealization. 'Aisling', for example, rewrites the Gaelic *aisling* sub-genre, which in earlier centuries had become the forum for surreptitious attacks on the colonizing English. The word "aisling" means dream or vision; during the poet's vision the unearthly woman Cathleen ni Houlihan, a personification of Ireland, would appear, and as both mother and lover, would demand that her men rise up and free her from suffering. Muldoon's vision is rather less deceived. The poem's protagonist, "making [his] way home late one night", staggers into a snow drift even though it is summer: the seasonal disturbance reflects times out of joint, an upheaval in the natural order. There he comes across an alluring woman, her eyes speaking of "a sloe-year", and her mouth "a year of haws". He begins a standard *aisling* formula for identifying his "goddess", before slipping into less conventional, more contemporary possibilities:

> Was she Aurora, or the goddess Flora,
> Artemidora, or Venus bright,
> or Anorexia, who left
> a lemon stain on my flannel sheet?
>
> It's all much of a muchness.
>
> In Belfast's Royal Victoria Hospital
> a kidney machine
> supports the latest hunger-striker
> to have called off his fast, a saline
> drip into his bag of brine.
>
> A lick and a promise. Cuckoo spittle.
> I hand my sample to Doctor Maw.
> She gives me back a confident *All Clear*.

Exaggerating the undercurrent of sexual enticement often found in the traditional *aisling* genre, Muldoon's protagonist has casual sex with the Cathleen figure, and remains indifferent to her real identity: "It's all much of a muchness". The lemon juice of 'The Frog' here returns as a "lemon stain", a discharge symptomatic of venereal disorder. After this brief dalliance the protagonist attends the hospital for a check-up (and provides a sample which, oddly, sounds more like sperm than urine), before being given the "*All Clear*" by a Doctor Maw who, despite the sinister undertones of her name, benignly replaces the voracious Cathleen ("all clear" is also an announcement of safety after bomb alerts). By contrast the hunger-striker's more committed relationship with the captivating Cathleen-Anorexia results in near self-destruction. Having called off his fast he is taken to the Royal Victoria Hospital: Victoria is implicitly the colonizing counterpart to Cathleen. After finally betraying the fanatical commands of his republican vision, the anorexic hunger-striker will be nursed back to health in what is — nominally at least — enemy territory.

As poems like 'The Frog' and 'Aisling' suggest, one of Muldoon's greatest achievements in *Quoof* is to have developed a style capable of conveying the Troubles in all their farcical tragi-comedy, as well as their undoubted horror. Something of this stylistic range is exhibited by Muldoon's expressed intention to purge himself of a public vocabulary employed by "the kennings of the hourly news bulletins".[4] The language of 'The More a Man Has the More a Man Wants', in particular, emphasises the inadequacy of such vocabulary. The narrative is dotted with official catchphrases: "legally held shotgun", "single high-velocity shot", "exit wound". Muldoon shows how this jargon is oddly collusive, insofar as it starts by describing, but soon comes to mask, obscenity. In 'The More a Man Has' these phrases are renovated like clichés: "You could, if you like, put your fist / in the exit wound / in his chest"; that throwaway "if you like" transforms a sensational description into a physical possibility, almost an invitation. The poem elsewhere portrays the aftermath of a car-bomb with cold-blooded, almost comic precision:

> Once they collect his smithereens
> he doesn't quite add up.
> They're shy of a foot, and a calf
> which stems
> from his left shoe like a severely
> pruned-back shrub.

Bizarrely, Clair Wills has argued that even here Muldoon is repeating the "dead official language of the media",[5] but it would be an odd report indeed which conveyed information about the success (or, in this case, failure) of the effort to collect together the victim's "smithereens". Wills is much more perceptive when suggesting that Muldoon deliberately raises issues of linguistic decency. To say that the description is tasteless is to beg the question of whether, in such circumstances, good taste is possible or even desirable. Muldoon employs cliché to grotesque effect: the local councillor's parts "add up" to less than the whole; the phrase "shy of a foot" sounds ridiculously coy; and the verb "stems" leads naturally, in fact organically, to the "severely / pruned-back shrub". While Heaney withdraws from atrocity into the abstract decencies of Art and Life, 'The More a Man Has' derives its horrific power from a dispassionate voyeurism which records the mundane, the magical and the obscene alike.

The councillor's fate foreshadows the explosive finale of 'The More a Man Has', but also picks up on other mutilations in *Quoof*. Throughout the volume the body is a fragile, even precarious device, scarred by cigarette burns ('Yggdrasill') or a pistol pressed hard against the victim's flesh ('The Sightseers'). More extremely, 'Blewits' describes a woman lying "on the bed / of her own entrails" — a gruesome distortion of the self-inwoven simile; and 'The Hands', "after the German of Erich Arendt", tells of a farmer whose hands are cut off by the Guardia Civil. The title of 'The Right Arm' seems to promise something similar — the mangled left-overs of some mutilation or explosion; in fact it employs a technique first seen in the early poem 'February', where the cliché of "wearing her heart on her sleeve" comes to suggest mutilation. 'The Right Arm' recalls Muldoon's childhood home in Eglish, and the shop run by his father. The boy plunges his arm into the sweet-jar for the last piece of clove rock. Pondering this apparently innocuous childhood memory, the adult narrator continues,

> I would give my right arm to have known then
> how Eglish was itself wedged between
> *ecclesia* and *église*.
>
> The Eglish sky was its own stained-glass vault
> and my right arm was sleeved in glass
> that has yet to shatter.

Muldoon specifies that the "right arm" is "sleeved in glass" to renew the cliché of "giv[ing] my right arm"; the phrase almost evokes a snared animal, gnawing off a limb. The poem is about entrapment: Eglish, from the Irish for "church", is jammed — etymologically rather than alphabetically — between two foreign words also meaning "church", so that its character is rigidly fixed by its name. Like earlier poems such as 'Clonfeacle', 'The Right Arm' is an example of the Gaelic *dinnseanchas* genre, but now the place-name's equation with its roots ensures only confinement. Even the clove-rock exudes religious significance, by echoing the hymn "Rock of Ages, cleave to me". The poem's final stanza, presenting an image of further entrapment within an already constrictive church-like vault, depicts the child lured by nothing more than a few treats, and the adult, once the trap has been sprung, still unable to escape his religious upbringing.

'The Right Arm' is a lament for lost innocence. But while in *Mules*, poems like 'The Merman' and 'Duffy's Circus' had demanded the cognitive leaps of an adult perception ("I watched a man sawing a woman in half"), 'The Right Arm' epitomizes Muldoon's developing ability to combine songs of innocence and experience in a single vision. For example *Quoof*'s opening poem, 'Gathering Mushrooms', begins with the poet's childhood memories of his father's mushroom shed, and of a tablecloth left sodden on the washing-line. This scene is recalled during a September evening "fifteen years on", as the poet and his unidentified companion go "tripping" — in more ways than one — through "Barnett's fair demesne", "thinking only of psilocybin". They pass the poet's father, who constitutes the one symbol of continuity, representing an unchanging dedication to the soil: fifteen years on, he still wears the "same old donkey-jacket / and the sawn-off waders", picking mushrooms "till kingdom come". Meanwhile the companion suddenly hurtles "towards the ever-receding ground", into an outbuilding where he discovers the poet's *alter ego*, "though my head had grown into the head of a horse". Straight from the horse's mouth comes a demand for a fanatically committed poetry:

> *Come back to us. However cold and raw, your feet*
> *were always meant*
> *to negotiate terms with bare cement.*
> *Beyond this concrete wall is a wall of concrete*
> *and barbed wire. Your only hope*
> *is to come back. If sing you must, let your song*
> *tell of treading your own dung,*
> *let straw and dung give a spring to your step.*
> *If we never live to see the day we leap*
> *into our true domain,*
> *lie down with us now and wrap*
> *yourself in the soiled grey blanket of Irish rain*
> *that will, one day, bleach itself white.*
> *Lie down with us and wait.*

Like 'The Right Arm', this passage builds up images of entrapment: behind one concrete wall is another, this time topped with barbed wire. The inverted centaur is another addition to Muldoon's extensive equine catalogue; it prepares for the talking horses of *Madoc* and *The Prince of the Quotidian*, while also remembering Swift's humourless, self-righteous Houyhnhnms and Muldoon's own centaurs. The speaker of this final stanza makes a virtue of suffering, seeking a pledge of ever deeper allegiance to "our true domain". Loyalty to one's place is transformed into a demand for absolute subservience to the republican cause, although the joyful buoyancy promised by the phrases "a spring to your step" and "leap / into our true domain" is belied by the relentless trammelling of "song", and the dirty protests' bestial realities: excrement smeared on the walls and floors, and only a "soiled grey blanket" for covering. Muldoon's reasons for juxtaposing his childhood home with this nightmarish, drug-induced vision now become evident: calls for the poet to "come back" and represent his people offer only debased, corrupted versions of his "true domain". The "outbuilding" parallels the father's mushroom shed, but psilocybin (an hallucinatory drug present in the Liberty Cap and other mushrooms) provides entry into a world far removed from that of the poet's father: the half-horse's euphemistic "dung", obsessively smeared and trodden, echoes earlier mention of the "horse manure" used as fertilizer for commercial mushroom production; the companion runs "into the maw / of a shimmering, green-gold dragon", with this rapacious image rewriting the "Wagon after wagon" of fertilizer which had "bluster[ed] in" to the father's mushroom shed like "a self-renewing gold-black dragon"; and finally, the "soiled grey blanket of Irish rain" evokes the tablecloth hand-embroidered by the poet's mother and left "sodden" on the washing line. In each case, aspects of the poet's rural background are sullied, travestied and misappropriated by inveigling Republican appeals to "Come back to us".

The list of hallucinogens in *Quoof* is extensive, ranging from glue to psilocybin, peyote to frog "venom". Almost recapitulating Aldous Huxley's *The Doors of Perception*, Muldoon has argued that "the world is hallucinogenic";[6] *Quoof*'s original epigraph had consisted of a similar quotation from the same text, which eventually found its way instead into 'The More a Man Has the More a Man Wants' ("I saw no mountains ..."). And in 'Gathering Mushrooms', mention of "the wood-pigeon's concerto for oboe and strings, / allegro, blowing your mind" subtly acknowledges one of *Quoof*'s more disreputable drug-related sources: *The Sacred Mushroom and the Cross*, by John Allegro, argues that the first Christians were, in Muldoon's own words, a group of "mushroom-eating hippies",[7] and that the Bible is a coded textbook for mushroom worship. However, the tone of 'Gathering Mushrooms', and of *Quoof* as a whole, shares less in common with this or with *The Doors of Perception* than with Huxley's companion volume, *Heaven and Hell*: as Huxley suggests, "visionary experience is not always blissful. It is sometimes terrible. There is hell as well as heaven".[8] Hallucinogens in *Quoof* usually access a world which is brutal and grotesque. Even references to non-hallucinogenic mushrooms are charged with horror: the deadly poisonous Destroying Angel is transformed into a woman at a literary party; and 'Blewits', a poem named after a harmless edible mushroom, describes a woman sexually mutilated "by blewits, or by chanterelles" (the chanterelle being, of course, another kind of edible mushroom). Only in 'Trance' does a drug-induced vision seem anything other than disgusting: like 'Gathering Mushrooms', the poem juxtaposes innocence and experience, merging Muldoon's earliest memory — of Christmas Eve, 1954 — with hallucinations provoked by the Fly Agaric mushroom and by "mind-expanding urine". In the first of three seven-line stanzas the poet's mother opens the scullery door to empty the tea-pot, and in the third she "slams the door / on her star-cluster of dregs". The hallucinatory middle stanza occurs in the moments between these actions:

> A wind out of Siberia
> carries such voices as will carry
> through to the kitchen —
>
> Someone mutters a flame from lichen
> and eats the red-and-white Fly Agaric
> while the others hunker in the dark,
> taking it in turn
> to drink his mind-expanding urine.
> One by one their reindeer
> nuzzle in.

Muldoon's verbs are unusual, but exact: "mutters", "hunker", "nuzzle". The poem's weird vision becomes less strange if the voices have been carried all the way from Siberia. Although the Fly Agaric is deadly poisonous in large quantities, the dried caps were once eaten as an intoxicant in some areas of Lapland and Siberia. (Fly Agaric is thought to be "soma", the mushroom of divine strength and immortality; this provides another, slightly more tangential, connection between Muldoon and Huxley, whose "soma" is the "perfect drug" of *Brave New World*.) Father Christmas therefore links the poet's childhood home with the hallucinogens of Siberia and Lapland: the mushroom's "red-and-white" is also the "red-and-white" of Santa briefly glimpsed disappearing up the chimney. Given Muldoon's evident predilection for all things equine, Santa's gift could hardly be more wonderful: a "new rocking-horse / as yet unsteady on its legs".

'Trance' compares, even substitutes, the magic of a young child's Christmas fantasies with the adults' drug-illuminated world. This ability to encompass the rival perspectives of innocence and experience in a single vision undoubtedly constitutes Muldoon's most significant advance on the cynical lyrics of *Why Brownlee Left*; it is a technique employed again and again throughout *Quoof*. As 'Gathering Mushrooms' suggests, the poet's father often symbolizes continuity between these visions. 'Cherish the Ladies', for example, announces itself as "my last poem about my father", where, as Edna Longley has pointed out, "last" could mean either latest or final.[9] The father is portrayed filling the cattle's drinking trough, but the poet suspects the reader would be better entertained by racier material:

> Such a well-worn path,
> I know, from here to the galvanized bath.
> I know too you would rather
>
> *I saw beneath the hedge to where the pride*
> *of the herd, though not an Irish*
> *bull, would cherish*
> *the ladies with his electric cattle-prod.*

After this italicized stanza, the poem returns just as suddenly to the father filling the cattle-trough. The poet briefly offers some debased hedge-school learning, a detour from the father's "well-worn path". But the father is ultimately inescapable; while the urban voyage of 'Immram' was ostensibly motivated by the desire to "find out more" about the absentee parent, in the lyrics of *Quoof* he is usually the point of departure and return. Nowhere is this more obvious than in 'The Mirror', from the Irish of Michael Davitt and subtitled "in memory of my father"; the poem implies that even after death the father never abandons the son. As the speaker struggles to re-position a "monstrous old Victorian mirror" on the wall, he imagines his father breathing through it: "*I'll give you a hand, here*". The father holds the mirror steady while the son drives home the nails.

Perhaps the best-known example of the father's continuing influence, and his ability to bridge phases of innocence and experience in the poet's life, comes in the title poem, 'Quoof'. Muldoon explains in his introduction to the volume for the Poetry Book Society that he had wondered for a long time about the etymology of "quoof", presuming it was one of his father's words. His father, however, claimed that "he first heard it from us, his children".[10] 'Quoof' therefore becomes an enigma, a word without a source; it is apparently a familial nonce-word. But as the poem immediately makes clear, there is no question about its meaning:

> How often have I carried our family word
> for the hot water bottle
> to a strange bed,
> as my father would juggle a red-hot half-brick
> in an old sock
> to his childhood settle.
> I have taken it into so many lovely heads
> or laid it between us like a sword.
>
> An hotel room in New York City
> with a girl who spoke hardly any English,
> my hand on her breast
> like the smouldering one-off spoor of the yeti
> or some other shy beast
> that has yet to enter the language.

This is archetypal Muldoon: an irregular sonnet, half-rhymed throughout, but aided by the subtlest of assonantal echoes — the sestet, for example, offers city, hardly, any, my, yeti, shy, yet to. And as John Kerrigan notes in the *London Review of Books*, the poem is "a little breathless, like [Muldoon's] voice on the Faber tape" (Muldoon's reading style is so extraordinary that it almost warrants a chapter in itself). Syntax is also exploited: the poem opens with what sounds like a question, or even a rhetorical brag about sexual adventure; and the final stanza lacks an active verb in the main clause, with the frozen tableau emphasising the absence of human interaction. In terms of the volume's thematic strategies, 'Quoof' represents *in extremis* the juxtaposition of childhood innocence and cosmopolitan sophistication. Clair Wills has stated that the poem signals "above all the desire to create in poetry a private, intransitive world, to experience the world of poetry as a paradise, an Eden, untainted by the corruption of the real".[11] However, this is to miss the point about Muldoon's "family word", which does at times act as a barrier between potential lovers, but can also be taken into "lovely heads". Despite Wills's argument, innocence and experience are not kept as discrete entities: "quoof" is a "shibboleth" (Muldoon's own description),[12] and like all shibboleths it incorporates as well as excludes. The word selects sexual partners willing to enter the poet's inner world, while barring those — like the girl who speaks "hardly any English" — who will not or cannot.

Reference in 'Quoof' to the yeti prepares for the title of the following poem: 'Big Foot'. One aspect of Muldoon's achievement usually neglected by critics is his genius as an 'animal' poet. The yeti and Big Foot join a mythical bestiary — inhabiting the gap, often exploited by Muldoon, between the real and the imaginary — which already includes centaurs and mermen, and to which *Quoof* also adds a unicorn; 'My Grandfather's Wake' from *Meeting the British* offers a "man-ox" and a "fish with three gold teeth", as well as "a nine-banded armadillo" — not mythical, but given its location, perhaps almost as peculiar — "found wandering in Meath / sometime in the 1860s". As even the most cursory examination of poem titles indicates, the animal kingdom provides Muldoon's most common subject matter, and most frequently exploited store of metaphors and images: 'Thrush', 'Thinking of the Goldfish', 'The Radio Horse', 'Behold the Lamb', 'Hedgehog' (*New Weather*); 'Mules' (*Mules*); 'Beaver', 'The Salmon of Knowledge', 'Mink', 'The Frog' (*Quoof*); 'Wolves', 'Bears', 'Pandas', 'The Ox' (*The Wishbone*); 'The Coney', 'Chinook', 'Brock', 'The Fox' (*Meeting the British*); 'Capercaillies', 'The Panther' (*Madoc — A Mystery*); 'Oscar' — the name of Muldoon's dog — and 'Cows' (*The Annals of Chile*).[13] Even leaving aside the ubiquitous horses, this list still fails to do justice to the all-pervasiveness of animal imagery in Muldoon's work. But as the centaurs, man-oxen and mermen might indicate, Muldoon is most interested in the anthropomorphic potential of the animal world, the possible transformations from human to bestial and vice versa. Animal imagery is as crucial to 'The More a Man Has the More a Man Wants', for example, as water imagery had been to 'Immram'; while following the adventures of a terrorist on the run, the poem emphasises how human values are replaced by brute instinct. Elsewhere in *Quoof* animal metaphors are employed to continue the sexual quest augured by the title poem. The title of 'Beaver' plays on some well-known slang concerning the bestial nature of female genitalia: as John Allegro records in *The Sacred Mushroom and the Cross*, Pliny observed that if the beaver "gets hold of part of a man's body it does not release its bite before the fractured bones are heard grinding together", to which Allegro coyly adds that this belief "has originated from a piece of earthly humour concerning the female organ".[14] In Muldoon's poem the addressee is instructed to "Let [himself] in by the leaf-yellow door" and step over the various women ("as you would across a beaver dam") who block his way to the stairs, until he reaches his "new room with its leaf-yellow floor". This insistence on "leaf-yellow" signifies a constant, and apparently arbitrary, sexual imperative which ignores the "flour-bag white" and "turkey-red" of other women littering the way to the spawning ground. The journey from the "leaf-yellow door" to the "leaf-yellow floor" ensures that this quest is virtually circular — and possibly foreshadows the "lemon stain" of venereal disorder in 'Aisling' — while removing the "door" which offered the possibility of escape from the cycle.

Distinctions between mankind and other animals are frequently blurred during *Quoof*'s sexual quest. In 'The Salmon of Knowledge', for example, the salmon leaves behind the "inch-to-the-mile // world of the eel" (reminiscent of Ted Hughes's pike, "A hundred feet long in their world")[15] but also, more bizarrely, leaves behind "the unquenchable oomph / of her whip, her thigh-length boot // on the other foot, / her hackled gulp of semen", before ending with mock-Keatsian uplift: "his name is writ in water". Similarly 'The Unicorn Defends Himself' switches from a Flemish tapestry on the hunt of the unicorn — which is challenged by a hunting-hound from the front and a spear tip from behind — to an analogous scene from the "Lower East Side": the unidentified addressee once "swallowed a radar-blip / of peyote" and later awoke between "two bodies, true, / one wire-haired and one smooth". In 'The Destroying Angel' women are not only deadly poisonous fungi, but also cockatoos who "perch on your left epaulette". The poem's horror is brought home by a lethal stanza break:

> Another gin and Angostura bitters
> and you are part of her dream
>
> kitchen's ceramic hob,
> the bathtub's
> ever-deepening shades of avocado,
> the various whatnots,
> the row upon row of whodunnits...

This obviously corresponds to the repulsion at domestic life most clearly evidenced in *Mules*, and spelt out by Muldoon's admission in a review from 1981 that he is prejudiced against "ordinary domestic life, the tedium of which ... is precisely what most of us

A Moral For Our Times: *Quoof*

spend most of our days trying to avoid or postpone".[16] But poems such as 'Aisling', 'Beaver', and 'The Destroying Angel', taken together, have occasionally raised questions over whether *Quoof* is a misogynistic volume.

If its treatment of women were examined in isolation, *Quoof* could perhaps be considered misogynistic. However, such a conclusion would travesty an interlocking volume which is never "a very likeable or attractive book in its themes".[17] As Muldoon admits, *Quoof* does indeed

> present some less than attractive aspects of the relationship between men and women. *Quoof* is a book which deals with violence and the underside of various aspects of the world — but to present those is not to align oneself with a particular point of view about women ... Some of those poems are about nasty moments — they're not attractive ... It's too easy to write poems that are likeable. I'm interested in disturbance and in what's upsetting.[18]

Pursuing hints from *Why Brownlee Left*, *Quoof* is more misanthropic than misogynistic; it never spares humanity, whether male or female. Undoubtedly, some of its "nasty moments" are very nasty indeed. In 'Blewits', for example, the female victim is "fist-fucked all night / by blewits, or by chanterelles, / until the morning that never comes"; by transforming men into mushrooms, the poem balances the female destroying angels elsewhere in the volume. That finicky indecision regarding the mushrooms' exact identity is apparent also in the "plate of blue-pink trifle / or jelly sponge" of 'A Trifle', and the "juice of freshly squeezed limes, / or a lemon sorbet" in 'The Frog': each case typifies *Quoof*'s dispassionate voyeurism, conveying an almost obscene concern with "trifles" amidst violence or danger.

The epigraph of *Quoof*, from Knud Rasmussen's *The Netsilik Eskimos*, prepares for a volume where both women and men are shape-changers: it tells of a "shaman" who turns herself into a man and marries her adoptive daughter; she transforms her genitals into a wooden sledge, and makes herself a penis out of a willow branch; and she makes a black-headed dog out of "a lump of snow she had used for wiping her end". The influence of shamanism on the volume is most evident in the long concluding poem, 'The More a Man Has the More a Man Wants', but in 'Glanders' a character called Larry Toal is described as the "local shaman". Compared with the epigraph's "old foster-mother" Larry is a poor relation, always telling how he "came within that of the cure for glanders /

from a Suffolkman who suddenly went west" — "glanders" being a disease affecting (inevitably) horses. Besides shamanism, the "foster-mother" also foreshadows several poems in *Quoof* where women are sexually dominant. In 'Sky-Woman', for example, the woman "hoik[s]" off her blouse and straddles the speaker "like Orion" (with the hint of another sex change). More and more he must "make do with her umlaut", as she turns her back on him "to fumble with / the true Orion's belt". Mention of the "umlaut" seems most likely a reference to anal sex, particularly given a similar hint in 'The Unicorn Defends Himself', and the request in the earlier poem 'Something of a Departure' for the woman to "take it like a man". William Wilson has even suggested that such poems set out to "masculate" women;[19] and certainly Muldoon's interest in sexual hybrids — as indicated by 'The Bearded Woman, by Ribera', for example — is carried over into *Quoof*'s epigraph. Wilson is on safer ground when noting the frequent association between women and textuality in Muldoon's poetry: the mother reads Proust ('The Mixed Marriage') or Rupert Brooke ('Ma'); she instructs her son to read Masefield's 'Cargoes' ('Profumo' from *Meeting the British*); Emily "rave[s] about Camus and the twenty-third psalm" ('The Girls in the Poolroom'); the woman in 'Whim' is first seen "poring over" Standish O'Grady's translations of the Cuchulain myth; the sky-woman offers the poem's speaker only an "umlaut" for his sexual pleasure. 'Kissing and Telling' from *Quoof* even merges this association with the volume's interest in hallucinogens: the woman reads aloud from *A Dictionary of Drugs*. Whether or not there are biographical reasons for this insistent combination of women and texts — the most obvious explanation would be Muldoon's "bookish" mother — in most cases the result is female empowerment. In 'Kissing and Telling', for example, the woman makes "wine of almost everything", including the anonymous men "she found out on the street"; male identity is eroded, as the male speaker acknowledges that "you might just as well be anyone". Despite the poem's title, kissing and telling remains only the weakest of threats: "I could name names. I could be indiscreet". Discretion, of course, means separateness as well as secrecy; however, the names which the speaker would let slip — and, in a sense, join with — are not of the woman but only of other, irrelevant males who have heard her mantra "*to promise nothing, to take nothing for granted*".

'Kissing and Telling' is one of thirteen sonnets in *Quoof* — provided, that is, a sonnet is simply defined as a fourteen-line poem; additionally, 'Gathering Mushrooms' and 'The More a Man Has' consist of sonnet-stanzas. Muldoon has argued for the sonnet being "an organic form", comparing its attraction to that of the iambic pentameter, the duration of which corresponds roughly to the period that "most of us hold our breath". The sonnet's organic quality has been attributed by Muldoon mainly to its "turn": "You establish something, then there's a slight change";[20] the appeal of such finesses supports his view that the chief function of poetry is to alter the way we look at the world.[21] Not all the sonnets in the volume exploit a turn from octet to sestet, but when they do, their most common shift is from generality to a specific instance: from "so many lovely heads" to one particular "girl who spoke hardly any English" ('Quoof'); or from the monotony of another bomb alert to the memorable "blue-pink trifle / or jelly sponge" ('A Trifle'). In '*from* Last Poems' Muldoon even alludes consciously to sonnet conventions. Not only do the numbered fragments go together to make up a sonnet, but three of them — IV, VII and XIV — relate to the sonnet's line numbers: so the poem opens with a quatrain (IV), is followed by three further lines (VII), and concludes with a section labelled XIV. However, the only sonnet in *Quoof* which really supports Muldoon's explanation of the form's popularity is 'The Sightseers':

> My father and mother, my brother and sister
> and I, with uncle Pat, our dour best-loved uncle,
> had set out that Sunday afternoon in July
> in his broken-down Ford
>
> not to visit some graveyard — one died of shingles,
> one of fever, another's knees turned to jelly —
> but the brand-new roundabout at Ballygawley,
> the first in mid-Ulster.
>
> Uncle Pat was telling us how the B-Specials
> had stopped him one night somewhere near Ballygawley
> and smashed his bicycle
>
> and made him sing the Sash and curse the Pope of Rome.
> They held a pistol so hard against his forehead
> there was still the mark of an O when he got home.

The rhyme-scheme fuses octet and sestet: for example "Ford" is finally picked up by "forehead", and "shingles" rhymes with "B-Specials" and "bicycle". However, the sonnet's turn certainly alters any perception of Ballygawley, if not of the world, as innocence gives way to experience. The octet sets up a jauntily idyllic scenario: the family crowded into an old banger one summer Sunday, specifically not to mourn the dead, but to delight in Ballygawley's new roundabout. The sestet darkens this perception, as day is replaced by night, and the roundabout's "O" becomes the "O" of a pistol pressed hard against Uncle Pat's forehead.

For all its ingenuity, in technical terms 'The Sightseers' still seems tame beside 'The More a Man Has the More a Man Wants', which is simultaneously a homage to the sonnet and an act — or series of acts — of organized violence against it. 'The More a Man Has' is a marvel, quite simply one of the greatest post-*Quartets* poems in English. Its fourteen-line stanzas conduct endless variations on the form, so much so that at times the poem almost seems like a sonnet sequence specifically designed to show off Muldoon's apparently infinite technical resources: it is no coincidence that the fifth line of the tenth stanza — "*for thou art so possessed with murd'rous hate*" — happens also to be the fifth line of Shakespeare's tenth sonnet. Muldoon can even reduce the sonnet to almost entirely monosyllabic lines: "*Just / throw / him / a / cake / of / Sunlight / soap, / let / him / wash / him- / self / ashore*". Jokes and jingles rub against metamorphoses, assassinations and explosions, while literary and pictorial allusions assist — and as often obscure — the narrative of terrorist adventure. Muldoon most admires in Byron his all-inclusiveness; the sonnet serves this function in 'The More a Man Has', accommodating the learned beside the slangy, the dignified and afflated beside the cynical and impure. And the poet's eye is as focused as ever: the adjective 'baggy-kneed', to describe a bear, is brilliantly unexpected; and elsewhere, a young girl "mumbles a primrose / Kleenex tissue / to make sure her lipstick's even". The surprise of finding such descriptions in a poem enhances the reader's delight that they should have been noticed in the first place. Just as extraordinary are the poem's verbs, many of which create the linguistic equivalent of cartoon effects: skedaddled, screeches off, hares, gobble, plonk, gnawing, lopes, noses round, hammer (up the stairs). Muldoon even consciously evokes cartoons — his baggy-kneed bear is also "animated" — the cartoon being a particularly appropriate genre for a poem, and volume, which stresses the anthropomorphic potential of animals and bestial characteristics of humans.

However, Muldoon's chief motive for the extensive animal imagery of 'The More a Man Has' is proclaimed in *Quoof*'s unprepossessing cover blurb, which darkly announces that "The last long poem is loosely based on the Trickster cycle of the Winnebago Indians"; Muldoon could be seen as merging the "mythical method" of 'Immram' with a celebration of native American culture first apparent in 'The Year of the Sloes'. In fact, Muldoon's humorous rewriting of his source soon allays any fear of bookish obscurity. The Winnebago Indian cycle recounts the adventures of Trickster, a shape-changer ostensibly created to destroy the evil spirits molesting mankind. This moral tag proves an excuse to enjoy Trickster's fantastical quest as he abandons his tribe and undertakes exploits as various as mistakenly eating his own intestines, having his huge penis whittled down by a chipmunk, changing sex at will, and almost drowning under his own diarrhoea. 'The More a Man Has' acknowledges the legend when it mentions a "Winnebago camper"; and the poem's forty-nine complete sonnet-stanzas duplicate in number the forty-nine sections of the Trickster cycle as recorded by the anthropologist Paul Radin, whose book *The Trickster: A Study in American Indian Mythology* (1956) is presumably Muldoon's main source. Following the Trickster-like terrorist Gallogly on his murderous quest, Muldoon not only exploits, but also comically distorts and even extends the exotic riches of the original. So whereas Trickster sends his detachable penis across a lake for sexual intercourse, when Gallogly's "cock rattles its sabre" he onanistically "tosses it off like a caber".

Gallogly embodies the animals with which Trickster — who at one stage believes himself to be a raccoon — is on speaking terms: he has "paws" and an "eagle eye", "squats in his own pelt", is led like a bear "by his own wet nose", "hare[s]" up the motorway, has a "bit between his teeth", "noses round" a bomb crater, gives the milkman a "playful / rabbit punch", appears as the bird-man Sweeney or a "game-bird", and his mole-like "velveteen shoulders and arms" help him dig out of a maximum-security prison. While stressing Gallogly's survival instincts, these examples, like the aquatic imagery in 'Immram', serve as constant reminders of the poem's source. More than 'Immram', 'The More a Man Has' is saturated with allusions to other texts: "as the crow flies" nods to Ted Hughes's earlier version of the Trickster myth; "North of Boston" announces the pervasive presence of Frost's poetry; and there are references to writers and artists as diverse as Heaney, the Gawain-poet, Huxley, Shakespeare, Bishop, Ovid, Hawthorne, Dante, Yeats, Picasso, Hopper, Pollock, Gertrude Stein, Lewis Carroll, and Robert Louis Stevenson. The significance of several allusions lies in Gallogly's polymorphic identity: they provide shifting disguises which assist a terrorist on the run, resourcefully adapting whatever means available to avoid capture. But with specific reference to the artists, John Kerrigan notes in his review of *Quoof* that the volume "needs no photographs — it illustrates itself". There are two poems about paintings (or prints) in *Quoof*: 'Mary Farl Powers *Pink Spotted Torso*' and 'Edward Kienholz *The State Hospital*'. 'The More a Man Has' can add "a shamrock after the school / of Pollock, Jackson Pollock"; "a woodcut / by Derricke"; a "picture by Edward Hopper / of a gas station" — which, providing the backdrop for the poem's final explosion, gives local violence what Edna Longley calls "the further context of a bleak modern nowhere";[22] and a celebrated painting by Picasso:

> Gallogly has only to part the veil
> of its stomach wall
> to get right under the skin,
> the spluttering heart
> and collapsed lung,
> of the horse in *Guernica*.
> He flees the Museum of Modern Art
> with the bit between his teeth.

Gallogly joins the long list of characters who are transformed, or half-transformed, into horses, while Muldoon also hints at connections between events in contemporary Northern Ireland and the Spanish Civil War; Picasso's *Guernica* takes its immediate inspiration from the artist's reaction to the bombing of the Spanish town.

The number of allusions in 'The More a Man Has' raises the vital question of whether Muldoon's poetry is, in John Carey's words, "tickled by its own knowingness", "packed to the gunwales with higher education". Even if commentators are also prepared to dismiss other masterpieces of twentieth-century poetry — *The Waste Land, The Cantos, The Dream Songs* — for the same reasons, most of the allusions in 'The More a Man Has', particularly those relating to Gallogly, can be defended on thematic grounds. Always camouflaged by allusion, Gallogly begins to suffer an identity crisis. Besides his animal manifestations as the bird-man Sweeney drinking from a foot-print in the mud, or the horse in *Guernica*, he actually embodies several characters simultaneously in an extended reference to Stevenson's *Treasure Island*:

> He seizes his own wrist
> as if, as if
> Blind Pew again seized Jim
> at the sign of the 'Admiral Benbow'.

> As if Jim Hawkins led Blind Pew
> to Billy Bones
> and they were all one and the same ...

This passage shadows an episode where Trickster uses only his right arm to kill a buffalo, a feast which the left then tries to steal: in the ensuing quarrel the left arm is badly damaged by the right. The self-division implicit in "seiz[ing] his own wrist" helps undermine Gallogly's terrorist obsession with tribal purity: when he is captured, his list of aliases includes Gollogly, Golightly, Ingoldsby, and English, that last name confirming the cultural mongrelism even of those most fanatically assertive of their antediluvian origins. Earlier, in a parody of Heaney's 'Broagh', Gallogly anxiously rehearses his tribal credentials:

> Gallogly lies down in the sheugh
> to munch
> through a Beauty of
> Bath. He repeats himself, *Bath*,
> under his garlic-breath.
> *Sheugh*, he says. *Sheugh*.
> He is finding that first 'sh'
> increasingly difficult to manage.
> *Sh*-leeps.

Heaney's 'Broagh' mentions "that last / *gh* the strangers found / dfffcult to manage",[23] creating a linguistic community to which Tom Paulin also refers when recalling the widespread belief during his childhood that "the *gh* sounds were impossible for anyone outside the North of Ireland to pronounce".[24] By means of a Biblical allusion, Muldoon stresses the sinister potential of such exclusivity: the Ephraimites were singled out and massacred because of their inability to pronounce "shibboleth"; instead they would say "sibboleth". In 'The More a Man Has' access to shibboleths is shown to be artificial: Gallogly becomes so concerned with his tribal identity that he imposes both "that last / *gh*" and "that first 'sh'" even on an innocuous word like "Bath". Gallogly is a republican terrorist, as well as being at least partly "English", but there is at least the suggestion that he might also be an undercover agent, relentlessly practising his accent.

Gallogly's shifting allegiances typify a poem in which even rival car hire firms, Hertz and Avis, can be switched and confused. His identity is in fact no more fluid than other characters', such as that of the American Indian, Mangas Jones, who is variously described as Apache, Mescalero, and Oglala Sioux. Female characters are equally perplexing. Muldoon has commented that

> In the aisling or 'dream-vision' which forms the middle section of the poem, Gallogly muses on his own mercenary past. He has made an abortive trip to the United States to buy arms, in the course of which he imagines himself to have killed a girl.[25]

This makes the poem's plot sound tidier than it actually is. There is no clean break between Gallogly's past and present; his musings surface intermittently, without warning and apparently without chronology. Gallogly's female victim is "Alice A." (as opposed to Alice B. Toklas), who turns out also, in one of her many manifestations, to be Lewis Carroll's mushroom-eating Alice in Wonderland. Just as Gallogly at one point instantly recovers from a near-fatal gun-wound, so Alice seems to come back from the dead: in a reference to *The Scarlet Letter*, the girl at the Aer Lingus desk "is wearing the same scent / and an embroidered capital letter *A* / on her breast". Hawthorne's Hester Prynne had been singled out and punished for adultery; this "capital letter *A*" therefore provides a connection between Alice and the adulterous Beatrice, the other (or more likely the same) important female character in the poem. Taking a swipe at Heaney's procedures, Muldoon portrays Beatrice's punishment for adultery:

> Someone on their way to early Mass
> will find her hog-tied
> to the chapel gates —
> O Child of Prague —
> big-eyed, anorexic.
> The lesson for today
> is pinned to her bomber jacket.
> It seems to read *Keep off the Grass*.
> Her lovely head has been chopped
> and changed.
> For Beatrice, whose fathers
> knew Louis Quinze,
> to have come to this, her perruque
> of tar and feathers.

Heaney's 'Punishment', famously, draws parallels between women in contemporary Northern Ireland who are tarred and feathered for consorting with British soldiers, and adulterous victims of judicial execution in Iron Age Jutland; in a powerful and brave conclusion, Heaney's persona admits he would "connive / in civilized outrage/ yet understand the exact / and tribal, intimate revenge".[26] Although the criticisms directed at *North*, by Ciaran Carson and Edna Longley in particular, are surely unjustified, Muldoon shares their anxieties. The stanza from 'The More a Man Has' suggests that self-righteous, authoritarian religion degrades and brutalizes women: as Longley points out, "'Chopped / and changed' not only darkens the light slanginess of everyday cliché, but visualises what it might mean"[27] — not least through its enjambement. There is even a hint that religion might at times be complicitous with terrorism. The lesson for today, "*Keep off the Grass*", not only prohibits soft drugs, but also plays on "grass" to hint again at Gallogly's ambiguous allegiances: he is perhaps the "grass" in question. Beatrice becomes an icon of suffering, a "Child of Prague — / big-eyed, anorexic"; her anorexia recalls mention of Anorexia in 'Aisling', so that when the traditional *aisling* formula is later repeated, the implication remains that Beatrice-Alice is the poem's ironic Muse, a Cathleen ni Houlihan for our times.

It is not only Beatrice and Alice whose identities merge in 'The More a Man Has'. Gallogly is pursued throughout the poem by an *alter ego*, Mangas Jones, who seems obsessed with his own anti-colonial vendetta:

> busily tracing the family tree
> of an Ulsterman who had some hand
> in the massacre at Wounded Knee.

These *disjecta membra* — a hand in a knee — evoke the "smithereens" of the local councillor blown to bits in a car-bomb assassination, while also preparing for the poem's explosive finale. Just as importantly, the parallel missions of Jones and Gallogly emphasise how one country's colonized can become another's colonizer. Passing through customs, Jones declares "A pebble of quartz" — an allusion to Frost's 'For Once, Then, Something' in which the persona glimpses down a well-shaft "a something white, uncertain" and wonders whether it could have been "Truth" or "a pebble of quartz".[28] Driven like Gallogly by outdated bigotries, Jones's quest is associated with a seductive substitute for "Truth". The obvious correspondence between the two characters even causes a fusion of identities. The deliberately ambiguous pronoun "he" opening the poem's third sonnet-stanza, for example, apparently refers to Jones, who in the previous stanza had arrived at Aldergrove Airport. This is bolstered by the assumption that Jones, following "the corridor's / arroyo" — a south-west American word meaning stream or brook — through the airport, might be led by the metaphor's logic to the "Stranmillis embankment" and its "once-sweet stream" (etymologically, Stranmillis comes from the Irish meaning sweet stream). However, "he" is not Jones: the "quorum" of glue-sniffing skinheads nearby "may not notice Gallogly, / or, if they do, are so far gone". Later Gallogly and Jones are apparently spotted together:

> 'I'll warrant them's the very pair
>   o' boys I seen abroad
> in McParland's bottom, though where
> in under God —
> *for thou art so possessed with murd'rous hate —*
> where they come from God only knows.'
> 'They were mad for a bite o' mate,
>   I s'pose.'

As eye-witnesses, the two unidentified speakers sound no more trustworthy than the skinheads, and their dialect is comically close to stage Irish. It is impossible to get beyond their accounts; the unconfirmed sightings epitomise a poem in which often the movements and motives of Gallogly and Jones can often only be guessed at. This enigmatic meeting also suggests that Muldoon is following the advice of his own Pancho Villa to "get down to something true, / Something a little nearer home": reference to the "pair / o' boys" "abroad / in McParland's bottom" remembers that the Muldoon family home was built on land bought from the McParlands of Collegelands.

Whereas the intentionally shaky plot of 'Immram' had at times seemed no more than a vehicle for Chandleresque asides and the poet's own dark obsessions, the incomprehensions and irretrievabilities of 'The More a Man Has' suggest a confused world of factions, splinter groups, follow-up searches, undercover agents, and at times, terrible brutality. ('The More a Man Has' must be crucial to any assessment of Ciaran Carson's poetry, which is heavily influenced by these elements). It is therefore missing the point to search for coherent plot development: characters merge, come back to life, shift from continent to continent and timescale to timescale, even transform themselves into animals to evade capture. Muldoon has described the poem's technique as "cinematic" or "quick-cutting",[29] but the brief glimpses afforded to the reader never allow a complete understanding. The props of Ulster terrorism recur in authentic, and disconcerting, detail: commercial gelignite, Kalashnikovs with filed-down serial numbers, mercury-tilt booby-traps, Armalites, Cortex, and, described with mesmerising precision, a seemingly unobjectionable black plastic bucket which is

> packed with fertilizer
> and a heady brew
> of sugar and Paraquat's
> relentlessly gnawing its way through
> the floppy knot of a Durex.

Even if 'The More a Man Has' gives us terrorist hardware and terrorist street-talk, it rarely gives us answers or identities. Councillors are blown up, arms stores are discovered, someone ominously breathes "Tell-tale" down the telephone, but perpetrators and their motives are never discovered.

Nowhere is this confusion more crucial than in the relationship between the male leads, Gallogly and Mangas Jones. When Gallogly prepares to escape from the high-security prison, he "juggles / his name like an orange", and "ogles / a moon that's just out of range"; this anagrammatical juggling confirms a nominal, even tribal, connection between Gallogly and, as he is finally labelled, the Oglala Sioux. The name Gallogly is a corruption of the Gaelic for a "foreign young warrior" — that is, a mercenary[30] — but when an unidentified "gallowglass" is blown up and killed at the poem's conclusion, the name incorporates both Gallogly and the Oglala Indian at the moment of death. It is significant that while some critics have argued that Gallogly dies, others have presumed that the victim is Mangas Jones: both interpretations are half right. The poem reaches its magnificent, breathtaking climax at a petrol station:

> It was this self-same pump attendant
> who dragged the head and torso
> clear
> and mouthed an Act of Contrition
> in the frazzled ear
> and overheard
> those already-famous last words
> *Moose ... Indian.*
> 'Next of all wus the han'.' 'Be Japers.'
> 'The sodgers cordonned-off the area
> wi' what-ye-may-call-it tape.'
> 'Lunimous.' 'They foun' this hairy
> han' wi' a drowneded man's grip

on a lunimous stone no bigger than a ...'

'Huh.'

This takes the fragmentation of the individual and the tribe, denied by both Gallogly and Jones in their vengeful quests, to a logically destructive conclusion. Muldoon's allusive genius ensures that the shattering of the body is paralleled by poetic splintering, as the passage makes fleeting reference to three poems by Frost, Bishop's 'The Moose' ("then there's a dim / smell of moose, an acrid / smell of gasoline"),[31] the myth of the Red Hand of Ulster, and *Dr. Jekyll and Mr. Hyde*. The oblique allusion to Stevenson's novel, set up by earlier mention of *Treasure Island*, helps confirm beyond dispute the dual nature of the victim. The "hairy / han'" evokes the pivotal moment in Dr Jekyll's testimony when he recalls his horror at waking to find that his hand has changed into the hand of Edward Hyde: "lean, corded, knuckly, of a dusky pallor, and thickly shadowed with swart hair".[32] Similarly the animal imagery associated with Gallogly ensures that the "already-famous last words" — presumably exploited and sensationalized by "the kennings of the hourly news bulletin" — refer to both Gallogly and Jones. The passage also alludes to Frost's pebble of quartz; the gallowglass's final grip is on the same "lunimous stone", which again unites Gallogly and Jones in refusing the "Truth". This reference to Frost joins with the myth of the Red Hand of Ulster, a fitting example of the centuries-old self-mutilatory battle for ownership of Ireland: it had been agreed between the commanders of two ships that the first to reach Ulster was entitled to rule, and one, seeing he was lagging, cut off his hand at the wrist and threw it to the shore. Muldoon highlights the cost of such fanatical sacrifice: the severed hand clings to the "lunimous stone" with a "drowneded man's grip" while the rest of the body has been blown to pieces. That final "'Huh'" (again borrowed from Frost) provides a contemptuous dismissal of what the fanatics have died for.

The word "lunimous", switching consonants like an earlier mention of "Vietmanese", or the etymological soup Gallogly-Oglala-gallowglass, wryly underlines a final lack of "illunimation": the poem's allusiveness might provide clues regarding the identity of the victim, but the killers and their intentions remain a mystery. 'The More a Man Has' shows how intricate Muldoon's parabolic techniques have become: his brilliant, brutal parable for contemporary Northern Ireland obliquely conveys the terrible "Truth" that in a violent sectarian society perspectives quickly become lost, motives and identities obscured, until ultimately it even becomes unclear who is killing whom, and why.

Notes

1. Heaney, S. *The Government of the Tongue* (London: Faber, 1988), xi.
2. Interviewed by Kevin Smyth, *Gown* (Queen's University, Belfast), 30 (7), May 1984, Lit. Supp., 5.
3. Gerald of Wales *The History and Topography of Ireland* (London: Penguin, 1982), 52. Written c. 1187.
4. Muldoon, P. 'Paul Muldoon writes ...', *Poetry Book Society Bulletin* 118, Autumn 1983, 1.
5. Wills, C. 'The Lie of the Land', *The Chosen Ground: Essays on the Contemporary Poetry of Northern Ireland*, ed. Corcoran, N. (Bridgend: Seren, 1992), 124.
6. 'A Conversation with Paul Muldoon', interviewed by Lynn Keller, *Contemporary Literature* 35 (1), Spring 1994, 21.
7. Introducing 'Gathering Mushrooms', *Ted Hughes and Paul Muldoon* (London: Faber Poetry Cassette, 1982).
8. Huxley, A. *The Doors of Perception and Heaven and Hell* (London: Grafton, 1977), 106. First published by Chatto & Windus (London) as separate volumes, in 1954 and 1956 respectively.
9. Longley, E. '"When Did You Last See Your Father?"', *The Living Stream: Literature & Revisionism in Ireland* (Newcastle-upon-Tyne, Bloodaxe: 1994), 172.
10. 'Paul Muldoon writes...', 1.
11. Wills, C. 'The Lie of the Land', 123.
12. 'Paul Muldoon writes ...', 1.
13. Muldoon's two children's books, *The O-O's Party* (Dublin: Gallery, 1980) and *The Last Thesaurus* (London: Faber, 1995), could be added to the list. *The O-O's Party* tells of the birds which attend a New Year's bash — alphabetized from the auk to the yellowhammer, while also remembering an absent friend, *Zosterops*. *The Last Thesaurus* recounts the last moments of a tiny, linguistically-gifted dinosaur: both imaginary and extinct, the Thesaurus is a fitting addition to Muldoon's bestiary.
14. Allegro, J. *The Sacred Mushroom and the Cross* (London: Hodder & Stoughton, 1970), 100.
15. Hughes, T. 'Pike', *Lupercal* (London: Faber, 1960), 56.
16. Muldoon, P. 'Ordinary People', review of *Close Relatives* by Vicki Feaver, *Times Literary Supplement*, 1 May 1981, 496.
17. 'A Conversation with Paul Muldoon', interviewed by Michael Donaghy, *Chicago Review* 35 (1), Autumn 1985, 85.

18. 'Lunch with Paul Muldoon...', interviewed by Kevin Smith, *Rhinoceros* 4, 1991, 89.
19. Wilson, W. 'Paul Muldoon and the Poetics of Sexual Difference', *Contemporary Literature* 28 (3), Fall 1987, 317-331.
20. Interviewed by Lynn Keller, 25.
21. *Muldoon in America*, interviewed by Christopher Cook, B.B.C. Radio 3, 1994.
22. Longley, E. 'No More Poems About Paintings?', *The Living Stream*, 240.
23. Heaney, S. *Wintering Out* (London: Faber, 1972), 27.
24. Paulin, T. *English Review* 2 (3), Feb. 1992, 29.
25. 'Paul Muldoon writes ...', 1.
26. Heaney, S. *North* (London: Faber, 1975), 38.
27. Longley, E. 'Poetic Forms and Social Malformations', *The Living Stream*, 197.
28. Frost, R. *The Poetry of Robert Frost*, ed. Latham, E. (New York: Holt, Rinehart & Winston, 1969), 276.
29. Interviewed by Michael Donaghy, 81.
30. 'Paul Muldoon writes ...', 1.
31. Bishop, E. *Complete Poems* (London: Chatto & Windus, 1991), 173.
32. Stevenson, R.L. *Dr. Jekyll and Mr. Hyde and Other Stories* (London: Penguin, 1979), 88.

Something Else Again: *Meeting the British*

An early draft of *Quoof* had been provisionally titled *Last Poems*. At first, there seems little reason to suspect Muldoon of any Rimbaud-like intention to abandon poetry, especially since '*from Last Poems*' provides the obvious source of Muldoon's initial choice; furthermore, the title echoes the line in 'Cherish the Ladies' referring to "my last poem about my father", where "last" means latest as well as final. Even the most cursory glance at Muldoon's publication record after *Quoof* would confirm there is no break in his output: Gallery Press issued his twelve-poem pamphlet *The Wishbone* the following year (1984); at least another dozen poems, not subsequently collected, were printed in British and Irish journals between 1983 and 1987; and the full-length volume *Meeting the British* appeared after a gap of just four years. In the meantime Muldoon had edited the *Faber Book of Contemporary Irish Poetry*, and arranged an edition of his *Selected Poems*. In literary terms, the years leading up to the publication of *Meeting the British* have been some of the most productive of Muldoon's career to date.

The poetic onrush recorded in the bibliography, however, can be deceptive. For a time after *Quoof* was published, Muldoon apparently did feel that his significant work was behind him. A masterpiece, *Quoof* represented the pinnacle and the culmination of Muldoon's early style; it was not for a time clear to the poet how his work could continue to improve and develop. The fact that so many poems written immediately after *Quoof* remain uncollected perhaps reflects not only Muldoon's low opinion of them but also a temporary lack of poetic direction. Certainly *The Wishbone* had proved a wrong turning: gnomic, cryptic, at times impenetrably private, the poems dissatisfied Muldoon so much that only five of twelve are carried forward into *Meeting the British*. These years also brought a number of major upheavals in Muldoon's life: the breakdown of his relationship with Mary Powers; the death of his father and sale of the Collegelands home; and his decision to leave an increasingly demanding job at the B.B.C., chiefly due to the realization that "if I continued to work in television I'd probably never write another poem". What must have been an unhappy, unsettling period ended when Muldoon met Jean Hanff Korelitz; the couple later moved to the United States and were married there in 1987. *Meeting the British* had been completed and published before Muldoon's emigration, but it is presumably no coincidence that, after the disturbances of previous years, a high number of the volume's poems were written in the settled environment of Dingle, County Kerry, where Muldoon and Korelitz lived from January to September 1986.

The poems in *The Wishbone* and *Meeting the British* are shaped by personal events from these years: despite their frequent refuge in obliquity, they constitute Muldoon's most autobiographical work before *The Annals of Chile*. Not that *The Wishbone* (nor, for that matter, *Meeting the British*) could ever be considered confessional in tone. The pamphlet is dedicated to Mary Powers, and several poems chart the end of their relationship: "around that time I was trying to write a couple of poems that brought to its logical conclusion the idea of leaving, that were treading a very thin line between what you can put in and what you can leave out".[1] By his own admission Muldoon at times leaves out rather too much. 'Bears', for example, reads like "a series of notes for a poem":[2]

> I ought to begin with Evelyn Waugh's
> 'How old's that noise?'
>
> when you wander arbi-
> trarily into *Le Déjeuner sur l'herbe*.
>
> Wahl, Wahl, Wahl,
> your great-great-grandmother's wail
>
> who froze to death in a cranberry patch
> among the Pennsylvania Dutch.
>
>   *
>
> Yaddo. Your father consecrating priests
> while Lowell and Roethke
> made like bears and beasts.
>
>   *
>
> I can no more calm your dutiful outcry
> than the luncheon-guest
> who dutifully clasps you to his breast.

Without a detailed knowledge of Mary Powers's family history, this does not even provide enough clues to seem enigmatic: it helps to know, for example, that "Wahl" was the maiden name of Powers's mother. The causes of Powers's "dutiful outcry" are unclear, although Evelyn Waugh's "'How old's that noise?'" (which comes not from a novel but from a conversation between Waugh and Powers's father, the writer J.F. Powers), connects her wail with the wail of her great-great-grandmother. Powers's father met Roethke and Lowell at Yaddo during 1947-8. He "consecrat[es] priests" imaginatively, because his stories often centre on Catholic priests. Apart from these obscurities, the poem has some nice technical touches: "arbi- / trarily", for example, is "mimetic of its own enjambement";[3] and 'The Bears', along with seven other poems from *The Wishbone*, pursues Muldoon's obsession with the sonnet form. However, the reference to Manet's *Le Déjeuner sur l'herbe* remains abstruse; the painting, famously, depicts a naked woman enjoying a picnic outdoors with a group of men. Besides preparing for the demise of the great-great-grandmother, it seems the allusion probably hides some private sexual connotation; but as Muldoon comments, "the poem resides around the asterisks",[4] hinting at autobiographical significance while ensuring it leaves out more than enough to avoid self-revelation.

'Bears' is an interesting failure — interesting partly because it embodies all the weaknesses and none of the strengths of *The Wishbone*. That Muldoon should be conscious of the poem's defects so soon after publishing it suggests a poet experimenting with new forms, seeking to avoid repeating the unrepeatable *Quoof* but without yet managing an assured new style. Nevertheless, despite all these false starts and tentative explorations, it would be mistaken to see *The Wishbone* as anything other than a coherent collection, if only in miniature. Muldoon's flirtation with minimalistic utterance tempts the cliché "pared to the bone", a cliché which *The Wishbone*'s title and subject matter also seem determined to evoke. 'The Lass of Aughrim', for example, tells of an Indian boy who strikes up on a flute, or rather, "on what was the tibia / of a priest / from a long-abandoned Mission". In 'The Marriage of Strongbow and Aoife' Ireland's "whole ox" is brought in on a spit, and a metaphorical "double-edged knife" is slipped between the speaker's ribs. The title poem reduces a festive frozen chicken to the remains of what Michael Hofmann describes as "some Dantesque atrocity": "the wishbone like a rowelled spur / on the fibula of Sir — or Sir —". And 'The Ox', undoubtedly the most impressive of the seven poems not collected in *Meeting the British*, constitutes an almost complete ravaging of the body:

> They had driven for three hours non-stop
> that April afternoon

>   to see the Burren's orchids
>   in bloom.
>
>   Milltown Malbay. They parked
>   in front of the butcher's shop.
>   'A month too early. I might have known.'
>   'Let's find a room.'
>
>   They reversed away from the window.
>   To the right hung
>   one ox-tail,
>
>   to the left one ox-tongue.
>   'What's the matter? What's got into you?'
>   'Absolutely nothing at all.'

That Muldoon adopts many of the same organizational procedures in *The Wishbone* as in his full-length volumes is confirmed by subsequent mention of "Ireland's whole ox" in the following poem, 'The Marriage of Strongbow and Aoife'. This connection makes his reasons for dropping a poem as perfect as 'The Ox' from *Meeting the British* all the more inexplicable. The tight-lipped style of *The Wishbone* is wholly appropriate to a poem which, by recording the minimal communications of the two protagonists, conveys the tensions between them far more powerfully than full-blown histrionics could ever do. Lured by the promised glory of "the Burren's orchids / in bloom", the couple find desolation and vacuity where they expected abundance. Their limited exchanges just pad out nothingness: "'Absolutely nothing at all'". Like the ox, their relationship has lost virtually all its substance.

Even if *The Wishbone* is, by Muldoon's exacting standards, a failure, 'The Ox' and perhaps 'Emily', among the uncollected poems, deserve a wider currency than can be offered by a pamphlet published in a limited edition of 750 copies. But the fact that Muldoon carries over five poems from *The Wishbone* into *Meeting the British* does create difficulties for the structure and coherence of the larger volume. It is of course dangerous to speak of creative "periods" when discussing an active writer, let alone one still in his mid-forties. Nevertheless, *Meeting the British* already gives the impression of being transitional: the poems from *The Wishbone*, and others written in the cryptic *Wishbone* style, sit uneasily alongside more pellucid lyrics. Muldoon must have determined, after the achievement of *Quoof*, to try something new; but like *The Wishbone*, *Meeting the British* is a testament to his not yet knowing what the something new should be. Reviewers tried to hide their disappointment, with limited success. So while John Lucas could herald a volume "head and shoulders above anything else so far published this year", and William A. Wilson welcomed Muldoon's "best work to date", William Scammell — a self-proclaimed admirer and (at times) imitator — had to admit deep dissatisfaction, and "Muldoon-deaf" John Carey, in a devastating attack, announced that "If all previous literature vanished, Muldoon's poetry would instantly suffocate".

Part of the problem with *Meeting the British* is caused by the long concluding poem, '7, Middagh Street'. Muldoon's earlier volumes had ended on a technical high, each with a poem more radical, sophisticated and adventurous than any of the shorter lyrics. '7, Middagh Street', by comparison, is a failure. The poem comprises seven monologues, each spoken by a different inhabitant of the house in New York where a motley crew of writers and artists congregated for a Thanksgiving dinner in 1940; beginning with Auden, it also takes in Gypsy Rose Lee, Benjamin Britten, Chester Kallman, Salvador Dali, Carson McCullers and Louis MacNeice. As Edna Longley has pointed out, each monologue "takes off from the concluding word or phrase of its predecessor",[5] so that '7, Middagh Street' is, in effect, a corona in form. But after the Chandleresque drug-trafficking of 'Immram', and the shape-changing terrorist yarn of 'The More a Man Has', a poem peopled by characters holding forth on the rôle of poetry and the responsibilities of artists is, to be frank, a little dull. Allen Ginsberg, notoriously, once dismissed Frost's 'Home Burial' as nothing more than "a couple of squares yakking at each other"; an unsympathetic reader might conclude that '7, Middagh Street' consists of squares yakking at themselves.

Despite taking their cues from each other, and sharing many artistic and sexual concerns, the poem's characters speak into the ether. The absence of dialogue creates a strangely rambling and dehumanized effect, which, coupled with the poem's circular structure, comes unintentionally close to reconstructing the purgatory of Beckett's *Play*. And even when monologues do seem to engage with each other, the results are disappointing. For example Muldoon's 'Wystan' — perhaps more accurately, Muldoon's Lowell's 'Wystan' — and 'Louis' come into conflict over the relationship between art and politics. Wystan states his case by beginning with an attack on Yeats:

> As for his crass, rhetorical
>
> posturing, 'Did that play of mine
> send out certain men (*certain* men?)
>
> the English shot...?'
> the answer is 'Certainly not'.
>
> If Yeats had saved his pencil-lead
> would certain men have stayed in bed?
>
> For history's a twisted root
> with art its small, translucent fruit
>
> and never the other way round.

The Auden of '7, Middagh Street' is, according to Muldoon, "on the cusp",[6] his major work finished, and the relative inferiority of his American poetry ahead of him. However, Muldoon puts into his mouth some good Audenesque jokes at the expense of Yeats's rhetorical bombast, not least that emphasis on the phrase "certain men". The criticisms of Yeats — who had died the year before — do fairly reflect Auden's own views at this time: art's "translucent fruit" growing out of history's "twisted root" is an organic version of the argument that "art is a product of history, not a cause", as Auden's "counsel for the defence" states in 'The Public v. the Late Mr William Butler Yeats' from 1939.[7] Muldoon's MacNeice is less sure that poetry makes nothing happen, arguing that it "not only can, but must". He recounts that Auden has set himself up as a "stylite" — like a Dutch master "intent only on painting an oyster" — before pointing out that "the very painting of that oyster / is in itself a political gesture". The section's unusually gauche rhyming couplets do nothing to allay the suspicion that although Wystan and Louis might seem to hold opposing beliefs, they are really in complete agreement: it all depends on how broadly the word "political" is defined. Muldoon has explained his own position:

> It may not make any great impression on the Richter scale, but ideally a poem should change the world. That's a rather grand thing to say. I'm not talking about a cure for cancer or Aids, or a solution to the Irish problem (as it's called), not a vast social impact. But I never go into a poem knowing where I'm going to end up. I always, I hope, make some discovery, however tiny; I come out the other end looking at some aspect of the world in a modified way. So that one doesn't look at

a hedgehog again, for example, in quite the same way. It's either a modest ambition or a huge ambition, and I think in that sense poetry must make something happen.[8]

Apparently Muldoon is siding with MacNeice, as they resist Auden's claim, from 'In Memory of W.B. Yeats' (1939), that "poetry makes nothing happen". In fact this passage underlines the flatness of the supposed controversy between Wystan and Louis; neither poet, surely, would have found much to quibble about in Muldoon's generalized formulation of the rôle of poetry.

'7, Middagh Street' promises to become a favourite in theoretical assessments of Muldoon's work. Terry Eagleton hailed it as "an ambitious meditation on the recurrent Irish theme of art and politics", examining "the problem of how neither to overprivilege or underrate the political relevance of art". Though hardly so specifically Irish as Eagleton suggests, such issues are worthy of debate, and are indeed debated *ad nauseam*. However, '7, Middagh Street' fails to dramatize them in an enlivening way: the terms of Eagleton's praise are extra-poetical, as if Muldoon's poem were an academic tract. For once Muldoon has exchanged parabolic strength for direct statements, even if these statements have been filtered through other artists. As a result, '7, Middagh Street' cannot be defended against John Carey's criticism that the poem "seems less interesting than its raw material". in 'Wystan' Muldoon has drawn extensively from Humphrey Carpenter's *W.H. Auden: A Biography*, but as Carey claims, "If you have not read Carpenter, the poem is virtually unintelligible; and if you have, it seems superfluous". 'Immram' and 'The More a Man Has', while deploying the "mythical method", never demanded knowledge of their sources. For all their allusions, both poems are, besides much else, gripping adventure yarns, reflecting Muldoon's admiration for Buchan, Stevenson, Chandler and the like. By comparison '7, Middagh Street' is static. Wystan opens the poem with an account of his arrival in New York:

> Quinquereme of Nineveh from distant Ophir;
> a blizzard off the Newfoundland coast
> had, as we slept, metamorphosed
>
> the *Champlain*'s decks
> to a wedding cake,
> on whose uppermost tier stood Christopher

and I like a diminutive bride and groom.
A heavy-skirted Liberty would lunge
with her ice-cream
at two small, anxious

boys, and Erika so grimly wave
from the quarantine-launch
she might as truly have been my wife
as, later that day, Barcelona was Franco's.

The passage begins with a line from Masefield's 'Cargoes', a poem which serves as one of the organizing elements of *Meeting the British*. Far from changing the way one looks at the world, the rest merely rhymes what Carpenter had already recounted:

> On the morning of 26 January 1939 the snow was falling heavily in New York City. It was the coldest day so far that winter ... About the middle of the day news came that, in Spain, Barcelona had fallen to Franco ... This was the day on which Auden and Isherwood arrived in New York. 'There they stood in the driving snow', recalled Isherwood, remembering how he and Auden looked up at 'the made-in-France Giantess with her liberty torch, which now seemed to threaten, not welcome' ... Erika and Klaus Mann, who now lived largely in the U.S.A., met them on the quarantine launch ...[9]

More is lost than gained in Muldoon's syntactically awkward version: not only has it become obscure to any reader unfamiliar with Auden's biography, but even the new additions — such as the "ice-cream" of the Statue of Liberty's torch — are worn-out, imaginative failures. The 'Immram Mael Duin' and the Trickster cycle of the Winnebago Indians had unleashed a seemingly boundless creativity; considerably less distanced from the opening section of the finished poem, Carpenter's biography seems only to have stifled Muldoon.

The biographical detail is not confined to 'Wystan'. While several celebrated artistic occasions, such as the Auden-MacNeice journey to Iceland, or Dali's spat with Breton and the surrealists, are mentioned in passing, elsewhere the poem often descends into personal gossip: and unfortunately, the gossip is not even interesting. Even Gypsy Rose Lee, recalling reactions to her first striptease, fails to inspire:

> 'I loved the act. Maybe you'd wanna buy

> Sam?' asked Nudina, over a drink.
> Nudina danced with a boa
> constrictor that lived under the sink
> in the women's room. 'He's a dear.'
> 'So *this* is a speakeasy,'
> Mother whispered. We'd ordered beer
> and pizza.
> 'Don't look now,' said Nudina, 'but Waxey's
> just come in.' 'Waxey?' 'A friend of mine
> from Jersey. Runs applejack
> through special pipelines
> in the sewers. Never even been subpoenaed.
> But let's get back to discussing the serpent.'

It is of course Muldoon's intention to present the reader with such private, almost overheard, narratives, which is why the poem offers first name terms with 'Wystan' *et al*. But the poem's strings are too visible, with the puppet-like characters seeming little more than parodies of themselves: so the easiest target, Chester Kallman, renowned for being Auden's promiscuous lover and his collaborator on various libretti, switches all too predictably from *Der Rosenkavalier* to "cunts, or fresh, young cocks". Nor does Muldoon ever manage to create the intimacy needed to tolerate the characters' arcane references: as John Kerrigan has suggested, the poem's obscurities "have an elaborate bookish whimsy which promises a long way round to empty-handedness".[10] '7, Middagh Street' is much more successful when it abandons the exclusively private sphere, and instead presents the tensions and interrelations between the individual and the public sphere of world events: the date of Auden's arrival in New York, for example, is notable for being the date Barcelona falls to Franco; Auden's father is remembered tending "the British wounded" in Egypt, Gallipoli and France, with the happy effect of leaving his son to play "Isolde to my mother's Tristan"; Westminster debates Auden's desertion to the States, as a minister confuses him with the tennis-star H.W. Austin; Dali recalls an anarchist taxi-driver who had asked him to choose between Spanish and Catalan flags; and MacNeice reminisces over his father's refusal to sign the Ulster Covenant. Only at these moments do personal details come alive poetically and begin to escape their biographical strait-jackets.

John Kerrigan may have been justified in calling '7, Middagh Street' a "partial failure",[11] particularly after the unqualified successes of 'The More a Man Has'. Nevertheless, in terms of Muldoon's poetic development '7, Middagh Street' is an intriguing poem. One of its achievements is to exorcise, or at least to torment, the ghost of Yeats. It has become a critical truism that MacNeice and Kavanagh, in very different ways, rendered the influence of Yeats safe for a subsequent generation of Irish — particularly, it seems, Northern Irish — poets; and Muldoon's slangy, free-wheeling style has meant he has remained less susceptible to any lingering effects than a poet like Derek Mahon (who has confessed he would need a lobotomy to rid himself of the Yeatsian line).[12] Although Yeats is almost never a stylistic presence in Muldoon's poetry, Yeatsian preoccupations are mocked or rewritten in several poems from *Mules*; similarly 'Under Saturn', an interesting uncollected poem published in 1981, takes off from, and at the expense of, Yeats's poem of the same name. Yeats's poetry is so pervasive in '7, Middagh Street' that at times he seems like the eighth member of the household. Wystan spoofs the excesses of 'Man and the Echo' ("Did that play of mine ...?"). And Gypsy remembers how she was told never to "give all thy heart", because — adapting Yeats's 'A Coat' for striptease ethos and for Muldoon's implicit Apology — "there's more enterprise in walking not quite / naked". When she reads in the *Daily Worker* that "'Striptease is a capitalistic cancer, / A product of the profit system'", Gypsy has recourse to Yeats again: "Perhaps we cannot tell the dancer / from the dance". Carson ends her monologue with a line from 'In Memory of Eva Gore-Booth and Con Marciewicz' — "two girls in silk kimonos" — which Louis, taking over, gratefully vandalizes: "Both beautiful, one a gazebo" (the Yeatsian rhyme is "gazelle", but the word "gazebo" occurs later). Imagining himself asperged with kerosene, Louis gives the "voice of Sir Edward Carson" a line from the same poem, "'Bid me strike a match and blow'"; in doing so he equates Yeats with the man partly responsible for the partitioning of Ireland. Finally, misquoting Yeats slightly, Louis states that "In dreams begin responsibilities", before abandoning the ideal for the brutally real: "it was on account of just such an allegory / that Lorca / was riddled with bullets". These examples combine a celebration of Yeats's legacy with a hooligan attitude to his poetry, as lofty allusions are placed in unflattering or comically inappropriate contexts. '7, Middagh Street' is a surreptitious elegy for Yeats; but it also confirms earlier hints that Yeats's chief function in Muldoon's poetry is to provide a figure of fun, ridiculously pompous.

When MacNeice leaves an all-night drinking session "by the back door of Muldoon's", Muldoon playfully reminds us that while any resemblance to persons living or dead is not coincidental, all the characters have been fictionalized to a greater or lesser extent, and manipulated to serve his own preoccupations. The reasons for Muldoon's interest in the Middagh Street mélange at this stage in his career are not hard to guess: at a basic level, the poem prepares for his own emigration to the States. Two of Muldoon's earlier long poems, 'The Year of the Sloes, for Ishi' and 'Immram', had already been set in the States, along with much of 'The More a Man Has'; Muldoon has observed that "many people in Ireland look as naturally — in many cases more naturally — west as east".[13] But even if the trans-Atlantic poetic ground of '7, Middagh Street' offers no surprises, the poem stresses that geographical displacement need not entail an emotional amnesia towards Irish origins. The insistent Yeatsian allusions, however disrespectfully they are treated, act as a pledge of continuity with (to put it in grandiose terms) an Irish poetical tradition. And while Auden insists that "we are all now dispossessed", MacNeice ends '7, Middagh Street' — insofar as a corona can be said to end — with an obsessive concern for roots: five of Louis's seven sections mention Ireland, even as they range in cosmopolitan fashion through Reykjavik, New York, Oxford and the Spanish Civil War. Wystan himself heads back to an origin of a kind:

> The roots by which we once were bound
>
> are severed here, in any case,
> and we are all now dispossessed;
>
> prince, poet, construction worker,
> salesman, soda fountain jerker —
>
> all equally isolated.
> Each loads flour, sugar and salted
>
> beef into a covered wagon
> and strikes out for his Oregon,
>
> each straining for the ghostly axe
> of a huge, blond-haired lumberjack.

Mick Imlah, writing in the *Times Literary Supplement*, was the first reviewer to point out that *Meeting the British* plays variations on the consonantal pattern "rgn": organza, arrogance, oregano, Arigna, Aragon, Oregon and so on. The word "origin", like the theme to the *Enigma Variations*, is never voiced, only implied and approximated. Auden therefore imagines striking out for a sexual Oregon-origin, in search of the phallic "ghostly axe" of a Paul Bunyan figure. Besides Wystan and Louis, the poem's other Europeans, Salvador (Dali) and Ben (Britten), speak persistently of events in their respective home countries. The characters in '7, Middagh Street', typifying Muldoon's approach throughout *Meeting the British*, focus all the more intently on their origins when they appear to have abandoned them.

One sort of origin which fascinates Muldoon is the name. From the "Jonsonian, emblematic" names of *Mules*, to the pre-ordained destinies of Coulter and Brownlee, to the restrictions of the *dinnseanchas* genre (the inescapably church-like Eglish, for example), names in Muldoon's work hold a Platonic power which confines and determines character; name is fate. Significantly, the resourceful shape-changer Gallogly can shift from alias to alias, his character and his allegiance in permanent flux. Others fare less well in their efforts to avoid the name's hegemonic influence. In '7, Middagh Street' MacNeice is told by a "one-eyed foreman" who "had strayed out of Homer" — presumably via the bigotries of Joyce's 'Cyclops' — that his is "a Fenian name":

> As if to say, 'None of your sort, none of you
>
> will as much as go for a rubber hammer
> never mind chalk a rivet, never mind caulk a seam
> on the quinquereme of Nineveh.'

The prejudice is misplaced because, as Muldoon has pointed out, the name MacNeice goes back at least as far as the pre-Fenian king Conor MacNessa; of course, the important point is that names make the individual vulnerable to sectarian abuse and exclusion. Muldoon has commented that "the name as just the word on its own, doesn't exist, as a signifier ... but in fact it has connotations that it cannot itself allow for. It exists in other realms".[14] But as Muldoon's MacNeice discovers, the name, more importantly, has connotations that the individual cannot allow for, and that shape his or her destiny.

The fixation with origins in *Meeting the British* is not confined merely to individual or nominal levels. On a material level, Muldoon's poetry at this time becomes increasingly concerned with the influence, often even the despotism, of the source over its products. The residuary bodies which linked the poems in *The Wishbone* are carried over into the longer volume, with new instances added. Muldoon even manages to poke fun at his own grotesque obsessions: Louis describes a sailor who "played a melodeon / made from a merman's spine"; and this, together with Carson McCullers's reference to "the rotting / carcasses of two pack-mules", cleverly evokes earlier poetry ('The Merman' and 'Mules') to emphasise Muldoon's new dissecting and decaying vision. Significantly, *Meeting the British* is avidly carnivorous: "Ireland's whole ox on a spit"; a "spider-crab's / crossbow and cuirass"; a "frozen chicken" replete with "*Paxo* sage and onion"; "medallions of young peccary"; lobster; octopus, squid and conger; oysters and clams; crawfish and turkey; even a Dali painting includes "a raw beef-steak". The dominance of sea-food in this list perhaps befits a volume which is transitional in more ways than one. But most of these examples are described in a context which could not be further from what Craig Raine calls the "paunchography" — gluttonous descriptions of food — of a writer like Hemingway.[15] They belong to the same category as the priest's tibia which serves as a flute in 'The Lass of Aughrim', or the seats of Rolls Royces "upholst- / ered with the hides of stillborn calves" in 'The Toe-Tag'; any sensory pleasure derived from the end product is tainted by an overpowering knowledge of its origins.

'Sushi' enacts and exemplifies this constant debate in *Meeting the British*: whether products should be judged transcendent of their origins. The poem establishes the "rgn" pattern even in its first line: "'Why do we waste so much time in arguing?'"; at its midriff 'Sushi' contains a sexual reference to the "erogenous / zones of shad and sea-bream"; and it ends with the theologian Scotus Eriugena. The "arguing" is interrupted by a mysterious, eclectic meditation on the nature of God, which distracts the poet from his companion's despairing attempts at communication, and is crammed with variations on the established consonantal pattern:

> *Is it not the height of arrogance*
> *to propose that God's no more arcane*
> *than the smack of oregano,*
> *orgone,*
> *the inner organs*
> *of beasts and fowls, the mines of Arigna,*
> *the poems of Louis Aragon?*

This pernickety intellectual dispute captures the different philosophies of two men, often confused with each other (Muldoon jokingly confuses them in 'Madoc'), who are named in the poem's final line: Duns Scotus and Scotus Eriugena. The latter, also known as John the Irishman, believed that God does not transcend the natural world, and located the divine origin — or "rgn" — pantheistically within all things; whereas Duns Scotus held that God is too "arcane" for human reason and promoted faith above intellect. The poem's speaker and the sushi-bar's master chef are divided along analogous lines. In a moment of insight, the speaker notices how an apprentice has "scrimshandered" a rose's "exquisite petals" out of "the tail-end of a carrot", concerning himself with the artwork's material origins rather than its completed form; the master-chef, however, is a man "unlikely to confound" the philosophers, and he only appreciates what Duns Scotus called the *haecceitas* — "thisness" — of the finished product, treating the apprentice's creation as if "it might have been alabaster or jade", its lowly source irrelevant. The conflict of opinions, like the conflict between the poem's speaker and his partner, remains unresolved; however, the sushi-bar, filled with the "erogenous / zones" of fish and the "roe" of sea-urchins, and making no efforts to distance or disguise the source of the food it serves, is an appropriate setting for a philosophical debate whose moral and aesthetic considerations inform *Meeting the British* as a whole.

If *Meeting the British* is a voracious volume, its voracity borders on disgust: 'Salvador' evokes "the boudoir / in the abattoir", emphasising the mixture of desire and repulsion which typifies other references to meat. The partner in 'Sushi' upbraids the poetic persona with the accusation that "'It's as if you've some kind of death-wish'"; and certainly the preceding poem, 'Something Else', suggests a sensibility much possessed with death, whether animal or human. 'Something Else' seems to engage in a gentle tussle with Seamus Heaney's 'Away from it All', in which the first person tells of a meal of lobster, shared with a friend. Heaney's persona recalls how "quotations start to rise // like rehearsed alibis", and alludes rather extravagantly to Czeslaw Milosz's *Native Realm:*

> *I was stretched between contemplation*
> *of a motionless point*
> *and the command to participate*
> *actively in history.*
>
> 'Actively? What do you mean?'[16]

This exchange is not unlike the derision aimed by Muldoon's Auden at Yeats's self-important rhetoric. The appropriation of Milosz's

Something Else Again: *Meeting the British*

grand quotation, when placed in a practical context, becomes merely foolish. Whatever the friend's identity, he clearly sounds like Muldoon, whose own 'Something Else', describing a similar scene, has its mind on other matters:

> When your lobster was lifted out of the tank
> to be weighed
> I thought of woad,
> of madders, of fugitive, indigo inks,
>
> of how Nerval
> was given to promenade
> a lobster on a gossamer thread,
> how, when a decent interval
>
> had passed
> (*son front rouge encor du baiser de la reine*)
> and his hopes of Adrienne
>
> proved false,
> he hanged himself from a lamp-post
> with a length of chain, which made me think
>
> of something else, then something else again.

The poem's technique is extraordinary. In effect it is a sonnet with a line and a half tacked on. Were the poem to end with "chain", its rhyming would be regular: *abba cddc eff eef*. As it is, "think" chimes with "tank" and "inks"; and "chain", preceding a heavy caesura but no longer at the end of a line, still picks up "*reine*" and "Adrienne" while preparing for the final "again". The sonnet's surplus, avoiding the finality of a full stop after "chain", suits a poem which begins by trying to blot out the lobster's imminent death but finds itself, through a process of analogic association, headed fatally towards another death. The persona cannot allow himself to stop at this fourteenth line: it hardly matters what the "something else, then something else again" happen to be, so long as they distract attention from thoughts of mortality.

'Something Else' is also an inquisition into the nature of memory and the creative impulse: Muldoon's partial reading claims that it is about "the inability to capture a moment except in the archaeological sense — well that's even a metaphor for the capturing of the moment, you know, seeing the dog curled with its litter under the table at Pompeii".[17] This quotation is more appropriate to

'Chinook', which actually employs the Pompeii metaphor, than to 'Something Else'; the "fugitive inks" which quickly disappear are only one small link in thought-processes impelled — as Muldoon's usually seem to be — by analogy. The prose piece 'Ontario', which opens the volume, displays the same shaping imagination as 'Something Else', when it recalls a conversation in a disco in Ontario with a girl who had lost a contact-lens:

> — Did you know that Spinoza was a lens-grinder?
> — Are you for real? [...]
> — A lens, I went on, is really a lentil. A pulse.
> Her back was an imponderable, green furrow in the ultra-violet strobe.
> — Did *you* know that Yonge Street's the longest street in the world?
> — I can't say that I did.
> — Well, it starts a thousand miles to the north, and it ends right here.

The proliferation of vegetables is no doubt in part a response to the presence of Muldoon's brother, who "wrote a thesis on nitrogen-fixing in soya beans" and "now works for the Corn Producers' Association of Ontario". Muldoon's own knowledge of vegetables seems, in its way, no less impressive and esoteric. Although lenses were so called because shaped like a lentil, this backward quest for origin obfuscates empirical reality in favour of the logic of a quirky etymology — "a lens" is definitely not "really a lentil". And a "strobe" is only tangentially a "pulse", even though one triggers mention of the other. For someone who spends time wondering "where the Plough stopped being the Plough and became the Big Dipper" (then something else, then something else again) the girl's impatient put-down, swapping the abstract for the concrete, is the perfect riposte. Self-critically, Muldoon opens *Meeting the British* with a humorous attack on his own analogic procedures.

In a volume so concerned with origins that a "lens ... is really a lentil", and a seat is upholstered, in exacting detail, with "the hides of stillborn calves", the emphasis on residuary bodies — whether they have been prepared for consumption or for burial — comes as no surprise. The effects can be loving as well as bizarre or revolting, however. So Muldoon's delicate elegy for his father, 'The Fox', unflinchingly recalls "your face / above its bib / pumped full of formaldehyde"; in this death-repose the father seems "engrossed",

> as if I'd come on you
> painfully writing your name
> with a carpenter's pencil
>
> on the lid
> of a mushroom-box.
> You're saying, *Go back to bed.*
> *It's only yon dog-fox.*

Poised and economical, 'The Fox' is a poignant elegy, particularly in the subtle way it expresses sympathy for the father's "painful" near-illiteracy. It is through the memory of the body — "corpse" would be irretrievable, too distant — that the father's continuing powers of protection are stressed. The son has been alarmed by "the geese / on John Mackle's goose farm", but his father, even after death, offers reassurance. When the son mentions that "You lay / three fields away // in Collegelands / graveyard", his direct address, together with the innocuous verb "lay", suggests both an emotional and physical proximity. The residuary body, surviving mortality, provides a crucial and comforting bridge between the living and the dead.

A body — that of a "month-drowned Aranman" — turns up in 'The Toe-Tag' as well; and the poem's title comes from its description of an "indigo-flowering cactus" like "a big toe with its tag". Similarly Wystan recalls coming across a Japanese spy, shot during the Sino-Japanese War, who had been buried under boulders; "one of his feet stuck out", for a "brindled pariah" to gnaw on. Another elegy from *Meeting the British*, 'The Soap-Pig', indicates that the relics of the dead need not always be bodily leftovers. Beginning with news of the death of a colleague at the B.B.C., Michael Heffernan, 'The Soap-Pig' is, according to Muldoon's Faber blurb, "a meditation on a bar of soap"; more exactly, "an amber, pig-shaped / bar of soap" given by Heffernan to Muldoon as a Christmas present "from what must have been 1975". In interview Muldoon has discussed the poem at some length:

> The character in the poem, the main speaker is, I suppose, more like me than is often the case. It seems to me very candid, which is a very risky business also, in the sense that, as is often the case with elegies ... it's as much about my response to Michael Heffernan, whom the poem is mostly about. It's almost in danger of seeming to be more about me and seeming self-absorbed and self-engaged. I suppose *that's* the risk the poem takes — it's always on the edge.[18]

Muldoon acknowledges the common elegiac difficulty of achieving a balance between the mourner and the mourned. This time it is the soap-pig, a residuary body of a kind, which connects Muldoon and Heffernan, and prevents the poem from becoming "self-absorbed and self-engaged". So while the poet recounts drinking sprees which would end with his "throwing up / at the basin", or "successive flits" from his wife to various bachelor pads and finally to (and from) Mary Powers, accompanying him through all these upheavals is the soap-pig: it finds a temporary home with Powers's collection of "porcelain, glass and heliotrope" pigs, but as another relationship begins to fall apart, it is flung "in a fit of pique" into the back yard. Its final resting place is the "wash-stand" of Muldoon's family home, where it is "squatt[ing]" when news comes through of Heffernan's death. Heffernan is intricately bound up with the soap-pig. It is all the poet can think of when he hears of his friend's death, as well as being the starting-point for later reminiscences:

> I could just see the Jesuitical,
> kitsch-camp slip-
> knot in the tail
> of even that bar of soap.
> For this was Heffernan
> saying, 'You stink to high heaven'.

The soap-pig is also the point of return. After undergoing surgery, Heffernan is given "a tiny, plastic valve" which "would no more dissolve" than the soap-pig. And when he deliberates on the Platonic reality of chairs and tables, either he or Muldoon — it isn't clear which — deduces that "the mind's a razor / on the body's strop" (one wonders by what criterion this was chosen as Muldoon's one entry in *The Penguin Dictionary of Twentieth-Century Quotations*). This metaphor brings the poem back to the soap-pig, in a powerful conclusion:

> And the soap-pig? It's a bar of soap,
>
> now the soap-sliver
> in a flowered dish
> that I work each morning into a lather
> with my father's wobbling-brush,
> then reconcile to its pool of glop
> on my mother's wash-stand's marble top.

Brought into use only after Heffernan's death, the soap-pig finds its place among other *mementi mori* and relics of the dead: the father's "wobbling-brush" and the mother's "wash-stand". These are all elements which support and sustain "the mind's ... razor"; but only the soap-pig is impermanent. The elegy for Heffernan is therefore composed as a more lasting monument, to replace the soap-pig once it has dwindled to a tiny sliver.

The six-line stanza of 'The Soap-Pig' rhymes *ababcc*. It is not entirely unrealistic to suggest that the stanza form constitutes a deliberately modest version of the eight-line Byronic stanza (*abababcc*), in the same way as the ten-line stanza of 'Immram' consciously extends its Byronic model. In 'The Soap-Pig' Muldoon's verse dwindles like his subject matter. The technique of 'The Wishbone' — as well as the pamphlet to which it gives its name — reflects a similar narrowing of range. Recording a Christmas spent alone with his father at their family home, Muldoon begins with a bleakly economical inventory of absent relatives: "Maureen in England, Joseph in Guelph, / my mother in her grave". In such desolate circumstances the father and son even watch the Queen's message to the Commonwealth "with the sound turned off". Given the poignancy of Hemingway's title, the father's choice of films is unsurprising:

> He seems to favour *Camelot*
> over *To Have and Have Not*.
>
> *
>
> Yet we agree, my father and myself,
> that here is more than enough
> for two; a frozen chicken,
> spuds, sprouts, *Paxo* sage and onion.
>
> *
>
> The wishbone like a rowelled spur
> on the fibula of Sir— or Sir—.

At first there seems no reason why the penultimate stanza should begin with the word "Yet". However, there is no *non sequitur*: even though the father favours *Camelot*, he and his son "agree", in one sense, to enact *To Have and Have Not*. Paradoxically, excess only emphasises lack: the prospect of a meal which is "more than enough / for two" is meant to raise spirits, while the underlying causes of this abundance are too painful to be acknowledged. Nor does

Camelot provide any refuge. In the final couplet it returns only to infect the feast: the image of cannibalism overwhelms the tiny promise of wish-fulfilment normally associated with the wishbone.

The wishbone's relation to the chicken is, in the scheme of *Meeting the British*, similar to the tibia-flute's to the missionary, or even the soap-pig's to Michael Heffernan; the remains of the animal and human dead clutter the volume. 'The Mist-Net' goes further than most when reducing the legacy to nothing more than "his mother's dying words: / *You mustn't. You mustn't*". But elsewhere the relics are physical, at times infused with an emotional force which, as in 'The Fox', unites living and dead once more. Another elegy for Muldoon's father, 'The Coney', employs dream logic to transport the poet suddenly back into the midst of "last year's pea-sticks / and cauliflower-stalks":

> This past winter he had been too ill
> to work. The scythe would dull
> so much more quickly in my hands
> than his, and was so often honed,
> that while the blade
> grew less and less a blade
> the whetstone had entirely disappeared
> and a lop-eared
> coney was now curled inside the cap.

Like the soap-pig, the whetstone offers a temporary link with the dead, before diminishing and disappearing. The "lop-eared coney" which materializes in its place is a surreal, supernatural Bugs Bunny, addressing the poet as "chief"; he swaggers along the "diving-board", before jumping into the "swimming-pool" of a septic-tank. 'The Soap-Pig' reports that Michael Heffernan had "breezed into Belfast / in a three-quarter length coney-fur"; balancing this reference, Muldoon's coney is "flayed" by the swimming-pool's "pack of dogs". The wonderful and the gruesome co-exist in this dream-world. The coney would "parade and pirouette like honey on a spoon", before throwing out a final invitation:

> 'Come on in, Paddy Muldoon.'
> And although I have never learned to swim
> I would willingly have followed him.

Having taken his father's place, the poet is confused with Patrick. Once the whetstone's link between father and son has shrunk into nothingness, Muldoon is tempted to follow the flayed coney, but also, implicitly, to dive in after Paddy Muldoon himself.

Together with 'The Coney' and 'The Fox', the dedication to *Meeting the British* clearly announces Muldoon's commemorative priority: "In Memory of Patrick Muldoon 1910-1985". However, two poems also mention Muldoon's grandfather, as if the death of his surviving parent has increased the importance of fixing and retaining family memories from further back. Not long before his father's death Muldoon did in fact make recordings of Patrick's family reminiscences, presumably so they would not be lost. Yet *Meeting the British* never indulges in a hammed nostalgia. What is noticeable about 'My Grandfather's Wake', for example, is how little it conveys of the event described by the title. It begins with references to a painting and a film: Wyeth's *Christina's Dream* and Malick's *Days of Heaven*. These very different works share prairie-houses and cornfields in common, and also, according to Muldoon, the "little barge" of a freshly-dug grave. After a detour via New England graveyards, the poem returns to an Ireland marked by the peculiarities of its fauna: a nine-banded armadillo, a man-ox, and a fish with three gold teeth. Only the final four lines seem to relate directly to the wake itself:

> Our cow chained in the byre
> was a galley-slave from *Ben Hur*
> to the old-fashioned child of seven
> they had sent in search of a bucket of steam.

This nautical theme echoes back to the "trireme" houses of Wyeth and Malick which ride on their sea of grain. At the same time the lines show how the child's imagination transforms the humdrum realities of his environment; in this metamorphosis, as well as in the specific allusion to triremes, the poem contains an early hint of 'Yarrow' from *The Annals of Chile*. There is of course more than a suggestion that the "child of seven" "sent in search of a bucket of steam" has been deliberately kept out of the way while the adults enjoy their get-together at the wake. But the poem's strength derives from its honesty; rather than seeking weepy-eyed melodramatics, it presents a child caught up in his fantasy world, seemingly indifferent to the death of a distant grandfather.

'My Grandfather's Wake' is surprising for what it leaves out: memories of the grandfather; descriptions of his appearance; the cause of death; and the reactions of relatives. 'Brock', a subtle elegy both for Muldoon's father and his grandfather, is only slightly more informative: it provides the briefest "glimpse" of the grandfather's "whiskers // stained with tobacco-pollen". Just as the child of 'My Grandfather's Wake' transforms a cow into a galley-slave, so in 'Brock' badgers and humans seem virtually indistinguishable; the anthropomorphic potential of the animal kingdom, a constant theme particularly in *Quoof*, now almost constitutes evidence of metempsychosis. 'Brock' is also intriguing because, like 'Something Else', it sets itself against a Heaney poem — this time, 'The Badgers'. Reviewing *Quoof*, Neil Corcoran memorably commented that "if there were an opposite to the word 'buttonholing' it would describe the characteristic stance of a Muldoon poem"; but in fact *Meeting the British* joins with *Quoof* in signalling what seems Muldoon's growing urge to button-hole the elder poet. *Station Island*, published between *Quoof* and *Meeting the British*, seems to have pleased and irritated Muldoon in equal measure. In the *London Review of Books*, he welcomed it as Heaney's best work since *Wintering Out*, while providing a slightly petulant list of criticisms for Heaney to heed in future. Muldoon's praise can be as pointed as his disapproval: it is impossible not to wonder about subtexts when 'Widgeon', a poem dedicated to and undoubtedly impersonating Muldoon (as well as adapting a story told to Heaney by Muldoon), is singled out for special approval. 'Brock' overlaps with Heaney's 'The Badgers' at several points. Heaney's poem begins one evening in a friend's garden: "half-lit with whiskey", the unidentified friend (who is apparently Michael Longley) associates the badger with the "murdered dead"; picking up the hint from his companion, Heaney's speaker wonders whether it could have been "some violent shattered boy / nosing out what got mislaid / between the cradle and the explosion". Later he dismisses the badger as "pig family", before reverting once again to a more anthropomorphic understanding:

> How perilous is it to choose
> not to love the life we're shown?
> His sturdy dirty body
> and interloping grovel.
> The intelligence in his bone.
> The unquestionable houseboy's shoulders
> that could have been my own.

'The Badgers' comes round in this conclusion to Heaney's perennial theme: the poet's relationship with his home community. Muldoon's 'Brock' shares Heaney's uncertainty as to whether the badger is just pig family, or something much more:

> I would find it somewhat *infra dig*

> to dismiss him simply as a pig
> or heed Gerald of Wales'
> tall tales
>
> of badgers keeping badger-slaves.
> For when he shuffles
> across the esker
> I glimpse my grandfather's whiskers
>
> stained with tobacco-pollen.
> When he piddles against a bullaun
> I know he carries bovine TB
> but what I *see*
>
> is my father in his Sunday suit's
> bespoke lime and lignite,
> patrolling his now-diminished estate
> and taking stock of this and that.

Like Heaney's poem, Muldoon submerges the scientific under the instinctive; both poets "know" the badger is a mere "pig", but "what [they] see" are its human associations. In a clever juxtaposition Muldoon lumps together the badger's porcine origins with Gerald of Wales' observations of badger setts, as if the techniques of modern scientific classification possessed no more validity than Gerald's bizarre naturalism. Even though the realities of "bovine TB" are enough, finally, to engulf earlier suggestions of metempsychosis, the badgers still seem to represent a kind of living relic, almost a mnemonic, of the poet's father and grandfather.

With its examinations of loss, and search for residual comforts, *Meeting the British* is preoccupied with transience. 'Gold', for example, detects a hidden barb even in Robert Frost's panegyric for Kennedy's Inauguration: while Frost hails "*A golden age / of poetry and power*", his work elsewhere reminds the reader that "Nothing gold can stay".[19] Such public references merge with details from the life of Gerard Quinn, the poem's dedicatee and the man chiefly responsible for Muldoon's appreciation of Frost's sly, multi-layered quality. Quinn, a teacher, is described reaching for his "blue pencil"; as Clair Wills has observed, blue pencils are used by writers so that corrections do not show up in printing.[20] Quinn is initially described wearing a soutane, but this too proves impermanent; he would later abandon his calling. The disparate examples from Quinn's life are linked with allusions to Marilyn Monroe, to Soutine's *Hare on a Green Shutter*, to Frost's poetry, and to Kennedy's short-lived presidency, through a shared emphasis on the ephemerality of existence. Not that *Meeting the British* ever requires any such reminders. More elegiac than Muldoon's previous volumes, it contains another group of laments which, rather than mourning the dead, dwell instead on the collapse of the poet's relationship with Mary Powers. Taken together with the sequence recording the marriage break-up in *Why Brownlee Left*, these poems confirm Muldoon as a poet of departures, inspired more by love's decline than by its delights. 'The Soap-Pig' hurtles through references to "Anne-Marie" and "Mary", and in doing so, considerably foreshortens any impression of the length of the relationship with each woman; while 'The Ox' (from *The Wishbone*), apparently describing the end of Muldoon's affair with Mary Powers, lingers morosely on the breakdown in communication between the couple; and 'Sushi' presents difficulties in yet another relationship. The sonnet 'Gone', addressed to an ex-lover who is presumably Mary, shares thematic procedures with other poems in *Meeting the British* which detect relics of the dead in the world around them. But this time the couple's "function" is to "forget" the reminders of their past relationship, from "the smell of an apple-cannery" and "talcumed catkins", to "the subcutaneous / freckle on a cue-ball" and — with an ideogrammatical link — "the story of O. Henry". Henry's story is an acute and humorous parable about the dangers of failed communication:

> what should we make of that couple
> we never quite became,
> both turning up one lunch-hour
>
> in an auction-room
> to bid, unwittingly, against each other
> for a set of ten Venetian goblets?

While the couple must forget the shared, private connotations of apple-canneries and the like, the question which concludes the poem perhaps asks whether O. Henry's story should survive this selective amnesia, both as a salutary warning and as reassurance that their break-up was the correct and necessary decision. The poem's title, 'Gone', is the auctioneer's cry after a sale; but it also constitutes emphatic confirmation that the relationship itself is "gone".

The following poem, 'Paul Klee: *They're Biting*', also describes a relationship which is "gone", although it remains reluctant to divulge the identity of the addressee. The residuary body is another

Something Else Again: *Meeting the British* 143

of the volume's sea-creatures, a "waist-thick conger" which advises the poet regarding a postcard, from an ex- or would-be lover, depicting Klee's painting:

> The lake supports some kind of bathysphere,
> an Arab dhow
>
> and a fishing-boat
> complete with languorous net.
>
> Two caricature anglers
> have fallen hook, line and sinker
>
> for the goitred,
> spiny fish-caricatures
>
> with which the lake is stocked.
> At any moment all this should connect.

In Forsterian terms, what the painting "connect[s]" with is the poet's personal life and immediate circumstances. There is a plane sky-writing "I LOVE YOU" over Hyde Park when the postcard arrives, but the emotion is resisted. As Edna Longley has pointed out, Muldoon merges two clichés: to fall for (someone), and to fall "hook, line and sinker".[21] The poet, however, does neither: he is "given the word" (another cliché) by a conger "mouthing NO" from a fishmonger's window. There is one more cliché which remains latent: understanding the conger's fate and appreciating its warning, the poet refuses to rise to the bait.

Apart from a passing reference in 'The Soap-Pig', the volume's only explicit mention of Mary Powers occurs in 'The Marriage of Strongbow and Aoife', carried over from *The Wishbone*. Besides identifying its addressee, the poem stands apart in other ways; most conspicuously, it places the couple's resentments in the context of ancient Irish history. The speaker announces that he "might as well be another guest / at the wedding-feast / of Strongbow and Aoife MacMurrough" as watch Mary struggling to "get to grips" with a spider-crab. Strongbow was the Norman conqueror of Ireland, who had been offered Aoife's hand in marriage if he would help her father, the King of Leinster, defeat his Irish enemies. This union is seen as a betrayal, serving up Ireland to the foreigners:

> A creative pause before the second course

>   of Ireland's whole ox on a spit;
>   the invisible waitress
>   brings us each a Calvados and water-ice.
>
>   It's as if someone had slipped
>   a double-edged knife between my ribs
>   and hit the spot exactly.

Like 'Something Else', the poem exceeds its end-rhyme: "spot" rhymes with "spit", but has been buried in the line; Ronald Marken has even suggested that the rhyme is internal because it mimics the knife slipped between the speaker's ribs.[22] The poem exploits other sonnet conventions: as Marken points out, the eighth and ninth lines — "A creative pause before the second course // of Ireland's whole ox on a spit" — constitute "a turn within a turn within a turn". The sonnet traditionally "turns" within these lines; the eighth line itself announces "a creative pause before the second course"; and line nine describes Ireland's ox turning on a spit. Despite these "turns", the poem seamlessly blends the wedding-feast with the couple's low-key meal; they are linked by images of sublimated violence, and, in particular, penetration. Meat-eating is a savage process in *Meeting the British*. The speaker suffers a fate similar to that of "Ireland's whole ox" or the spider-crab; the double-edged knife between his ribs is Mary's knife, finally breaking into the crab's soft meat.

Meeting the British does not confine itself to an exclusively Irish history and mythology. The slightly overlong 'Bechbretha', for example, encompasses allusions to "local king[s]" such as Bricriu Poison-Tongue and Congal the One-Eyed, but also introduces the wonderful *Bechbretha* ("the Brehon judgements / on every conceivable form / of bee-dispute, / bee-trespass and bee-compensation", as Muldoon helpfully explains); with the assistance of two modern politicians, Merlyn Rees and Enoch Powell, it is the British, however, who finally claim the bees for themselves, draping hives in the Union Jack. The poet announces to his audience that "90 per cent of British bees / were wiped out by disease / between 1909 and 1917" — suggesting obvious parallels with the Great War — but his audience ignores such arcane knowledge in favour of the cheap theatricals of politicians. Merlyn Rees calls for order, and reaches

>   into his mulberry cummerbund.
>   'This,' he said, 'is the very handkerchief
>   that Melmoth the Wanderer
>   left at the top of the cliff.'

Something Else Again: *Meeting the British*

The winners of this particular "bee-dispute" are obvious; Muldoon implies that the excesses of political rhetoric will always defeat more considered approaches.

The volume's title poem ranges further afield in its meetings with the British: the poem focuses on Pontiac's Rebellion against the British in the 1740s. Like 'The Mixed Marriage' from *Mules*, Muldoon awakens the readers' expectations with an apparently loaded title, only then to surprise them by avoiding contemporary Ulster and describing instead an historical event over two hundred years old. 'Meeting the British' is an account, from the Indian viewpoint, of how the British crushed the Ottawa Indians by undertaking what the blurb calls "the first recorded case of germ warfare". From *New Weather* onwards, Muldoon has remained aware of parallels between the respective fates of the Irish and the native Americans: his response to Bloody Sunday had been to write 'The Year of the Sloes, for Ishi'. But as he states in interview, the differences are as important as the similarities:

> It would be naive of me to say that there's no parallel. There is a sense in which the Irish culture was ... not exactly decimated, but certainly, the history of England and Ireland has not been a happy one. Now I don't think I'd want to go to the extent, of course, where one would say that this was absolute genocide — as one might say of what happened in North America.[23]

Although Muldoon excuses neither set of colonizers, his comments are reminiscent of Kipling's famous exchanges with Roosevelt. While Roosevelt lectured him on the British Empire's treatment of 'natives', Kipling would retaliate that if only the British had acted as ruthlessly as the New World colonizers, there would no longer be any natives to mistreat. 'Meeting the British' is therefore, according to Muldoon's own formulation, at once distanced from the recent history of Northern Ireland and parallel to it. The persona has a retrospective knowledge of British perfidiousness which no Ottawa could possess: the British ingeniously despatched the rebellion by giving the natives "six fishhooks / and two blankets embroidered with smallpox".

For all these skirmishes with the British, Muldoon is never a political poet in the narrow sense; he does not consider it any function of his poetry to tell the reader which way to vote, or even which way he himself votes. Asked in interview about his politics, Muldoon has replied that "I don't think it matters. I don't think it's of any interest".[24] Yet sandwiched between two poems with broadly political resonances — 'Meeting the British' and 'Bechbretha' — 'Crossing the Line' is perhaps the closest Muldoon has come to expressing an opinion about a contemporary political event: the 1985 Anglo-Irish Agreement. Typically, Muldoon does not refer explicitly to the Agreement. So despite its obvious application to the Irish border, and its general use as a phrase meaning to commit or over-commit oneself, "crossing the line" in this case contains two primary and distinct meanings: it is a sea-faring term referring to the equator; and a term in television — the poem is set in a television studio — which describes the technical mishap where left and right sides are suddenly switched. Two rival commanders, aboard a ship, dine on "medallions of young peccary", while "their flunkeys / hand each a napkin / torn from the script of a seven-part series / based on the *Mabinogion*". The eleventh-century *Mabinogion* tales are undoubtedly among the masterpieces of Welsh literature; significantly, the tales often centre on ancient wars between Britain and Ireland. There is no doubt, however, about the specific event described on the makeshift "napkin[s]",

> Where Pryderi's gifts of hounds and horses
> turn out to have been fungus.

Given his obsession with horses and mushrooms, this transformation could almost have been undertaken with Muldoon in mind. Pryderi was a Welsh king, who at one time had been given an incomparable herd of swine (Muldoon's commanders dine on peccary). The magician Gwydion duped Pryderi into swapping them by offering some illusory horses and hounds; only after the exchange had been made and Gwydion had returned home did Pryderi realize he had been tricked. The *Mabinogion* therefore provide the rival commanders with an unhappy forewarning of the dangers of making deals. Muldoon leaves tantalizingly unsaid the result of Gwydion's betrayal: Pryderi raised an army and marched north towards his enemy's lands; the two men met in single combat, and Gwydion, by magic as well as strength, defeated and killed Pryderi. Nor does the poem announce which of the rival commanders is the betrayer and which the betrayed; the televisual connotations of the title imply that the men might at any moment swap positions.

Despite its many strengths, *Meeting the British* is a dissatisfying volume. It contains poems which unquestionably belong among Muldoon's best work — 'The Marriage of Strongbow and Aoife',

'The Wishbone', 'The Fox', 'The Soap-Pig', 'Something Else', 'Paul Klee: *They're Biting*' — and often powerfully embodies Muldoon's perennial themes of violence, mutilation and the fragility of the body. At times it also predicts Muldoon's later development: his cautious interest in autobiography, for example, is an important step towards the relative candour of *The Prince of the Quotidian* and *The Annals of Chile*. Yet even ignoring what Ciaran Carson — a friend and admirer — has condemned as Muldoon's "crossword puzzle" strategies,[25] the volume contains too many fillers. So for example, when 'Profumo' ends with Muldoon's mother ordering him to go away and read Masefield's 'Cargoes', the poet, of course, is vicariously prompting the reader to do the same thing: not alone in *Meeting the British*, the poem sacrifices any dramatic impact merely in order to bolster the volume's larger structures. As William Scammell argued in the *Irish Review*, while the best poems are certainly worth preserving, it would have been preferable had Muldoon enlisted them as an impromptu supplement to his *Selected Poems* (published a year previously), and fastidiously discarded all the others.

Notes

1. 'An Interview with Paul Muldoon', interviewed by Clair Wills, Nick Jenkins and John Lanchester, *Oxford Poetry* III (1), Winter 1986-7, 18.
2. *ibid.*, 18.
3. *ibid.*, 19.
4. *ibid.*, 19.
5. Longley, E. 'The Room Where MacNeice Wrote "Snow"', *The Living Stream: Literature & Revisionism in Ireland* (Newcastle-upon-Tyne: Bloodaxe, 1994), 265.
6. 'An Interview with Paul Muldoon', interviewed by Lynn Keller, *Contemporary Literature* 35 (1), Spring 1994, 26.
7. Auden, W.H. *The English Auden* ed. Mendelson E. (London: Faber, 1977), 393.
8. *Muldoon in America*, interviewed by Christopher Cook, B.B.C. Radio 3, 1994.
9. Carpenter, H. *W.H. Auden: A Biography* (Boston: Houghton Mifflin, 1981), 253.
10. Kerrigan, J. 'Ulster Ovids', *The Chosen Ground: Essays on the Contemporary Poetry of Northern Ireland*, ed. Corcoran, N. (Bridgend: Seren, 1992), 253.

11. *ibid.*, 252.
12. Quoted by Johnson, D. *Irish Poetry After Joyce* (Notre Dame: University of Notre Dame Press, 1985), 24.
13. *Muldoon in America*, 1994.
14. Quoted by Wills, C. 'The Lie of the Land', *The Chosen Ground: Essays on the Contemporary Poetry of Northern Ireland*, ed. Corcoran, N. (Bridgend: Seren, 1992), 24.
15. Raine, C. 'Bad Language: Poetry, Swearing and Translation', *Thumbscrew* 1, Winter 1994/5, 38.
16. Heaney, S. *Station Island* (London: Faber, 1984), 16-17.
17. Quoted by Wills, C. 'The Lie of the Land', 138.
18. 'Lunch with Paul Muldoon', interviewed by Kevin Smith, *Rhinoceros* 4, 1991, 85-86.
19. Muldoon gives a fuller account of Frost's undercutting in interview with Michael Donaghy: "Frost says that the new administration welcomes in a 'golden age of poetry and power / Of which this noontide's the beginning hour'. Now noon is the peak of the day. If the beginning is the peak of it, the rest is a kind of decline. Then consider the phrase 'golden age'. The word 'gold' as it occurs throughout Frost is almost inevitably pejorative." 'A Conversation with Paul Muldoon', interviewed by Michael Donaghy, *Chicago Review* 35 (1), Autumn 1985, 84.
20. Wills, C. 'The Lie of the Land', 137.
21. Longley, E. 'No More Poems About Paintings?', *The Living Stream: Literature & Revisionism in Ireland* (Newcastle-upon-Tyne: Bloodaxe, 1994), 241.
22. Marken, R. 'Paul Muldoon's "Juggling A Red-Hot Half-Brick In An Old Sock": Poets In Ireland Renovate The English-Language Sonnet', *Eire-Ireland* 24 (1), Spring 1989, 90.
23. *Muldoon in America*, 1994.
24. Interviewed by Michael Donaghy, 85.
25. 'Ciaran Carson interviewed by Frank Ormsby', *The Linen Hall Review* 8 (1), Spring 1991, 8.

Parallel to the Parallel Realm: *Madoc — A Mystery*

"What I want to write", Muldoon has confessed in interview, "are beautifully pellucid, simple lyric poems".[1] 'Madoc — A Mystery', the 246-page title poem of Muldoon's sixth full-length collection, is an ugly, opaque, sprawling epic, spanning two continents and half a century, while offering a potted history of Western philosophy from Thales to Hawking along the way. Muldoon explains the discrepancy between poetic intent and finished product in terms of a lack of volition: eighteen months in the making, 'Madoc' is a poem which, he says, "needed — without my sounding too corny about it I hope — to write [itself] through me".[2] Nevertheless, the structure of the volume signals not so much a new departure as a huge shift in emphasis. Even using the crudest measurements, it is clear that the long poems ending Muldoon's collections gradually become more intrusive: while *New Weather's* 'The Year of the Sloes, for Ishi' provided just four pages out of forty-seven, by the time of *Meeting the British* the long concluding poem, '7, Middagh Street', filled twenty-five of the sixty pages. Madoc accelerates this development: the seven works in part one constitute less than one-twentieth of the volume, having been reduced to the poetic equivalent of an overture. They introduce some of the major themes which will be fully expressed and elaborated in 'Madoc' itself.

This first section of Madoc relates teasingly to the longer poem. Alerted by the volume's subtitle — *A Mystery* — one might expect the opening prose passage, 'The Key', to offer some kind of clue or revelation. Certainly, a key reappears with conspicuous significance in 'Madoc' itself: "That teeny-weeny key. Bear it in mind". But as might be expected from Muldoon, 'The Key' obscures as much as it illuminates. The piece describes how the protagonist "ran into Foley six months ago in a dubbing suite in Los Angeles"; Foley was "half-way through post-production on a remake of *The Hoodlum Priest*". Remakes, rewrites, repetitions, mimicries, copies, xeroxes are all integral to Muldoon's 'Madoc': Southey, for example, wrote an epic also called *Madoc*, alluded to by its namesake on several occasions; and the colonizing exploits of Muldoon's Pantisocrats are anticipated by the Madoc legend itself, which records how a twelfth-century Welsh prince of that name sailed away from his country's civil war in search of a quieter land, returning only once to collect fresh supplies and adventurers for his colony before vanishing for good. 'The Key' provides further instances of duplication: the protagonist recalls how he sat through the first version of *The Hoodlum Priest* (itself a "copy" of a true story) three or four times, scrutinizing the crowd scenes for his cousin, who had appeared as an extra. This "identity parade" parallels the sequence Foley is busy working on:

> a police line-up, in which the victim shuffled along, stopped with each suspect in turn, then shuffled on. At a critical moment, she dropped a key on the floor. Foley was having trouble matching sound to picture on this last effect.

Foley is presumably named after Jack Foley, who perfected a technique subsequently known as "foleying": matching sound effect with picture. By contrast the protagonist is less concerned with synchronization than with a diachronic search for origins. He wants to "say something about the etymology of 'tuxedo'", which was named after a country club in Tuxedo Park, New York; even the O.E.D. fails to mention that the club's name was taken in turn from an American Indian place-name. A reference to "mesquite", from another native word — *mizquitl* — bolsters the suggestion that by emphasising linguistic borrowings and deprivations, 'The Key' prepares for the physical dispossession of the American Indians in 'Madoc'.

In another example of copying, the word "mesquite" seems to prompt the persona, by his own admission, to begin to "'misquote'" himself:

> *When he sookied a calf down a boreen*
> *it was through Indo-European.*
> *When he clicked at a donkey carting dung*
> *your father had an African tongue.*
> *You seem content to ventriloquize the surf.*

Foley swallowed whatever it was;

> *Still defending that same old patch of turf?*
> *Have you forgotten that 'hoodlum' is back-slang*
> *For the leader of a San Francisco street gang?*

Muldoon has commented that the risk in writing this versified direct speech is that some people may believe he was trying to write well.[3] In fact the passage is deliberately bad: the persona misquotes himself partly because he sounds like an awful Muldoon, thumping out terrible, stilted couplets. Yet there is an inherent paradox in misquoting oneself — all such self-misquotations are, naturally, original quotations as well. This encapsulates the division between Foley and his visitor, who fanatically traces the (presumably misquoted) root-sounds back to their distant origins, and characterizes his companion's job as merely "ventriloquiz[ing] the surf". Foley is intrigued more by the rootless slang of street-talk: "hoodlum" originated in San Francisco around 1870, although its early history is obscure. (Muldoon is also playing a joke on his own name: "hoodlum" is very nearly "back*wards*-slang" for "Muldoon"). Despite the accusation that he has abandoned his Irish origins — the word "boreen" specifically locates the father in Ireland — Foley might even be seen as adopting a Muldoon-like approach to the civil wars of his homeland. The street-fighting and gang warfare of San Francisco and of *The Hoodlum Priest* are powerful analogues and, to a degree, duplications, of life in modern Ulster. The exchange with Foley, although "remarkable for its banality", throws the protagonist (to use the unspoken cliché) out of sync: "These past six months I've sometimes run a little ahead of myself, but mostly I lag behind, my footfalls already pre-empted by their echoes". 'The Key' may not provide the solution to the mystery of 'Madoc', but its temporal disruptions do match the organizing — or more exactly, disorganizing — strategies of the longer poem; the quotation, the xerox, the remake often precede and predict their originals, stealing their authority.

There are several aquatic allusions in 'The Key': the cousin is called Marina; Foley wears "an ultramarine tuxedo" and emerges from his sound booth "like a diver from a bathyscope"; his job is characterized as "ventriloquiz[ing] the surf". Perhaps these references connect with other poems in part one of *Madoc* which are also concerned with having crossed the Atlantic and left Northern Ireland behind. 'Tea', for example, is in part a poem about Muldoon's emigration to the States:

> I was rooting through tea-chest after tea-chest
> as they drifted in along Key West
>
> when I chanced on 'Pythagoras in America'...

These tea-chests are, improbably enough, the flotsam of the Boston Tea Party, washed down-coast to Florida two centuries later. They are also the containers for packing possessions — in this case, books

— for the crossing to the States. So with his luggage still arriving, the poet's hospitality cannot yet extend very far:

> All I have in the house is some left-over
>
> squid cooked in its own ink
> and this unfortunate cup of tea. Take it. Drink.

The poem's concluding imperatives hint at sacramental connotations, echoing the Last Supper. But the squid also recalls the sea-food prevalent in *Meeting the British*; given that the tea is made from a tea-leaf caught up among the poet's books, the squid's "ink" develops unpleasant connotations of printer's ink. 'Pythagoras in America', the essay by Lévi-Strauss which the poet "chance[s] on" as he roots through the tea-chests, is about eating as well. Noting how Pythagoras, a vegetarian, forbade the consumption of fava beans on the grounds that they served as a dwelling place for the souls of the dead, Lévi-Strauss goes on to examine why, under certain circumstances, Pythagoras lifted the prohibition. However obliquely, this relates 'Tea' to the disgustedly carnivorous appetites of *Meeting the British*, and even the volume's hinted interest in metempsychosis — the belief in the transmigration of souls from one body to another (Pythagoras is once said to have stopped a man beating a dog because he could recognize in its yelps the cries of an old friend). But 'Pythagoras in America' is integral to the themes of 'Madoc' too; like 'Making the Move' from *Why Brownlee Left*, or 'Profumo' from *Meeting the British*, 'Tea' gives Muldoon the opportunity to sneak a mention of useful sources for the long concluding poem. *Madoc — A Mystery* is just as voraciously carnivorous as Muldoon's preceding volume, and beans are also served up; nevertheless, 'Madoc' still manages to find evidence of a Pythagorean colony in the States. The section of 'Madoc' entitled '[Pythagoras]' — each of the poem's sections is named parenthetically after a Western philosopher — refers to the Roanoke Rood, a "scorch-marked lump of wood" covered in mud except for the mysterious word "CROATAN". This was the only sign left by Raleigh's lost colony, which had disappeared by the time he returned with new supplies and settlers (like Madoc before him). 'Madoc' toys extensively with the word and its possible meanings, before concluding that it should read "Not 'CROATAN' not 'CROATOAN', but 'CROTONA'" — Crotona being the location of Pythagoras's educational colony and ideal community in Italy. 'Tea' accordingly manages to balance symbols of emigration from Europe to the States

Parallel to the Parallel Realm: *Madoc — A Mystery*

against the most resonant image (the Boston Tea Party) of American rejection of foreign political influence.

Other poems in part one also focus on emigration to the States. 'The Panther', for example, shows the poet exploring the history and environment of what is to become his new home ground:

> For what it's worth, the last panther in Massachusetts
> was brought to justice
> in the woods beyond these meadows
> and hung by its heels from a meat-hook
> in what is now our kitchen.
>
> (The house itself is something of a conundrum,
> built as it was by an Ephraim Cowan from Antrim.)

This augurs the summary and brutal "justice" of 'Madoc', while also underlining some of the disastrous effects caused by the settlers on the natural habitat. Later in the poem, the flagstone under the meat-hook reveals "the smudge of the tippy-tip" of the panther's nose; the "tippy-tip" suggests less a savage beast than an innocent, even cute, victim, ruthlessly slaughtered. But even if the panther's ghostly return implicates the poet as a colonizer, the architectural history of the house still ensures — in another case of duplication — that it has the potential to become a home from home. By contrast 'The Briefcase' seems much more homesick for the North. Dedicated to Seamus Heaney, the poem imagines that the eelskin briefcase will revert to its animal origins, slinking through a culvert and along the East River to the open sea, taking with it "the first inkling of this poem" — a clear instance of footfalls pre-empted by their echoes; no doubt there is also a sly allusion to Heaney's 'Lough Neagh Sequence', in which the eel is described as a "gland" which "drifted / into motion half-way / across the Atlantic" before making its way "two hundred miles in- / land" via the rivers and estuaries of Ireland. Muldoon's specific reference to the East River fixes his New York location while perhaps drawing attention to the briefcase's intended eastward direction: Ireland. As Michael Hofmann has pointed out, 'The Briefcase' therefore serves as a kind of Chaucerian envoi, but with the opposite wish: Stay, little book. The sonnet's rhyme scheme (*abcdefgfgedcba*) supports this conclusion, by creating what Lucy McDiarmid calls a "watertight poetic form": the central quatrain is surrounded by five symmetrical rhyming lines on each side.

'The Briefcase', like 'The Key', seems to promise, but makes no effort to deliver, clues to the mystery of 'Madoc'. A valise surfaces several times in the longer poem's narrative, without ever quite divulging its significance. Yet it has found its way back to Ireland, and finally turns up in the dome of Unitel West, situated "half-way between Belfast and Dublin". Other poems from this first section also parade an apparent relevance to 'Madoc' while giving up their "keys" no more willingly. The title of the couplet 'Asra', for example, even evokes one of the central characters of 'Madoc', Samuel Taylor Coleridge, whose Asra poems were inspired by his love for Sara Hutchinson. Like Coleridge's coded and indirect dedications to an illicit love, Muldoon's two-liner gives little away:

> The night I wrote your name in biro on my wrist
> we would wake before dawn; back to back: duellists.

The image of the lovers as "duellists" with all the division and hostility that it implies, is perfect. The first line, however, excludes the reader like the worst of Muldoon's *Wishbone* poems; while its meaning is clear enough, without extra-poetical assistance the only person who might understand the event's significance is the unidentified addressee. By calling the poem 'Asra', Muldoon highlights its deliberate obliquity and private connotations; in fact, only the mention of "biro", a modern word for a modern invention, proves the poem is not ventriloquized through Coleridge himself.

There are further connections with Coleridge in 'Cauliflowers', a distorted sestina commemorating Muldoon's father and uncle. The poem opens with an epigraph from the *National Enquirer*, which reports how light-producing bacteria, taken from the mouths of fish, have been added through gene-splicing to the plants of carrots, cauliflowers and potatoes so that they glow in the dark; as Muldoon has observed of the *National Enquirer*, "all kinds of strange things are reported in this wonderful 'organ', I think, would be the word for it".[4] 'Madoc' quotes Coleridge reporting a similar discovery by a M. Haggern, who one evening perceived "*a faint flash of light repeatedly dart from a marigold*"; Coleridge conjectures that "*there is something of electricity in this phenomenon*". 'Madoc' later extracts the poetic product of Coleridge's arcane reading:

> 'Tis said, in Summer's evening hour
> Flashes the golden-colour'd flower
>   A fair electric flame:
> And so shall flash my love-charg'd eye
> When all the heart's big ecstasy
>   Shoots rapid through the frame.

'Cauliflowers' is therefore another duplication; Muldoon, like Coleridge, is fascinated by the dubious possibility of *"plants that glow in the dark"*. However, besides its Coleridgean parallels, 'Cauliflowers' seems to have little bearing on 'Madoc'. The poem represents Muldoon's earliest published experimentation with the sestina, a form which will become integral to 'Yarrow' from *The Annals of Chile*; but as that later poem confirms, it is a form Muldoon moulds, even vandalizes, as thoroughly as he does the sonnet. In a conventional sestina, the end-words are unchanged in every stanza. Two examples from 'Cauliflowers' suffice to indicate the flexibility Muldoon introduces into what is normally one of the more rigid poetic forms: Regan, the surname of Muldoon's uncle, becomes "regain", "jerkins", "jerry-can", "Oregon" and "original"; "market" reappears as "make out", "mud-guard", "scorch-marked", "Magritte's", "Margaret", and finally, "unmarked pit" (curiously, "scorch-marked" does provide a passing link with 'Madoc', in which the Roanoke Rood is described as "scorch-marked"). Despite this formal freedom, 'Cauliflowers' still strains to deliver its end- or rhyme-word: so lovers are conveniently overheard murmuring "light / of my life", because "light" is an end-word. Incorporating an unsurprisingly irregular envoi, the poem's conclusion rises above such clumsiness:

> My father going down
> the primrose path with Patrick Regan.
> All gone out of the world of light.
>
> All gone down
> the original pipe. And the cauliflowers
> in an unmarked pit, that were harvested by their own light.

Muldoon takes a line from Vaughan — "They are all gone into the world of light!" — but revises it so that death, far from accessing a radiant paradise, implicitly consigns the poet's father and uncle to a darkness similar to the "unmarked pit" of the cauliflowers.

'Capercaillies', like 'Cauliflowers', pre-empts and draws particular attention to certain details in 'Madoc'. When the poem specifies that the speaker and "St Joan" are staying in "Room 233" of a hotel "somewhere north of Loch Lomond", the numerical reference anticipates a passage from 'Madoc' where Coleridge is led by a Seneca "Up a spiral staircase with precisely two hundred and thirty-three steps, each conjured from the living rock"; many Indian tribes believed that rocks were imbued with spirits and that they themselves were conjured from the earth of the Red Pipestone Quarry by the Great Spirit.[5] That there are are also two hundred and thirty-three sections in 'Madoc' indicates something more important than a play on Fibonacci numbers: in fact, there were two hundred and thirty-three native tribes in America at the time of the sub-continent's "discovery". 'Capercaillies' also broaches several other of the longer poem's preoccupations. It is, for example, representatively carnivorous:

> While their flesh is notably gamey
> even in bilberry-time, their winter tack's
> mainly pine-shoots, so now they smack
>
> of nothing so much as turpentine.

What gives this passage its shock value is the way in which the poem's celebration of the capercaillie — as a living creature — modulates into this gastronomic appreciation. Previously the capercaillie had been described in anthropomorphic terms, with the female "meekly back from Harrods" in her yellow gum-boots, and the male "a straggler from Hadrian's / sixth legion" or a "renegade Norman knight". These latter images of colonization befit what is arguably the most bizarre and wonderful of all British birds: the capercaillie was once native to the British Isles — never forgetting his equine preoccupations, Muldoon parenthetically informs the reader that "'horse of the woods', the name means in Gaelic" — but was hunted down to extinction, before being reintroduced from Sweden. The poem conceals one further, more playful instance of attempted colonization. Dillon Johnson has argued that if part one of *Madoc* constitutes a key to the title poem, then Muldoon's translations of Nuala Ní Dhomhnaill's poetry in *The Astrakhan Cloak* provide a key to a key: Muldoon inserts the phrase "the acrostical capercaillie" into his version of Ní Dhomhnaill's 'The Lay of Loughadoon' ('Loch a Duin').[6] 'Capercaillies' is certainly "acrostical": taking the first letter of each line, it reads "Is this a *New Yorker* poem or what". Besides its wry joke at the expense of the literary politics of an influential American magazine, the acrostic suggests an effort by Muldoon, however ironically intended or expressed, to assimilate himself into the poetic mainstream of his new homeland.

Although the poems of part one represent accessible introductions to the thematic complexities of 'Madoc', many reviewers ignored these initial pointers, and with few exceptions their responses to the longer poem ranged from the bewildered to the appalled. Grey Gowrie, in *The Telegraph*, considered Muldoon "a good writer suffering an acute attack of literature"; John Banville complained in the *New York Review of Books* that Muldoon had gone "too far — so far, at least, that I can hardly make him out at all"; even Michael Hofmann, a gifted poet-critic and one of Muldoon's greatest apologists, admitted feeling tempted "to throw the whole thing at a computer and say: 'Here, you do it'" (a reaction which Muldoon gleefully recounts in interview). Yet the origins of *Madoc* had seemed humble enough. Muldoon claims that both poem and volume started while he was preparing his edition of Byron:

> Byron's always taking out, not necessarily the heavy artillery, just the old musket and taking a pot shot at Southey ... then I started to think again about the pantisocratic scheme. Of course, that scheme didn't materialize. Then I thought, well, hey, what if it did?[7]

Byron's *The Vision of Judgement* and *Don Juan* are sources for 'Madoc'; Muldoon quotes directly from both. For more important reasons, however, the roots of Muldoon's poem go further back, beyond the Byron edition: 'Madoc' is, in a sense, the poem Muldoon had waited his whole career to write, merging a paean (and elegy) for the culture of the native American tribes with a fully orchestrated exploration of alternative lives. Coleridge and Southey rewrite not just their own histories, but also the course of subsequent national and international events, by crossing the Atlantic and founding a Pantisocratic community on the banks of the Susquehanna river. The historical reality had been more anti-climactic: the project was never fulfilled partly due to a lack of finances and partly because Southey began to argue, against the fundamental tenets of Pantisocracy, that servants should "do the manual labour, and that the women should have exclusive charge of the children and domestic work".[8]

'Madoc' is a philosophical poem, but with no consistent set of beliefs. The events described are filtered through a history of Western philosophy from 580 B.C. to the present day; and each of the poem's sections reflects, or is in some way shaped by, the presiding philosopher. The poem opens, for example, with '[Thales]', who maintained that the world originates in and is sustained by water, and that water accounts for every physical phenomenon; so in this section a series of alarms sends "a ripple" through the building, and a running man, juxtaposed with a frog "scrawl[ing] across a lily-pond", prepares to "[take] the plunge". In '[Anaximenes]', two sections later, water imagery has been replaced by air or, in this case, oxygen — for no other reason than that Anaximenes considered air the underlying principle of the world. No one philosophy is presented in 'Madoc' as more accurate or profound than any other; rather, Muldoon enjoys and exploits the myriad poetic possibilities offered by so many different ways of interpreting the world. His summaries of a philosopher's thought are often brilliantly apposite, and sometimes destructive: so Ayer's Logical Positivism is encapsulated, with comic aplomb, in the line "September 14th, 1836. Burr is incontrovertibly dead". Nor is the relationship between the supertitled philosopher and the text ever constant. Many sections pun on a name: '[Bacon]' serves up a boiled ham; '[Seneca]' recounts a creation myth of the Seneca Indians; '[Paine]' describes the death of Alexander Hamilton, shot "through the kidneys // and milty spleen"; Coleridge, Byron and Jefferson figure in sections which take their names; '[Burnet]', '[Clarke]', '[Berkeley]', '[Hartley]', '[Reid]', '[Hamilton]', '[Newman]', '[Putnam]', '[Russell]', '[Moore]' and '[Lewis]', remarkably, share their names with characters from 'Madoc'; and Henry O'Bail makes just three appearances — not coincidentally, in sections named after Boyle, Bayle and Boole.

This mad history of Western philosophy shares organizational strategies with previous templates employed by Muldoon: 'Immram Mael Duin' in 'Immram' and the Trickster cycle of the Winnebago Indians in 'The More a Man Has the More a Man Wants'. At a late stage Muldoon considered dropping the supertitles altogether, and has since expressed the wish that they should be read almost subliminally,[9] in the way the subtitles of a foreign language film might be. However, the philosophical references guarantee the sly multi-layered quality which Muldoon enjoys in Frost's work. They ensure that 'Madoc' raises "questions about the nature of reading",[10] and specifically they allow a multi-speed approach to the poem. As Muldoon explains,

> if I were advising someone how to read this book, I would say ... "Read it as a ripping yarn. Don't get too concerned about the other thing. If you want to get involved in the other thing, you can. And in fact there is a lot of it there. If you don't know who Burr or Blennerhassett is, well, you may have to go and find out. But that's okay. There are lots of things we have to go and find out. We have to go and find out what red, what wheel and barrow are, at some level."[11]

Parallel to the Parallel Realm: *Madoc — A Mystery*

'Madoc' is both a "ripping yarn" and, despite Muldoon's disingenuousness, a detailed philosophical poem. In fact there are thematic reasons for arguing that the supertitles are integral to the text of 'Madoc'. The poem is framed by a science-fiction setting from an alternative world of the future, where the Pantisocrats' crossing to the States has changed the whole course of world history. The Pantisocrats' adventures, which form the main body of 'Madoc', are retrieved from a descendant of Southey, named South, who has been fitted up to a contraption called a "retinagraph", so that "all that follows / flickers and flows / from the back of his right eyeball". The events of the poem are therefore ordered according to South's perceptions and preoccupations. He is, in Muldoon's words, "some kind of a Sunday philosophy buff", making sense of the world by filtering it through a "madcap history of Western thought".[12]

South's retina first glimpses the Pantisocrats, in '[Parmenides]', past a divide in the road between "the Way of Seeming and the Way of Truth" — a divide incorporating the section's presiding philosopher and Frost's 'The Road Not Taken'. Stressing its own artifice, 'Madoc' constantly draws attention to the presence of this other road or parallel universe, from the duplicated key and valise to Thomas Jefferson's "newly-modified polygraph" which

> will automatically
> follow hand-in-glove
>
> his copper-plate 'whippoorwill'
> or 'praise' or 'love':
>
> will run parallel to the parallel
> realm to which it is itself the only key.

Bringing the actual course of history — the road taken — to bear on the poem's parallel realm proves partially successful. Neither Coleridge nor Southey wholly evade their fate: just as the renegade bishop's calling in *Why Brownlee Left* catches up with him in old age, so the poets in their alternative lives die at the predestined time — Coleridge 1834, and Southey 1843. However, the poem's alternative "vision" of history remains precarious and unstable, flickering from "the back of [South's] right eyeball" as the retina verges on disintegration. Like 'Kubla Khan' to which it often alludes, 'Madoc' is a fragmented vision poem; and as befits a vision emitted from a disintegrating retina, many of its mysteries are insoluble. At times Muldoon misleads the reader; for example, a character called

MacGuffin, who later changes his name to Smith and then Magoffin, seems to possess enigmatic significance — unless, that is, the reader is aware that Alfred Hitchcock's term for a plot device was a "MacGuffin".[13] The poem finally seems to explode its fragile parallel universe and science fiction frame of "Unitel" (an "iridescent dome" revising 'Kubla Khan'), along with the retina which has both given birth to, and been produced by, this alternative history.

Like the most successful of Muldoon's earlier long poems, 'Immram' and 'The More a Man Has the More a Man Wants', the quest is central to 'Madoc'; its title, most obviously, refers to the legend of the Welsh prince who abandoned his barbarous country in search of a quieter land. The Madoc legend consistently provides a "parallel / realm" to the Pantisocrats' colonizing exploits, as they leave Britain to establish their utopia — or as it transpires, dystopia — in the New World. Part of the attraction for Muldoon no doubt lies in the legend's compliance with his expressed belief, in interview with John Haffenden a decade previously, that

> One of the ways in which we are most ourselves is that we imagine ourselves to be going somewhere else. It's important to most societies to have the notion of something out there to which we belong, that our home is somewhere else ... there's another dimension, something around us and beyond us, which is our inheritance.[14]

However, 'Madoc' reveals the strong moral drive which underlies so many of Muldoon's parables and evasions. It poses the question of how such an "inheritance" can be claimed without simultaneously disinheriting others. As Muldoon has acknowledged in interview, the Madoc legend is an appropriate test case, having been exploited in order to reinforce colonial claims: the legend was first given widespread currency by the Tudors, who emphasised their own Welsh pedigree in order to undercut the Spanish with a prior claim to the lands and riches of the Americas.[15] 'Madoc' attacks the fanaticism with which evidence of the Welsh prince's descendants amongst the North American tribes was hunted down and manipulated. The word "penguin", for example, was supposed an Indian word with Welsh origins, from *pen* ("head") and *gwyn* ("white"). In '[Whitehead]' Southey is suddenly disabused of this etymological fantasy, waking "in a cold sweat" to the terrible revelation that "penguins don't have white heads".

As part of this disinheriting of the natives, 'Madoc' explores how legend and language merge to become what Muldoon calls a "weapon of colonization".[16] In reaction, Muldoon has filled the poem (and, as "tuxedo" and "mesquite" from 'The Key' suggest, the volume too) with native American words, tacitly celebrating and commemorating a culture on the verge of being wiped out. The words fulfil a purpose similar to the water imagery in 'Immram' or the animal metaphors of 'The More a Man Has the More a Man Wants', providing a constant reminder of the natives' presence even as the settlers, searching for their own inheritance, dispossess and destroy them: squantum, kinnikinnick, manitou, mackinaw, wannigan, sachems, sagamore, mugwump, punk, cougar, raccoon, coyote, tomahawk, wigwam, quamash, caucus, powwow, skunk, woodchuck, hickory; Indian inventions referred to include the canoe, kayak, calmuet, catalite pipe, longhouse, hammock, toboggan, lacrosse, moccasin, and pirogue.[17] (As 'Capercaillies' has already highlighted, this celebration of native culture is even carved in stone, with each of the two hundred and thirty-three tribes represented by a step cut into "the living rock".) Ironically, tantalizing glimpses of the Welsh prince and his lost tribe are, in 'Madoc', as often linguistic as physical: Thomas Jefferson "finishes off a carafe // of his best Medoc"; the man-servant Shad, apparently inspired by the rhyme, first thinks of the Madoc legend while bending down to pick up a "mattock"; and the Irish stallion Bucephalus, another of Muldoon's talking horses, argues that the "nock" in Mount Monadnock is from the Gaelic *cnoc*, a hill, while failing to notice the clandestine presence of Madoc himself in the mountain's name. Bucephalus in fact pursues a colonizing agenda which would preempt even the Madoc legend:

> 'Were the secret of the ogam
> script on the edge of this standing stone
> known to the Reverend Samson Occom
> he would hold it in disdain.
>
> Yet his own people, the Mohegan,
> are the seed of the Celtic chieftain, Eoghan.'

Muldoon has acknowledged that most of Bucephalus's statements relate to the theories of the historian Barry Fell, who argues in *America, B.C.* that the Celts had arrived in North America centuries before: the Mohicans (or Mohegans), supposedly, can be traced back to a Celtic chieftain.[18] Bucephalus's claims, following Fell, rely for physical evidence on some stone scratchings which look a little like ogam, an ancient alphabetical writing system (from the old Irish *ogom*) used by the Celts. While denying the rights of the native tribes, the colonizers desperately search for and attempt to appropriate any evidence, no matter how dubious, which might bolster their respective historically- or mythically-based arguments for land ownership.

It is not just the profusion of native words which makes 'Madoc' linguistically curious. In 'Profumo' the poet's mother had ordered him to go away and read Masefield's 'Cargoes' ("Quinquereme of Nineveh from distant Ophir"). 'Madoc' proves the lesson in conveying verbal riches has been well learnt. The poem also contains Ulster dialect, the blissfully rambunctious diaries of the explorers Lewis and Clarke, the private language of Sara Fricker — "'Now your snouterumpater is a connoisorrow / who has lost her raspectabilberry'" — and any number of other neologisms and nonce-words: "rowdy-dow-dow", "furfurry", "camelopard", "laverock", "retinagraph", "Lasabers" and so on. Some passages are bejewelled, almost weighed down, with a seemingly endless supply of exotic polysyllables:

> October 25th. Though the sandstone bluffs and spurs
> give way, for the most part, to sparsely-
>
> wooded, deeply-fissured mesas
> redolent of wormwood, of the artemisia's
>
> turpentine and camphor,
> there's still the occasional, delicately-chamfered
>
> column of honey- or salmon-coloured querns
> surmounted, as here, by an obsidian cornice.
>
> Camphor and turpentine. Elk-slots. Bear-scats.

In such examples, there is a pleasure in linguistic exactness for its own sake. But while never forgetting the political implications, 'Madoc' also retains the excited sense of being a "frontier poem" in diction as much as subject matter: with language, as well as land, apparently up for grabs, anything seems possible. The poem's formal techniques are also varied: sonnets (about thirty in total) are juxtaposed with sections consisting of one or two lines, irregular quatrains with quotations from Southey, Lewis and Clarke, Catlin, Byron, Red Jacket *et al.* Quick cuts, reminiscent of the cinematic strategies of 'The More a Man Has', give the impression that numerous interlocking stories, all happening at once, are vying for supremacy. This polyphony of voices and registers in the poem delights in a cultural diversity; but it is a diversity which, the narrative bleakly illustrates, will give way to the futuristic vision of "Unitel", symbol of a monolithic international government.

'Madoc' contrasts two methods of colonization: the brutal and the assimilatory. For all the technical prowess which the larger canvas and larger ambition of 'Madoc' allows him to demonstrate, the consistency of Muldoon's obsessions can be gauged from 'Promises, Promises' in *Why Brownlee Left*, which retrospectively reads like a modest rehearsal for 'Madoc'. The poem records the musings of a member of Raleigh's Roanoke colony who foresees what will happen after their leader returns to the Old World for supplies and more people:

> He will return, years afterwards,
> To wonder where and why
> We might have altogether disappeared,
> Only to glimpse us here and there
> As one fair strand in her braid,
> The blue in an Indian girl's dead eye.

Or, as 'Madoc' later adds, an indecipherable scrawl on a lump of wood. But this is a typical disappearing act from *Why Brownlee Left*, because the colonizers have not, in fact, gone anywhere. The "dead eye" of the Indian girl may conceivably allude to an optical malfunction, but it also undoubtedly conveys overwhelming associations of fatality. Whereas the "eighty souls" of the Roanoke colony become assimilated into their environment, the speaker seems to suggest that Raleigh will only "glimpse" their fate in the natives' corpses. The same methods of colonization divide Coleridge and Southey in 'Madoc'. Failing to consider even the possibility of cultural assimilation, Southey is quoted from the preface to his own *Madoc* as believing the lost Welsh Indians retain "their complexion, their language, and in some degree, their arts". Muldoon spares the reader any more of Southey's *Madoc*, a poem alternately dull and repugnant, which becomes representative of a self-delusive pomposity: as Muldoon's Southey (repeating, as it were, the historical Southey) notes, "*Taylor has said it is the best English poem that has left the press since* Paradise Lost; *indeed, this is not exaggerated praise, for, unfortunately, there is no competition*". In Southey's poem Madoc is a Christian crusader overthrowing "foul idolatry", which is exiled and later punished by "Heaven's ministers of vengeance", that is, the "heroic Spaniard's unrelenting sword".

Muldoon's Southey is hardly portrayed more sympathetically than his historical counterpart. After Alexander Cinnamond, the Scots-Irish scout, abducts Sara Fricker (or given that "We doubt even that we doubt", helps her to abscond), Southey tracks him down and rams "the sheaf of goose-quills / into his eyes". Upholding the Old Testament injunction "an eye for an eye", Cinnamond later takes revenge by burning down the Pantisocratic settlement, raping Edith Southey, castrating George Burnett, and killing Berkeley Coleridge and Lovell — although the man-servant Shad, following his Biblical namesake Shadrach, is saved from the "fiery furnace". Southey loses an eye when nine months later Edith gives birth to South (Southey minus an 'ey', whose descendant will also lose an eye to the "retinagraph"). For the rest of the poem Southey's political apostasy grotesquely distorts the fundamental Pantisocratic tenets. Pantisocracy holds beliefs regarding the relationship between humankind and the land not dissimilar to those of native American tribes; so it is no coincidence that Southey's persecution of the natives begins when he builds a complex system of barricades round the settlement, and renames it "Southeyopolis". He soon bans certain native religious ceremonies, and becomes increasingly ridiculous in his despotism:

> Since he's suffering from a mild case of the flux,
> he's couchant on a tavelin
> of vairs and minivers. In his right hand is the valise,
> in his left the three-tined javelin
>
> with which he admonishes, from his litter,
> the Cayuga so slovenly as to have dropped his muzzle-loader.

When Southey wrongly suspects a revival of one of the proscribed religious ceremonies, he makes a scapegoat of South's old wet-nurse, sentencing her to twenty lashes; in the ensuing revolt, South follows the Cayugas "into the shadows", his destination "a matter of pure conjecture". Thereafter Southey's life becomes gradually more pathetic: he denounces his enemies to an empty "tree-girt auditorium"; and with his glories now reduced to the "scrofulous", "scabrous diadem" of his "lime-scaled pate", his settlement is breached and he is hacked to death by the "ram- / rods and switches and taws and tomahawks" "wielded by the ghosts of a thousand Cayugas".

Southey's bigoted understanding of Madoc as the Christian scourge of heathenism is related, in Muldoon's poem, to the iambic march "Te Deum", which gradually encroaches on what is a more natural and often native beat (as well as the poet passing time and skipping over narrative links) — "de dum". The Pantisocrats set sail from Bristol to the ambiguous chorus of "de dum, Te Deum"; the far-off sound of horses galloping, as Cinnamond and his troop return to exact their revenge on Southey, becomes an ironic "Te Deum. De dum. Te Deum. De dum. Te Deum"; and Southey's first inkling of the settlement's burning, when he is "struck" by a "strict, unseasonable, black snowflake", resounds to the fanatical chant of "Te Deum, Te Deum, Te Deum, Te Deum, Te Deum". Elsewhere the "Te Deum" chant takes on diabolic associations, becoming the chorus to a rhyme repeated by Southey as he returns from attacking Cinnamond:

> 'From his brimstone bed at break of day
> a-walking the Devil is gone
> to look at his snug little farm the Earth
> and see how his stock went on ...'

Southey's (and the Devil's) progress is immediately rendered, in '[Anselm]', "De dum, Te Deum, de dum, Te Deum, de dum". Southey's link with diabolic forces recurs later, from the title "The Satanic School" which, in his descendant's interpretation, groups Southey with Coleridge, and the settlement which Bucephalus describes as "Hell", to the evil spirits which continually molest him — possibly a Faustian theme, especially given that Southey must die at an appointed date — and which turn out in their final manifestation to be the Cayuga Indians he has exploited and suppressed.

Any hope of benign interaction between the two cultures fades as the more powerful Christians disinherit and destroy the indigenous religion. A beaver, sent as an "emissary" from the Great Spirit, becomes caught in two separate traps and gnaws "both drubs to the bone"; its skeleton reappears towards the end of 'Madoc' dragging itself "traps and all, / across the floor, along the bed; 'Put me out of my misery'". Perhaps the poem's most dignified passage is an extract from an actual speech by Red Jacket, which Muldoon quotes verbatim. Telling the whites that killing the son of the Great Spirit may well be "the merited cause of all your troubles and misfortunes", Red Jacket offers to reverse the colonization process and send "missionaries to teach them our religion, habits and customs". Yet against this larger plot of the settlers' ruthless greed and self-righteous brutality runs a sub-plot tracing Coleridge's efforts to find Sara Fricker; although this quest appears unsuccessful, he alone is finally granted an insight into Madoc's fate. Coleridge is first seen reaching into his pantaloons to take out "a small, sea-green vial", before being "overwhelmed by another pang of guilt"; his addiction to laudanum stresses a rift with Sara, who will probably never "make good the yards, feet and inches / between herself and S.T.C.". This provides tentative evidence that Sara leaves voluntarily, a supposition neither confirmed nor contradicted when after her disappearance Coleridge hears news of a white woman in a nearby town, and rides up a hill to observe through a telescope:

> While the white woman is being rogered
> by one Seneca tipped with chert
>
> she sap-
> sips
>
> a second.

What Coleridge witnesses may or may not be rape, and may or may not involve Sara. But whether forced or not, the scene seems to constitute a native ritual. An earlier section titled '[Seneca]' describes a Senecan Indian religious myth where a woman is impregnated by Wind and gives birth to two Trickster-like sons, Flint and Sapling. Now one Seneca is "tipped with chert" — a variety of quartz that resembles flint — while the woman "*sap*-sips" another (my italics). Muldoon has suggested that the primary "mystery" in 'Madoc' is what happens to Sara,[19] but despite all the enigmatic clues — including a herring not so much "salted" as, in all probability, red — Sara's fate remains undiscovered because like Madoc's adventurers she completely disappears into the native community; whereas Coleridge, Southey, Edith and Aaron Burr all die at the predetermined times, Sara's death date in 1845, as decreed by the parallel universe of regular history, is passed over without comment. Having witnessed the orgiastic scene, Coleridge seems to accept Sara's disappearance from the narrative. He begins to use her as a convenient excuse, as he falls in with the Lewis-Clarke expedition, or shifts from tribe to tribe and drug to drug, in a quest which incorporates nostalgia for past loves and a trail of clues hinting at the assimilated presence of the Welsh Indians.

The widely differing trajectories of Southey and Coleridge have prompted critics to seek out allegorical resonances. Edna Longley has even claimed that 'Madoc' is partly "an in-joke, with Southey and Coleridge representing Heaney and Muldoon in America".[20] Longley has remained better placed than most to observe periodic strains in the friendship between Heaney and Muldoon; but since she offers no clues as to possible resemblances, it would certainly seem more easily justifiable to detect elements of the Heaney-Muldoon relationship in *Shining Brows*'s portrayal of Louis Sullivan and Frank Lloyd Wright. Longley also endorses, though not *in toto*, Clair Wills's (almost exclusively) political reading of 'Madoc'. Noting that the Pantisocrats establish their utopia in Ulster, Pennsylvania, Wills argues that "Like the besieged Protestant community in Northern Ireland, Southey finds himself building walls in 'Ulster' to protect the illegitimate progeny [South] of an Englishwoman raped by an Irish mercenary".[21] This is reminiscent of Terry Eagleton's praise of *Meeting the British*: Wills at times risks reducing a 246-page poem to nothing more than an inquiry into Muldoon's views on the Northern Irish political situation. Nevertheless, her approach is partially supported by Muldoon himself:

> I could say, if I were the kind of person who would tell you straight up, 'Well, look. This is a poem about Ireland. This is a poem about the failure of Ireland, as a state.' It's not necessarily the first thing I'd say about it, but it's a perfectly legitimate thing to say about it. I was fearful when I was writing it that, in fact, it would be too obvious that that's what it was about, that the Ulster thing was growing too heavy-handed.[22]

Muldoon hedges in characteristic fashion, leaving it unclear, for example, whether the statement "It's not the first thing I'd say about it" refers to the hypothetical "I" who would "tell you straight up", or the cagey, elusive "I" of Muldoon himself. Yet he clarifies two important points: that during the composition of 'Madoc' he attempted to tone down the political analogue; and that the Ulster angle is one among many of the poem's layers.

Whatever their political implications, comparisons between Coleridge and Southey are obviously vital to the structural and thematic concerns of 'Madoc'. However, the parallel realm of history shapes the poets' destinies as well as determining their death-dates. Southey's self-aggrandizement and self-delusion, and Coleridge's decline into drug abuse, fulfil fates which are "very much like what happened ... in real life".[23] 'Madoc' still makes strong distinctions, on moral grounds, between the poets' fates, particularly by drawing implicit parallels with legends involving a

Good and a Bad Twin. When Coleridge remembers the Gog Magog hills of Wales, it is worth noting that some traditions consider Gog and Magog as twins (rather than the composite giant Gogmagog). This provides one possible overlap between Celtic culture and that of native Americans, who in 'Madoc' erect a statue to the Good Twin, and whose creation mythology draws on a similar dualism:

> Wherever Sapling runs, trees leap up behind him.
> Whenever he throws a handful of earth, living things
> rush off in all directions. Each winter, the animals are
> impounded by Flint in a cave of ice. In spring, Sapling
> sets them free.
>
>   *
>
> Sapling makes two-way rivers for easy canoe-journeys.
> But Flint undoes the work, causing rivers to flow,
> like this, in one direction only.

Coleridge is undoubtedly the Good Twin of 'Madoc'. While Southey barricades himself into his dystopian empire and seems increasingly self-parodic in his pomposity, Coleridge becomes an assimilable shape-changer. So much so that during the crucial years 1799 to 1805 he disappears from the narrative and into the native environment, his exact whereabouts an insoluble "mystery"; when questioned about these years his response is to tie an implicitly Gordian "knot" in "the waist-cord of his breeks". The name, so often restrictive in Muldoon's poetry, also illustrates Coleridge's freedom. The Pantisocrat Favell follows the example of earlier Muldoon characters such as Hunter, Archer and Brownlee, remaining "true to his name" by abandoning the settlement and heading off for "God-knows-where" on a "chestnut jennet": the obsolete *favel* means a pale-yellow horse. Coleridge, by contrast, avoids the constraints of his name by slipping from alias to alias on his quest: first Higgenbottom, then his old Light Dragoons disguise Silas Tomkyn Comberbache (which re-introduces his disastrous horsemanship), and finally "George Rex", from the initials G.R. etched on his penknife.

In his book *North American Indians*, quoted several times in 'Madoc', George Catlin notes that "'Medicine' is a great word in this country ...The word medicine, in its common acceptance here, means mystery, and nothing else".[24] The mystery at the heart of 'Madoc', heralded even by the poem's subtitle, is therefore not only

Sara's disappearance, but also Coleridge's gradual initiation in the mysteries of native culture. His journey is both self-medicinal and, perhaps, a cure for colonialism. Encountering his first hostile native, Coleridge brandishes "John Eliot's // Algonquian Bible / and quaveringly intones the name of 'Manitou'", a reaction both comic and impotent as he is irreverently hustled to the half-Scottish Mohawk chief, Joseph Brant. But already Coleridge's visionary powers have granted him insights denied the more prosaic Southey. A spaniel leads him "through the caverns of the Domdaniel" and "along a path / covered with grass / to a belt of blue beads, a bow made of horn" — a journey which foreshadows the mystical inner travels of the Senecan leader Handsome Lake and of Coleridge himself immediately prior to death. The belt of blue beads, recurring throughout Coleridge's quest, may also signify a Welsh Indian presence: according to Catlin, finding traces of ancient Welsh skills among the Mandans,

> these people have also, as a secret with themselves, the extraordinary art of manufacturing a very beautiful and lasting kind of blue glass beads, which they wear on their necks in great quantities, and decidedly value above all others that are brought among them by the Fur Traders.[25]

Coleridge first sees the blue beads in a laudanum-induced vision while Sara is being abducted, or helped to abscond. The beads come to be associated with Sara's disappearance, suggesting that her fate will — in another duplication — parallel that of Madoc: assimilated into the native community almost without trace. Unlike Coleridge, Southey never manages to grasp any insight into the "mystery". Catlin, for example, tentatively suggests that the Welsh word *mandon* — a kind of madder used as a red dye — might provide evidence that the Mandans were given the name by Madoc's tribe, impressed with their beautiful red dyes; earlier, unconsciously circling the theory, Southey relates how he "*carried Epictetus in* [his] *pocket till* [his] *very heart was ingrained with it, as a pig's bones grow red by feeding it upon madder*". Such clues combine with the series of plays on the word 'Madoc' to weave a Welsh presence through the text. But Southey, expecting Welsh purity to have remained unsullied by the savage idolatry of the natives, remains stubbornly imperceptive.

Coleridge, by contrast, makes numerous connections between the Welsh and the native tribes during his quest. He wonders why the blue beads and bow made of horn remind him "not of Sara, but Mary Evans" — Mary Evans having been his first love and herself of Welsh descent. Coleridge is finally forced to admit that Sara could be "anywhere west of the Missouri". But his search for lost love is actually consummated later, when the Spokane chief offers him the "use of" his wife in return for some kinnikinnick and a Sheffield knife; Coleridge is shocked before lovemaking by a heart-shaped tattoo on her "left teat" and "a Cupid's dart from, this can't be, EVANS". Presumably, Coleridge is following in the explorer John Evans's sexual wake; but the revelation also seems to offer him the opportunity of satisfying a nostalgic longing for Mary Evans. The Irish stallion Bucephalus, speaking from beyond the grave (having died of syphilis), announces elsewhere that

> 'I wanted merely to assure you that the name 'Evans'
> is akin to both 'Eoghan' and 'Owen
>
> Gwyneth', the father of Madoc,
> and that Madoc himself is, above all, emblematic
>
> of our desire to go beyond ourselves ...'

Bucephalus's theory that Madoc and Evans are "akin" would suggest that Coleridge has made love to a kind of Welsh Indian — or at least an Indian carrying Madoc's signature — no matter how arbitrarily the two pedigrees have been brought together. Since Madoc is "emblematic / of our desire to go beyond ourselves", Coleridge unlocks the mystery of Madoc by discovering that to locate what Muldoon has called the true "home" or "inheritance" requires not fidelity to a tribe or fixed identity, but escape from them.

Aside from Coleridge's example, 'Madoc' is a brutal poem. Beavers are trapped, horses are deliberately burnt to death, dogs have their throats cut, bears are shot, and the numerous references to animal furs and to the ruthlessness of the Traders are summed up by the poem's earliest, most phlegmatic example: "The woodchuck has had occasion / to turn into a moccasin". The savagery provides clear continuity with *Meeting the British*; but the world described in 'Madoc' holds the same disregard for human as it does for animal life. Alexander Cinnamond, for example, is first seen fondling "a tobacco- / pouch made from the scrotal sac / of a Conegosta"; later his trews are made from "the epiderms, de dum, / of at least four, maybe five, hapless Gros Ventre women". Cinnamond values humans, like animals, for raw materials and possible exploitation. Among the scalpings, murders, rapes and mutilations, Cinnamond's dispatching of Burnet, deliberately couched in a

Parallel to the Parallel Realm: *Madoc — A Mystery*

language all the more shocking for concealing obscenity, still stands out. Cinnamond's victim

> Dangles
> by one fretful ankle
> over the illustrious dung-hill.
>
> As to holding forth
> on the inherent worth
> of the earth,
>
> he would surely be on the brink
> of speech — were it not for the brank
> of his own prong.

"Brank" is an obsolete Scottish verb — meaning to restrain or bridle — which Muldoon transforms into a noun, with horrible effect. (The same fate is conveyed by employing a much more demotic diction in Muldoon's play *Six Honest Serving Men*, where a local I.R.A leader is said to have been found "with his bollocks / stuffed down his own throat like a bloody plug".) Such brutality is not only restricted to Cinnamond. But although Muldoon is careful to avoid any suggestion of Rousseauesque idealism in his portrayal of the native tribes, who even, at times, operate complicity with Cinnamond, he more often depicts the dignity of their culture. Assimilation and miscegenation are emphasised to undermine Southey's faith in tribal purity, and to explain why a search for genuine Welsh Indians is based on fatuous or bigoted notions of colonization. But Muldoon also intends to correct any false historical impressions which may still linger. 'Madoc', for example, announces "one or two things we should know" about the King of the Mohawks, Joseph Brant, including that he studied Hebrew, Latin and Greek in England, and that he was once interviewed by Boswell for the *London Magazine*. Brant offers Coleridge tea and scones, preserves and clotted cream, before tempting him into a philosophical discussion concerning free will.

As the moment of the retina's disintegration approaches, the poem's "vision" becomes ever more sketchy and incoherent. Guided by a cormorant and white coyote, both of which constitute aspects of a native religious symbolism and landscape, Coleridge returns to Southeyopolis. However, he apparently turns into a "wraith" after laying a hand on the shoulder of a nightmare-ridden Southey, who "wrangles the fiend across the room":

>   The wraith pokes its tongue in Southey's ear —
>   'Rhythm in all thought, and joyance everywhere' —
>   Before leaving only a singe on the air.

Presumably Coleridge's journey is only imaginary, and the two poets experience complementary visions which reveal vastly differing destinies — Southey, the Bad Twin, haunted by the forces he has repressed, and the good twin Coleridge assimilated into native culture. Having been nursed by natives in his final sickness, when his historically determined death-date arrives Coleridge "insinu- / ates himself through this crack into the vaults / of the Domdaniel. His familiar is a coyote made of snow".

Coleridge might be said to fulfil the Madoc legend. Yet his assimilatory achievement, gaining access even in death to a rich "inheritance" by going "beyond [himself]", finds a tragic footnote in the fate of native tribes. Three years later the Mandan villages "are ravaged by smallpox", and within another six years native culture has already dwindled to a curiosity, the stuff of stereotypes and ham theatricals:

>   An almost naked 'Mandan' in harlequin
>   red and black lozenges
>   manages only one shot from his squirrel-gun
>   before a raiding-party of 'Shoshones'
>
>   rush his buffalo-wallow
>   and wrestle him to the ground. His ululations are to no avail.
>   They take his scalp.

The scalp turns out to be a wig, and when the "'Mandan'" afterwards "washes off the lamp-black and vermilion paint, there's a fleur-de-lys on his shoulder blade" — the fleur-de-lys being the emblem of the "other" Prince of Wales. Rather than signifying a Welsh Indian, this fleur-de-lys merely identifies South, who had been given a deep "trifoliate" wound when interceding on behalf of his wet nurse. In one of the retina's final glimpses the Modocs, another tribe possibly descended from Madoc, are pushed to the Pacific and "systematically hunted down"; this austere reportage marks the annihilation of whole tribal cultures, including, possibly, Madoc's own descendants. While Southey believes that Madoc's band remains untainted by the savagery of the natives, the real savagery, which the exiles had managed to evade for seven hundred years, has caught up with them at last. At this point South's retina disintegrates, but there is no relieved awakening to the real world: the precarious parallel universe goes up in flames, reverting the course of history to that original and predestined, though horribly comparable, "Way of Truth".

Notes

1. *Muldoon in America*, interviewed by Christopher Cook, B.B.C. Radio 3, 1994.
2. *ibid.*
3. 'An Interview with Paul Muldoon', interviewed by Lynn Keller, *Contemporary Literature* 35 (1), Spring 1994, 18.
4. Introducing 'Cauliflowers', *Muldoon in America*, 1994.
5. McCurry, J. '"S'Crap": Colonialism Indicted in the Poetry of Paul Muldoon', *Eire-Ireland* XXVII (3), Fall 1992, 106.
6. Johnson, D. 'Poetic Discoveries and Inventions of America', *Colby Quarterly* XXVIII (4), December 1992, 209.
7. Interviewed by Lynn Keller, 15.
8. Quoted by Holmes, R. *Coleridge: Early Visions* (London: Hodder & Stoughton, 1989), 84.
9. Interviewed by Lynn Keller, 13-14.
10. *ibid.*, 13.
11. *ibid.*, 14.
12. *ibid.*, 11-12.
13. Hitchcock gives a MacGuffinesque definition of the MacGuffin in Truffaut, F. *Hitchcock by Truffaut* (London: Paladin, 1978), 191-193.
14. 'Paul Muldoon', interviewed by John Haffenden, *Viewpoints* (London: Faber, 1981), 141.
15. Interviewed by Lynn Keller, p. 17. See Williams, G. *Madoc: The Making of a Myth* (London: Eyre Methuen, 1979), 39-67.
16. 'Way down upon the old Susquehanna', interviewed and profiled by Blake Morrison, *The Independent on Sunday*, 28 October 1990, 37.
17. See McCurry, J. '"S'Crap": Colonialism Indicted in the Poetry of Paul Muldoon', 103.
18. Interviewed by Lynn Keller, 18.
19. 'Lunch with Paul Muldoon...', interviewed by Kevin Smith, *Rhinoceros* 4, 1991, 83.
20. Longley, E. *The Living Stream: Literature & Revisionism in Ireland* (Newcastle-upon-Tyne: Bloodaxe, 1994), 51.
21. Wills, C. *Improprieties: Politics and Sexuality in Northern Irish Poetry* (Oxford: Oxford University Press, 1993), 224.
22. Interviewed by Lynn Keller, 20.
23. *ibid.*, 11.

24. Catlin, G. *Letters and Notes on the Manners, Customs, and Conditions of North American Indians* (New York: Dover Publications, 1973), vol. 1, 35.
25. *ibid.*, vol. 2, 261.

The Poetry of Architecture: *Shining Brow*

"Always excepting da Ponte and Hoffmansthal", Craig Raine modestly prefaces his own work for opera, "the librettist ... is essential only as a flunkey".[1] Having taken the step of publishing *Shining Brow*, a libretto commissioned by Madison Opera and based on the life of the architect Frank Lloyd Wright, Muldoon might have been suspected of offering the flunkey's work in isolation, without the music's polyfilla on hand to conceal the slapdash craftsmanship often associated with libretti. Aware of the common prejudice against the genre, the Faber blurb promised something more: "a dramatic poem in its own right". However justified the claim, as a marketing ploy it proved unsuccessful: *Shining Brow* attracted only a small handful of reviews. Even the steadily expanding body of criticism dedicated to Muldoon's poetry has so far ignored or marginalized the libretto, apparently considering it nothing more than the interim work of a poet saving the bigger gesture for the "regular" volumes which sandwich *Shining Brow*: *Madoc — A Mystery* and *The Annals of Chile*.

Muldoon, certainly, does not share this view, having found the libretto form "thrillingly releasing";[2] *Shining Brow* is, as a result, one of his most ambitious and innovative achievements to date. Paul Driver noted in the *London Review of Books* that Muldoon's libretto is a kind of sestina, "accommodating within itself a whole host of prosodic and rhetorical forms"; recurring leitmotifs represent the operatic equivalent of the sestina's end-words. 'Yarrow', the long concluding poem of Muldoon's next major volume, *The Annals of Chile*, is made up of what Muldoon calls "intercut exploded sestinas";[3] *Shining Brow* is clearly a vital movement towards, and inspiration for, that formal experimentation, allowing Muldoon to assimilate into his poetry a Wagnerian operatic device which has shown how repetition can be used in ways "that wouldn't have occurred to [him] before".[4] Yet the libretto is much more than a stepping-stone. Despite his reservations concerning the élitism of opera, Muldoon unquestionably appreciates its *sui generis* potential:

> One of the great things about opera as an art form is that characters can quite happily come right up to the front of the stage and say 'I feel bad', 'I feel great', 'My heart is broken', 'My hand is frozen'; and somehow the over-the-top element in it I found really very exciting.[5]

Muldoon plainly disagrees with Auden's sloppy argument that opera must be necessarily melodramatic because "people do not sing when they're feeling sensible";[6] nevertheless, he does exploit the fact that the form allows more extreme modes of expression. For a poet whose voice in earlier work had predominantly couched itself in subjunctives and conditionals, the libretto grants a new freedom and directness of utterance, more explicit than anything previously attempted without the operatic camouflage.

Muldoon's involvement in the *Shining Brow* project had been motivated initially by the opportunity to collaborate with his friend, Daron Hagen, a young Wisconsin-born composer whom he has described as "extremely literate, very interested in language, very well read".[7] There was therefore never any question of the librettist subordinating his talents to those of the composer, in the way of a traditional operatic hierarchy. Working alongside someone as sympathetic as Hagen — to whom the libretto of *Shining Brow* is dedicated — Muldoon could ensure that poetry was given no less priority than music: as he has commented, "There was no way I was interested in writing a piece in which ciphers would trundle on and off the stage and utter a few banalities".[8] The terms of the commission generously avoided any unnecessary interference: Madison Opera had stipulated only that the production should focus on some aspect of Frank Lloyd Wright's life and work. At an early stage Muldoon decided to concentrate on the period from 1903 to 1914, "which are the years in which drama, in its broadest sense, occurred in Wright's life".[9] During these years Wright abandoned his wife and family for Mamah Cheney, the wife of a wealthy client; he built Taliesin — Welsh for "shining brow" — as a home for himself and Mamah. But in 1914, when the chef set fire to the house, Mamah and her children were killed in the blaze, and Taliesin destroyed. *Shining Brow* is largely based on historical incident, but there are a few embellishments and liberties: despite having read Wright's memoirs of this period, and other biographical sources, Muldoon and Hagen felt "less interested in veracity than verisimilitude".[10] So Wright and his "*Lieber Meister*" Louis Sullivan, for example, did not meet at their old haunt, the Cliff Dwellers' Club, on the day of the fire; the dates are made to coincide in the opera for dramatic effect. Similarly the characters, although based on historical counterparts, are set down and "left to look after themselves".[11] After collaborating on a detailed initial treatment which even incorporated gesture and movement onstage, Muldoon and Hagen completed *Shining Brow* over the following year, and in April 1993 the opera played to full houses in Madison for a pre-arranged run of three nights. A small provincial company, Madison Opera had still recruited a high-powered team to stage *Shining Brow*. Stephen Wadsworth, Bernstein's librettist for *A Quiet Place*, acted as producer and director; David Birn designed effective sets, jostling Louis Sullivan's proud formal architectural designs against Wright's earth-coloured, lopsided fronts; and Roland Johnson conducted the Madison Symphony Orchestra. The premiere was broadcast live on a Wisconsin classical radio station; but even nationally *Shining Brow* was one of the season's operatic highlights, attracting recording agencies and East Coast critics. The metropolitans were impressed, if more than a little patronizing. Praising the "plucky little company", the *New York Times* reviewer wondered how anyone could have foreseen that such a "daring venture" would happen in Wisconsin.

The text of *Shining Brow* differs in several respects from the libretto performed in Madison. A few alterations were made by the company to protect delicate sensibilities: Louis Sullivan's drunken "Another brandy, you son of a bitch" becomes "Another brandy, damn it"; and similarly, "Bring me that brandy, you little prick" is toned down to "Bring me that brandy, for Christ's sake". Muldoon had also allowed Daron Hagen to make any changes he considered musically helpful. Given the technical demands the libretto placed on the composer, it is greatly to Hagen's credit that such changes are kept to a minimum. However, his few revisions are always inferior. The "manacles of yarn" which Mamah Cheney has managed to throw off, for example, sound much more appropriately cumbersome than the comparatively dull "chains of yarn" in the performance version. And when Mamah sings about "what remains of my life", instead of "what remains of my empire", Hagen loses a half-rhyme with two words which together announce the extent and the decline of Mamah's "empire": chamber and November. As Paul Griffiths pointed out in the *New Yorker*, Muldoon's libretto is so subtly crafted that even the most minute alterations can prove disastrous. In the barbershop quartet of the second act, one of Muldoon's quatrains reads,

> Nineteen twelve. The Greeks and Turks
> fight a familiar duel.
> The Piltdown Men of Planter stock
> scuttle Irish Home Rule.

Intellectually, this is far more detailed than audiences are accustomed to expect from libretti. The Planters are Piltdown Men, fraudulently prehistoric in their beliefs (the Piltdown Man was a notorious archaeological con); and the verb "scuttle" prepares for subsequent mention of the Titanic foundering "on a berg". However, Hagen adds a definite article, and his music turns the quatrain into a couplet:

> Nineteen twelve. The Greeks and the Turks fight a familiar duel.
> The Piltdown Men of Planter stock scuttle Irish Home Rule.

This recalls the inert long lines of Muldoon's teenage poems: "scuttle" has lost its urgency; the half-rhyme Turks / stock, almost a phonetic anagram, has been swallowed up; and while "fight a familiar duel" had been familiarly anapaestic, Hagen blurs "familiar" into three syllables.

Such details raise the question of whether it is possible to do justice musically to the subtleties of the libretto. Most of Hagen's problems are caused by the fact that Muldoon's lines are compelled less by syllabics and phrasing than rhyme and half-rhyme. In act one, for example, a chorus of draughtsmen celebrates "the poetry of architecture". Two consecutive stanzas read as follows:

> The poetry of architecture
> is a poetry of tension;
> we take as our theme
> the brick and the beam
> and we add an extra dimension.
>
> But the poetry of architecture
> is not without its laws;
> there's someone at the bottom
> of every totem-
> pole: you can't make bricks without straw.

That additional "But" causes the chorus an awkward, hurried moment. Far more difficulty, however, is created by the rhythmical shift in the third and fourth lines; "we take as our theme / the brick and the beam" is perfectly regular and unproblematical, but "there's someone at the bottom / of every totem- / pole", especially when succeeded by a gaping caesura, demands that the composer ignore the half-rhyme and enjambement by following the phrasing. Despite some choral effort to stress "totem-", the lines sound banal and flat: "there's someone at the bottom / of every totem-pole". It is no criticism of Hagen's compositional skills to suggest that at such moments the music and poetry inevitably grate against each other. Muldoon's tinkering with the libretto, as a form which, like the sonnet, can be celebrated, wrecked and revolutionized all at once, is poetically innovative — but also, unfortunately, at times a musical curse. Elsewhere in the libretto Muldoon has even added what Paul Driver terms "'write protect' labels" which resist the music. When the draughtsmen sing that "We know pretty much exactly what he has in mind / when he mentions his 'pencil in his hand'", it is hard to imagine how the *cordon sanitaire* of the quotation marks could be adequately conveyed in musical terms. Hagen's solution is only partial: he camps up the whole couplet.

In other ways, undoubtedly, the libretto is musically enabling. Hagen's main influence, it soon becomes clear, is Leonard Bernstein; there are even conscious musical allusions to his work. But while retaining a unified tone, Muldoon has also prompted Hagen to capitalize on echoes of everything from Gilbert and Sullivan to negro spirituals, Britten and Richard Strauss to Shaker hymns and Julia Ward Howe. Hagen eagerly accepted these musical pointers, and even suggested that Muldoon add a barbershop quartet. Such collaboration, of course, carries attendant dangers for a composer unaccustomed to Muldoon's allusive genius: one reviewer argued unfairly that "Mr Hagen shows the talents of the pasticheur more than the knack and energy and enjoyment of the man who has to tell you a musical story, and has to tell it as his own". In fact a distinctive musical sensibility does emerge from Hagen's work — not least, in true Muldoon fashion, when he is alluding to others: the variations on a waltz from *Der Rosenkavalier* in the cocktail party scene, for example, are delightfully playful and just a little manic. No less powerful is a blues melody for a chorus of workmen. The song is an example both of the librettist determining the shape of the music, and of Muldoon being given the opportunity, via the freedoms of the libretto form, to expand his poetic range: "I've always wanted to write a blues poem", he has said, "And this was just a wonderful occasion when it was, I think, appropriate".[12] Although the song is interrupted both on the page and in performance, Muldoon has read it (but, interestingly, did not write it) as a complete poem:

> When I woke up this morning, I was still in my dungarees.
> I steadied myself at the washstand with a shot of Tanqueray.
>
> When the whistle blew at lunchtime, I opened my lunch-pail.
> It was completely empty. My mouth is full of nails.

> My mother was a Mohawk, my father used to stay out nights.
> That must be why I'm blessed with such a head for heights.
>
> They say the soul weighs about the same as a plumb-line and a plumb.
> That must be why there's a blood blister on my thumb.
>
> I'd sawn halfway through a plank. Now I can't see my mark.
> It's the fate of every carpenter to fade into his own woodwork.

The hexameter's lilt and predominantly monosyllabic lines together convey the melancholic resignation of the workers, who are the bottom of the totem-pole, the straw for Wright's bricks. They fade, rhythmically as much as metaphorically, into their own woodwork, exploited by Wright like all the other major characters. The lyrics also seem to contain a literary allusion to poems by Michael Longley and Seamus Heaney. Longley's 'In Mayo' ends with an image of "snipe the weight of the human soul", to which Heaney refers when, in 'A Kite for Michael and Christopher', he reports how "My friend says that the human soul / is about the weight of a snipe / yet the soul at anchor there, / the string that sags and ascends, / weigh like a furrow assumed into the heavens". Muldoon's workmen enter the theological fray, having heard that "the soul weighs about the same as a plumb-line and a plumb". However, while Longley's snipe and Heaney's kite soar exultantly, the souls of the suffering workmen are weighted down, earthbound in more senses than one.

This reference to poems by Longley and Heaney is symptomatic of a libretto which alludes heavily not just to musical but to literary sources. Homer, More, Dante, Goethe, Shakespeare, Donne, Keats, Tennyson, Dickens, Coleridge, Richard Hovey, and Yeats are all glanced at or quoted, and there are extensive Biblical and Arthurian references. At other times the suspicion of an echo lingers: Mamah's lines, "as seamstress calls to seamstress // across a mile-wide quilt", for example, sound uncannily like John Hewitt's "as moth that answers moth / across a roaring hill". In *Shining Brow* language (and music) is presented as worn and second-hand. Leit-motifs flit incessantly from mouth to mouth, driving the libretto forward with an unstoppable rhythmic impetus: when Catherine complains that she has not seen Wright "in a month", Louis Sullivan is roused from his brandy-sodden slumber only long enough to demand "Another brandy and *crème de menthe*". Often whole speeches are unknowingly repeated verbatim by different characters who seem trapped in a tangle of promiscuous words. These allusions and ventriloquisms relate to the opera's dominant themes of ownership and usurpation: although Wright often acknowledges his debts — "I borrowed those lines from a masque / by a certain Richard Hovey" — both Mamah and Louis Sullivan ask him on numerous occasions whether he means "borrowed" or "purloined". Accusing Wright of stealing his architectural theories "all to the greater glory of your name", Sullivan is particularly sensitive to his former protégé's magpie quotations; when Wright "borrow[s]" a phrase from Goethe, Sullivan announces that Goethe himself "purloined" the phrase, whether from Schelling or Tobler. And just as Sullivan traces the term "frozen music" from Schelling to Goethe to Wright, so the libretto mimics this family tree by borrowing from Heaney borrowing from Longley. No utterance, no inspiration, is original. Muldoon has borrowed — or purloined — an ensemble technique first perfected by da Ponte, to show that even when characters mean different things, they sound virtually the same:

Edwin: ⎧ For three long months I've tried to ease
Mamah: ⎨ For three long months I've been ostracized
Wright: ⎩ For three long months I've tried to loose

Edwin: ⎧ the pain of these nodes
Mamah: ⎨ but the nods
Wright: ⎩ the knot,

Edwin: ⎧ of gristle and keratin
Mamah: ⎨ and winks and twitching curtains
Wright: ⎩ the inextricable, Gordian

Edwin: ⎧ but have found no salve,
Mamah: ⎨ have only strengthened my resolve;
Wright: ⎩ knot that binds Mamah and myself.

Shining Brow is a working example of what *Madoc*'s 'The Key' calls "footfalls pre-empted by their echoes". Opinions, destinies, affections, seem already determined by the irresistibility of repetition and leitmotif. So when Catherine Wright, feeling neglected, reminisces with her husband about a time when "we ate roast chestnuts and pecans / and built upon the built-up dark", it is inevitable that eventually Mamah will share the same emotions and repeat the same speech, almost perfectly.

Pre-emptive echoes, of course, cannot be acknowledged without anachronism. Set between 1903 and 1914, *Shining Brow* makes no mention of Heaney, Longley and Hewitt, nor of a Muldoon poem with which it shares striking similarities: 'Madoc — A Mystery'. In its last lines *Shining Brow* even quotes 'Madoc': Wright hears a bird crying out "against oblivion" in his heart, and identifies it as "A siskin, or some such finch"; when in 'Madoc' Coleridge and Southey come into view, "A flock of siskins / or some such finches / blunders up from the Susquehanna". This is only the most blatant in a series of thematic cross-references: despite different settings and styles, both works explore colonization through a fusion of Welsh and native cultures. Wright marries these cultures in Taliesin, the house he builds for himself and Mamah. As Brendan Gill recounts in *Many Masks*, his biography of Wright,

> The Lloyd Joneses had been accustomed to giving Welsh names to their homesteads, and even as Wright was building his refuge he decided to call it Taliesin, after a legendary Welsh bard whose name Wright had encountered in a mask of that name by the American writer Richard Hovey ... According to Wright, the name meant, in Welsh, 'shining brow', and he intended his house to serve as the shining brow of the little hill on which it stood. 'Not on the hill but of the hill', he would say.[13]

Muldoon's Wright associates his architectural theories of integrity with a native aesthetic, arguing that "The Sioux and the Shoshone / might have taught the Greeks and Romans / a lesson in harmony"; this supposedly indigenous approach is complemented by Wright's Welsh origins, embodied in the name Taliesin.

There seems at first one vital difference between 'Madoc' and *Shining Brow*: whereas the earlier work flickers precariously from the back of an eyeball on the point of disintegration, *Shining Brow* apparently offers more stable foundations by embroiling poetry and architecture: just as Wright names his home after a poet, the Welsh bard Taliesin, so the title of Muldoon's libretto is a translation of the house's name. And the unfolding events of act one parallel the construction of a house for the Cheneys: Wright first meets Mamah when she and Edwin arrive to discuss the projected designs, and their subsequent affair emerges against the backdrop of *"the Cheney house, initially in mid-construction, though the building gradually materializes during the course of the scene"*. But the structural stability of *Shining Brow* turns out to be an illusion. Pondering the collapse of his marriage, Edwin later notes that "For everything that's built / something is destroyed"; this endless cycle of construction and destruction is confirmed by the libretto's journey from the design and gradual emergence of the Cheney residence, to Taliesin's destruction by fire and Wright's determination to rebuild it out of the ruins. In imitation, Muldoon loops his conclusion back round to the prologue: Wright ends *Shining Brow* with the line "So much. So much. So much ... So ..."; Sullivan opens the opera with "So much so, that even now I flinch". The cycle, of poetry and architecture, implicitly begins again.

The leitmotifs and the cyclical pattern of *Shining Brow* ensure that the various elements of Muldoon's libretto are, like Wright's designs, "all somehow integral". Wright is the prime mover of the cycle, and everything which occurs in *Shining Brow* is in some way related to, or caused by, his egomania. Even his casual adoption of the Indian cause reveals him as a thieving disinheritor, destroying others to create enough room for his own ambitions and desires. Both Catherine and Mamah mercilessly parody Wright's predilection for introducing native tribes at any opportunity: Muldoon has admitted that "some of the hokum that Wright talks about Indians is really commenting on some of the hokum I talk".[14] Oblivious to his wife's entrance, Wright states that Mamah has "pierced my heart like an arrowhead", to which Catherine sardonically asks, "Is it Minnetaree or Mandan?"; later Mamah, after she has displaced Catherine, unknowingly duplicates this exchange with Wright. And when Wright, temporarily reunited with his one-time *"Lieber Meister"*, compares him to an Anasazi, Sullivan replies,

> An Anasazi? You speak far better than you know.
> The Anasazi were eclipsed
> by the Hopi and the Navaho.

Ignorant of this barely muted grievance, Wright switches into theoretical automatic pilot to argue that "The Hopi, the Haida, the Huron, the Hunkpapa Sioux" could all have taught the Greeks and Romans "a lesson in harmony". The tendency to choose examples according to the demands of alliteration and assonance merely emphasises the artificiality of beliefs which even Mamah finds ridiculous: "I can't quite imagine the appeal to John Ruskin / of a few sticks covered with deer-skins".

This theme of usurping covers territory similar to that of 'Madoc', but in a more approachable and often more powerful style. Wright achieves a tragic stature much greater than Robert Southey, his counterpart in 'Madoc', can manage, because self-delusion is an integral part of his genius: while Southey is mocked for an arrogance far in excess of his meagre talents, Muldoon has observed that the general perception of Wright as "one of the great figures of twentieth-century art" is used in *Shining Brow* as "a given".[15] However, it is Wright's emotional range as much as his creativity that outstrips Southey's. Although Wright was, according to Muldoon, a man "entirely out of touch with his emotional life",[16] the libretto does give him passages of sheer lyric beauty. After Mamah's death, Wright is led from the tantalizingly elusive memory of her scent to an inescapable realization of his loss:

> And her scent? Was it musk?
> Not musk. Cedar perhaps. Perhaps night-scented stock.
> Not stock. Sassafras.
> Not sassafras. Maple.
> Not maple. Pine;
> the scent of a plain pine box
> where she'll lie in this hallowed ground.

Aspects of life and death, desire and destruction, are also, it seems, "all somehow integral" in *Shining Brow*. Even without the despairing inevitability injected by Hagen's setting, as Wright homes in on the death-scent, this is far from the "skittery elegy" Peter Sirr claimed to find in the opera. Such moments are more poignant, more delicate and reflective than anything Southey's tightly circumscribed character can ever muster. Although Wright is darkly portrayed, his combination of complexity and fallibility renders him deeply sympathetic: even those he mistreats — Sullivan, Ed Cheney, the draughtsmen and workmen — cannot help but admire or love him.

The other characters are destined to orbit around Wright. Louis Sullivan, for example, may match his genius, but cannot resist his charismatic pull. Sullivan's first speech portrays Wright as David to his Goliath; and he spends nearly the entire performance slumped in a "dimly lit corner, stage right", rousing himself occasionally to order another drink or complain about his displacement by Wright. Wright freely borrows or purloins from Sullivan, often repeating the central architectural tenet of his *Lieber Meister* that form must follow function. Yet Wright is generous in his praise, and meticulous in his acknowledgements. When the men finally meet at the Cliff Dwellers' Club, Wright announces that Sullivan was "the first to fire / my imagination", and cannot understand the causes of his tutor's enmity: "He knows only too well / how great I deem / him to be". Sullivan, at the same time, complains of being "damned with faint praise", and detects "malice in [Wright's] magnanimity". Muldoon does not choose between these differing accounts: the duet they sing together grants equal voice and validity to each side. Wright's difficult relationship with Sullivan borders on love. The desperate parries and circumlocutions of the two men, as they struggle to become reconciled, leave them "*motionless, as though reaching out to each other, yet unable to touch*".

Wright's relationship with Sullivan is obviously more multi-dimensional than that between Southey and Coleridge; one reason may be that Muldoon "had in the back of [his] mind some of [his] own relationships with other writers and other mentors".[17] Yet even here, parallels between *Shining Brow* and 'Madoc' are inescapable, because Muldoon again employs the trope of the bad twin. Wright recalls reading a newspaper report "of a man who complained of an ache in his chest" and was subsequently operated on: the doctors found a lump "of gristle and keratin" which had been "his own twin / whom he'd ousted in their mother's womb". The image of "gristle and keratin" becomes a leitmotif increasingly associated with Wright's victims: the beginnings of cuckold's horns on Edwin Cheney, for example, are "nodes" of "gristle and keratin". Wright apologizes to Edwin for having "borrowed" his wife, to which Cheney stoically responds, "You've already cost me the earth". Catherine also complains of a disinheritance, deploring the fact that Wright's family have "all been shut out by the wall / you've thrown up round yourself". Mamah at first believes that Wright represents the means to her "own enfranchisement", as she leaves behind her monotonous life of needlepoint and sets out with him for the promised inheritance of an "Avalon" in Europe. But having arrived, she lets slip an intractable admission that nothing at all has changed, despite her denying even the slightest "pang of guilt"

> for having followed my bent,
> as it were, from Boone, Iowa,
> and the monotony of needlepoint
>
> to the realm of Julia Ward Howe;
> as they say in Boone —
> or used to say — *per ardua*
>
> *ad astra*. Though I went to such great pains
> to throw off my manacles of yarn ...
> the truth is that my mouth is full of pins.

Mamah is forced to conclude that Julia Ward Howe is "dead and gone"; the failure of her own quest is confirmed by a connecting image — "the valley // of disenchantment / that runs from here to Chicago" — which chains her to the life she has struggled to evade. Her refuge in Wright only constricts her further, until finally she and her children are caught in the "labyrinth" of a burning Taliesin for ten hours without hope of escape, all "scream[ing] out in their torture". The Dantean *terza rima* of Mamah's lament is not coincidental; rather, to purloin Louis Sullivan's architectural precept, "form follows function". Reversing the trajectory of the *Divine Comedy*, Mamah crosses the water for her paradisiacal Avalon, before descending through the purgatorio of suffering and isolation in Berlin, to the infernal "depths of hell" in Taliesin.

Wright's own selfish quest is at times stereotypically artistic in its search for "a harder / and higher road" diverted from conventional mores. Following '7, Middagh Street' and 'Madoc', *Shining Brow* can be interpreted as the final section of a triptych examining the artist's social responsibilities. It is also the most successful, because bombastic discussions of Art and Life are undercut, and revealed as empty deceits. When Wright calls reporters to a press conference at Taliesin on Christmas Day, 1911, he publicly trots out rhetorical clichés about the artistic calling:

> So much for the 'conventional'. The average
> man may live by average laws;
> the artist, however, must forge
> in his own maw
>
> some new vision of order,
> an even more exacting moral code.
> The artist must take a harder
> and higher road,
>
> through the dark night
> of the soul towards a necessary light.

Muldoon has commented that one of the key differences between Wright and Sullivan is that the former was "a tremendous self-publicist".[18] Wright appropriates John of the Cross, as he elsewhere appropriates countless Old Testament references, to portray himself and his inspiration in impressively religious terms. In private Wright recognizes the fraud: "I have been a traitor / to my wife, my friends, to architecture".

Before the press conference, reporters wonder whether "the old fox" will show us a "clean / pair of heels", and become "Tired of all

> the Ostrogoths under Theodoric,
> might come sweeping back across the land.

Wright now interprets colonialism as the fall into a postlapsarian world of division where the "intricate / order" underlying all things has been obscured; he seeks the revitalization of a native culture, not to undo the injustices it has suffered, but so that Mamah's death can be reversed and revealed as an illusion. As Wright repeats her translation from Goethe, Mamah's disembodied voice ghosts him; but after her voice fades, Wright continues alone in *"the area we associate with* SULLIVAN*"*. He wishes the natives would reinstate their "intricate order", before finally admitting the irrecoverability of his loss and theirs:

> So much, then, for the domain
> of the Ottawa, the Ojibwa, the Omaha Sioux,
> the Potawottoman;
> so much for all that tittle-tattle:
> they have all gone into the built-up dark.
> Yet my heart goes out to Louis Sullivan.
> In the prairie of my heart, a little
> bird cries out against oblivion;
> I know, I know, I know, I know, I know.
> A shrike, perhaps. A siskin, or some such finch.
> So much. So much. So much ... So ...

Wright retains a penchant for alphabetizing native tribes, but now dismisses his theories as "tittle-tattle". Like Mamah, the Indians are "dead and gone", their disappearance into the "built-up dark" disproving the claim in Mamah's translation of Goethe that destruction "is itself a grand illusion". Facing his loss, Wright at last shows signs of escaping his egotism: his heart "goes out to Louis Sullivan". The bird crying out against oblivion is the incessant drive of Wright's heartbeat, a recognition of his survival and continuing vitality amidst disaster. Yet it still remains unclear whether Wright has appreciated the natural interdependence and mutuality exhibited as much by the technique as the subject matter of *Shining Brow*. His new understanding of "oblivion" may encourage greater empathy, or merely fuel the urge to expand his empire, whatever the cost.

The Poetry of Architecture: *Shining Brow*

pupil "How to achieve / a native architecture the natives might afford". Architecture is incriminated throughout *Shining Brow* in the sins of colonization. The impulse to build is an impulse towards expansionism, which in turn displaces or destroys precursors. Wright and Sullivan sing of their erstwhile ambition to "make [their] mark / on the clean slate of America", but constant references to the native tribes confirm that the slate, although not so "well-worn" as that of Europe, is still not as "clean" as the two men presume. Ultimately Sullivan and Wright, acknowledging their own rôles in the disinheriting of others, reach contrasting verdicts about the prospects for decolonization. In his last speech (or aria), after he realizes he can never be reconciled with his former pupil, Sullivan "cr[ies] out"

> from the Slough of Despond
> while the Mohawk, the Shawnee, the Delaware,
> under Thayendanegea, Tecumseh and Tammany
> come sweeping back across the land
> that was not 'borrowed' but 'purloined'.

Sullivan's continual quibbling over "borrow" and "purloin" takes on new significance, as he abjures the inheritance he has "purloined" from the native tribes and awaits its inexorable restoration: he is Hector "sighing for a sail" which will augur his own destruction. Like Carleton and Wright, Sullivan encompasses both victim and victimizer: the "lump in [his] throat" offers a reminder of his own part in colonial usurpation, while he has himself been swallowed up by Wright, his thunder stolen and his ideas purloined. Having realized that he and Wright "can never be reconciled", Sullivan looks to the prospect of the native tribes "sweeping back across the land" as a way of assuaging his own guilt and of fantasizing, through displacement, about the possible restoration of his own lost inheritance.

Wright's lengthy final speech also returns to his obsession with the ubiquitous natives, as he laments Mamah's death and persuades himself, through a merging of his supposedly American Indian theories of integrity and Mamah's translation of Goethe's 'Hymn to Nature' that Mamah lives on, her death no more than "a grand illusion". But whereas Sullivan admits no doubt in prophesying the return of the native tribes, Wright weakly substitutes this certainty for a mere wish:

> Would that the Osage, bows in hand,

He appears in all but two scenes; and even when he is not centre stage, the other characters remain preoccupied with his relationship to them. The only major character who falls outside Wright's control — although he is also, on one level, destroyed by Wright — is Carleton. Carleton is isolated from the others, and not only by race: his is a purely spoken rôle, unassimilable into the music and the leitmotifs which infect the other characters. Muldoon gives Carleton a speech which in style and tone is absolutely unlike anything else in *Shining Brow*; it takes as its model the proto-Irish poet, Amergin, whose famous incantation to Ireland begins, "I am the Wind that blows over the sea; / I am the Wave of the Ocean; / I am the murmur of the billows". Carleton's lines, although stylistically similar, are imbued with a terrible foreboding:

> I am a breast without a nipple.
> I am a watch-tower without a beacon.
> I am the gall in an oak-apple.
> I am the birch stripped of its bark.
> I am a raven swooping over the squadron.
> I am a hang-nail on a finger.
> I am the eye that looks askance.
> I am a flint that holds no spark.
> I am the rain falling at a slant.
> I am a half-moon-shaped gold torc.
> I am a sponge steeped in vinegar.
> I am the hart. I am the hind.
> I am the green and burning tree.
> I am the cloud no bigger than a hand.
> I will go down in history.

Carleton is not the only character to expand his identity until it fills the world: Wright and Sullivan compare themselves variously to David and Goliath, Achilles and Hector, the Master Builder, Taliesin, Percival, Christ, an Anasazi, Prometheus, an Irish High King, Leviathan, a noble stag, a pack of hounds and a hump-backed whale. But Carleton's world carries no learned, mythological connotations: his declamation encompasses, and even emphasises, imperfection, disease, death, obliquity. His culminating boast — "I will go down in history" — echoes the chorus "going down in history" from the barbershop quartet, and serves as a prophetic warning that, although he is a peripheral character, his actions will earn him a place in the annals alongside the likes of Amundsen, Canalejos, and Woodrow Wilson.

After Wright has laid Carleton off, Sullivan wonders with his old this tally-ho and view-halloo". But Wright relishes his suffering too much, and excessive pride even encourages self-portrayal as a lachrymose Christ: "I am a man of sorrow / and acquainted with grief". Throughout *Shining Brow* Wright veers between hunter and hunted, victimiser and victim. Mamah implicitly compares Wright to Actaeon, "a stag dragged down by his own hounds"; but Wright also acknowledges he has "torn down / much that was beautiful" (the phrase recalls Sullivan's observation, quoting Goethe, that the Irish are "a pack of hounds / dragging down every noble stag"). Wright might be both stag and hounds, but he is also, by his own admission, a "hump-backed whale" leaving nothing in his wake, and swallowing so many lumps of keratin and gristle that he finally likens himself to Taliesin trapping and destroying its inhabitants. His acceptance of some responsibility for events at Taliesin also identifies him with the chef Julian Carleton, the "Minotaur" in the labyrinth. Despite his expressed sympathy with the native tribes, Wright's first brush with a non-theoretical minority reveals a dismissive attitude:

> don't they have geese
> in Barbados
> or wherever it is Carleton purports
> to be from?

Mamah's more outspoken racism goes unchallenged by Wright, and prompts Carleton to ask why he should kowtow to someone who calls him a "cannibal" and a "nigger". The chef's anger explodes with apocalyptic consequences when Wright later has to "let [him] go" — that is, to use the crucial, unspoken cliché — *fire* him. The "gristle and keratin" of Carleton's Adam's apple, after he burns Taliesin to the ground and swallows hydrochloric acid, equates his actions with Wright's unthinking appetites. The leitmotifs create a network of responsibility and implication: when the maid claims that Carleton "lay in the maw of a hump-backed whale // like a lump of ambergris", the chef has become another of Wright's victims, doing to others (firing) as he has himself more metaphorically been done to.

Summarising his intentions, Muldoon has commented that in *Shining Brow* he "wanted to do something that was about something real, that was about real crisis, a series of crises, that was about strong emotions and disturbing aspects of the psyche".[19] While '7, Middagh Street' seems stilted in the way of a clever parlour game, the characters in *Shining Brow* are less ciphers than fully realized and distinctive individuals. Wright, of course, dominates the opera.

Notes

1. Raine, C. 'Preface', *The Electrification of the Soviet Union* (London: Faber, 1986), 9.
2. *Muldoon in America*, interviewed by Christopher Cook, B.B.C. Radio 3, 1994.
3. 'An Interview with Paul Muldoon', interviewed by Lynn Keller, *Contemporary Literature* 35 (1), Spring 1994, 9.
4. *ibid.*, 9.
5. Interviewed by Christopher Cook.
6. Auden, W.H. 'Notes on Music and Opera', *The Dyer's Hand and other essays* (London: Faber, 1963), 472.
7. Interviewed by Lynn Keller, 10.
8. *ibid.*, 5-6.
9. *ibid.*, 4.
10. *ibid.*, 5.
11. *ibid.*, 5.
12. *ibid.*, 10.
13. Gill, B. *Many Masks: A Life of Frank Lloyd Wright* (London: Heinemann, 1988), 217.
14. Interviewed by Lynn Keller, 19.
15. *ibid.*, 4.
16. *ibid.*, 6.
17. *ibid.*, 7.
18. *ibid.*, 7.
19. *ibid.*, 6.

Muldoodles: *The Prince of the Quotidian* and *Six Honest Serving Men*

Reviewing *The Prince of the Quotidian* and *The Annals of Chile* together in the *Sunday Independent* (Dublin), Seamus Heaney cleverly contrasted the works of a poet biding time and amusing himself — "Muldoodles" — with the impact of his very best poetry: "Mulboon". *The Prince of the Quotidian* is undoubtedly a "Muldoodle". Having resolved to write one poem a day during January 1992, Muldoon seems to have followed Robert Lowell's deceptively simple advice, "Why not say what happened?". So when, most days, nothing very much happens, Muldoon writes about nothing very much: "I spent the evening transferring the new Lloyd Cole / and *Cajun Classics* from CD to tape". Other times he worries about how dinner guests will get along; or eagerly announces on the telephone to Medbh McGuckian that his daughter's middle name will be Aoife. The action consists mainly of outings to the theatre or opera, an overnight stay in Binghamton to hear the Ulster Orchestra, and several trips to the countryside.

Muldoon at first had no intention of publishing *The Prince of the Quotidian*, but was persuaded by Peter Fallon at Gallery Press. Certainly, the pamphlet raises questions of value which could not be asked of his regular poetry; there are tempting analogies with Salvador Dali, scrawling shapes on a napkin. Yet it is missing the point to judge *The Prince of the Quotidian* by the same criteria as the rest of Muldoon's work. The pamphlet is composed in a minor key, and should be evaluated within these acknowledged limitations. It may not represent Muldoon at his most effulgent or ambitious, but it is never less than an interesting curiosity. From a poet whose published criticism consists of a handful of (mostly cranky) reviews, *The Prince of the Quotidian* promises to be a valuable source for Muldoon's views on the contemporary cultural scene. Gallery's blurb exploits this apparent candour as an important selling-point: "Sometimes intimate, sometimes socially critical, [*The Prince of the Quotidian*] shares some reflections, thoughts, ideas, and opinions (on U2, Field Day, and his own exaggerated 'exile') of a major poet". This is no doubt justified, but with an important caveat which Muldoon has stressed in conversation: as is the nature of journals, *The Prince of the Quotidian* expresses views which are often transitory and sometimes no more than an immediate reaction to particular circumstances. Muldoon observed in 1981 that "there is a place in poetry for opinion, but there's no place for the opinionated";[1] he now comes dangerously close to disregarding his own prohibition. *The Prince of the Quotidian* is the product of an absolutely ruthless, at times insulting, critical sensibility. After a night at the Metropolitan, for example, Muldoon declares *The Ghosts of Versailles*

> an opera so terminally *bouffe*

> even the Montgolfiers' hot-air balloon
> seems a leaden leitmotif —
> 'Where's the bouillon,
> never mind the beef?'

Elsewhere Czeslaw Milosz becomes "'Coleslaw' Milosz"; and "Doctor Heaney", "the great physician of the earth", is referred to as "waxing metaphysical", having taken to "'walking on air'" (this remembers Heaney's description of Muldoon having "practically achieved the poetic equivalent of walking on air").[2] Derek Mahon is also mentioned uncharitably: "That man with the belly like a poisoned pup / was once a strange child with a taste for verse". The second line is taken from Mahon's self-portrayal in 'Courtyards in Delft'; Muldoon goes on to allude to Mahon's drinking problems.

However hostile they seem, Muldoon's criticisms usually hit the mark. Brian Friel's "'vershin'" of *Three Sisters*, for example, sets out to prove that "Chekhov was more Irish / than a rush"; and the whole Field Day enterprise is dismissed as adding up "to so much less than the sum of its parts // like almost every Irish stew". Another poem is inspired by an objection to "the other Seamus", Seamus Deane's comment in the *TLS* that Muldoon is "'in exile' in Princeton". As would be expected, Muldoon fiercely rejects such grandiose terminology, but in the process he criticizes a more self-important, less meticulous poet:

> this term serves mostly to belittle
> the likes of Brodsky or Padilla

> and is certainly not appropriate of me; certainly not
> of anyone who, with 'Louisa May' Walcott,
> is free to buy a ticket to his emerald isle

> of choice.

Muldoon seems to have reacted with anger to Deane's piece: so much so that the next poem begins, "It seems that yesterday I let off so much steam / the snow melted". But he does draw a sober and crucial distinction between those writers forced into exile by authoritarian regimes, and those who, despite enjoying the pomp of self-proclaimed "exile", are free to live wherever they choose. Derek Walcott is irreverently confused with the author of *Little Women*, Louisa May Alcott; Muldoon also tacitly suggests that Walcott has unacceptably cashed in on his relationship with his own "emerald isle" of birth.

References to Muldoon's original emerald isle crop up throughout *The Prince of the Quotidian*, even though the poet expresses growing affection for his new environment: "the tidal marshes of Hackensack, / the planes stacked / over Newark, even the smell of cloves // and chloroform / that sweetens Elizabeth" — Elizabeth being the name of an industrial town in New Jersey. Muldoon has observed that "when I lived in Belfast ... I'm not sure if I had any better sense of what was going on there than I do now".[3] The extensive list of literary and musical allusions in *The Prince of the Quotidian* proves that geographical displacement has not entailed any cultural amnesia: among those mentioned are Heaney, U2, Brian Friel, Field Day, Swift, Sterne, Joyce, Yeats, Beckett, Mahon, Longley, Montague, the Ulster Orchestra, Deane, McGuckian and Ní Dhomhnaill. So close is Muldoon to Ireland that when a wave breaks "over a rock / somewhere west of Dingle", his windshield becomes "a tangle / of eelgrass and bladderwrack". And when he notes that his child's due date is 12 July, the wider significance of that date in Irish history inevitably intrudes. Grim bulletins from contemporary Ulster also reach the peripatetic poet. He is dismayed by news of two murders in the Moy, and later opens his freezer to find the "blood-besmirched / face" of one of the victims, Kevin McKearney, imploring him to visit his grave. Even the Ulster Orchestra, playing at Binghamton in New Jersey, is drowned out by a far cry from its homeland:

> Much as I'm taken by Barry Douglas playing Rachmaninov
> with the Ulster Orchestra
> I remember why I've had enough
> of the casuistry
>
> by which pianists and painters and poets are proof
> that all's not rotten in the state:
> amid the cheers and the cries of 'Bravo'
> I hear the howls of seven dead
>
> at a crossroads between Omagh and long Cookstown.

There is not only impatience and despair in this passage but genuine rage, which seems the more authentic because the poet does not seem to know whom or what it should be directed at. Muldoon's reaction may seem surprising to those who argue that he is a slick stylist, producing what Heaney calls "the sophisticated repose of *poésie pure*";[4] but as *Quoof* illustrates, it is when he seems dandyish and trifling that, paradoxically, Muldoon's poetry becomes most responsible. Distinctions between art and life are casuistic, because the disease of the Troubles has managed to corrupt even the most exquisite music, diminishing its palliative properties.

Muldoon's negative and often grumpy evaluations of so many of his contemporaries in *The Prince of the Quotidian* are to some extent mollified by the fact that he saves the most cruel criticisms for himself. In interview he is notoriously concessionary and self-effacing, always tagging statements with a humble disclaimer which can range from the straightforwardly modest ("it's not as if I have any particular wisdom in these matters") to the jokily dismissive ("my time might have been better spent playing billiards").[5] But Muldoon reserves much stronger self-opprobrium for poetic expression. In 'The Soap-Pig', for example, he admits to having been craven and self-regarding (Michael Heffernan even tells him, in a roundabout way, "'You stink to high heaven'"); and he confesses that "Many's an Arts Club / night with Barfield and Mason / ended with me throwing up / at the basin". In 'The Ox' and 'Sushi' he is stubbornly moody, ignoring his female companion's increasingly despairing attempts at communication. *The Prince of the Quotidian* voices still more explicit criticisms against Muldoon, which eventually are fully articulated in 'Incantata' and 'Yarrow', the two long poems from *The Annals of Chile*.

The pamphlet may at times portray Muldoon as sour and temperamental, but the fiercest attacks are targeted at the poetry rather than the man. One poem lists unfavourable descriptions of Muldoon's work — "'humdrum', 'inadequate', // 'inconsequential journalese', 'a klieg light / masquerading as the moon'" — before sending out a warning to readers and critics who might be foolish enough to "look for a pattern in this crazy quilt / where all is random, 'all so trivial'". Only St Erasmus, martyred by having his viscera "cranked out by a windlass", would undertake such a project, exhorting "the windlass-men to ever greater zeal": Muldoon implies that the dedicated critic of his poetry must be masochistic. Later in the sequence, even this put-down is put down. When another of Muldoon's talking "horsehead[s]" drops in — complete with parachute, like the mules in the

Korean war — to read the work in progress which will become *The Prince of the Quotidian*, his diagnosis is brutal:

> 'What's with you, *a mhic*?
> Apart from the 'eel-grass and bladderwrack'
>
> there's not an image here that's worth a fuck.
> Who gives a shit about the dreck
> of your life? Who gives a toss
> about your tossing off?' 'I know, I know, but ...'
>
> 'But nothing: you know it's dross;
> you know that 'Erasmus' stuff is an inept
> attempt to cover your arse;
>
> leave off your laundry-lists and tax-returns
> and go back to making metaphors ....'

As in 'Gathering Mushrooms', the horse-head is an *alter ego*, bestial but seductive. The passage expresses Muldoon's sincere doubts about the worth of *The Prince of the Quotidian*; but on another level it is marvellously disingenuous. Despite the four-letter invective, the passage is as guilty as "that 'Erasmus' stuff" of cunningly pre-empting criticism.

However, the horse-head's dismissal of *The Prince of the Quotidian* as "dross" still needs to be challenged. The pamphlet certainly encompasses the "dreck" of the poet's life, but its "crazy quilt" does also show signs of a larger patterning; not least in the last two poems, which abandon the journal form by consciously rounding off the sequence. Many of Muldoon's usual preoccupations are repeated throughout: Ireland, literature, music, film. And recurring motifs and cross-references occasionally provide something more structured. While the Erasmus poem, for example, quotes the criticism that Muldoon's work is "trivial", the word is later powerfully re-deployed after the poet hears, amidst the applause for Barry Douglas and the Ulster Orchestra, the "howls of seven dead" at the crossroads between Omagh and Cookstown: "The 'trivial' happens where 'three roads' meet. / Does St Augustine // 'trivialise' the sack of Rome?" This replies to those casuists who argue that "pianists and painters and poets are proof / that all's not rotten in the state"; it also defines the sphere and the nature of Muldoon's own so-called triviality.

Yet *The Prince of the Quotidian* is undoubtedly at its best when most closely following its title, as Muldoon explores the fixtures of his everyday life. '7, Middagh Street' had prepared for emigration; Madoc was still fashioning a response to a new landscape and environment; despite all the references to Ireland, *The Prince of the Quotidian* is the work of a poet now settled on a new home ground, growing more and more to love Hackensack's tidal marshes, "the planes stacked / over Newark", and the industrial towns in New Jersey. Muldoon even feels more at home than his wife, who being a native New Yorker, considers it "heresy" that he should reply to a questionnaire from *Who's Who in New Jersey*:

> has she forgotten Zabinski, cut down in a barber's chair
>
> in Brooklyn or darkest Queen's?
> I bring this up over dinner at George Pitcher and Ed Cone's.

Like several poems from *The Wishbone*, this requires a detailed knowledge of family history (more detailed, in fact, than Muldoon himself possessed: the poem is apparently based on a misapprehension). Zabinski, or Zabin, was thought to be a distant relative of Muldoon's wife; his chief claims to fame are that he fixed a major baseball series, and was later killed by the mafia. The poem mocks an insular New York mentality which even considers "Brooklyn or darkest Queen's" to be dangerous foreign territory. Muldoon subtly implies that it is he, and not his American wife, who feels a strong sense of belonging in New Jersey.

The extent of this belonging can perhaps be gauged by the number of signposts casually mentioned by the poet as he alternately "zoom[s]" or "putter[s]" around New Jersey and neighbouring states: the Holland Tunnel, Brooklyn, Queen's, Hackensack, Newark, Elizabeth, Washington Crossing, New Hope and Lambertville are all referred to within the first five poems. Specific pubs and restaurants are singled out; and because Muldoon names, but offers no further details about, the friends he encounters during the month, he creates an impression of a closely-knit social circle which would have seemed altogether less intimate had the friends remained anonymous. Even the frustrations of a teaching career do not disrupt the overriding impression of satisfaction and personal contentment: Muldoon manages to make a funny poem out of marking papers for a seminar he taught on Irish literature, as he incorporates some of the students' worst misquotations and misunderstandings. He also finds space to include himself — despite the squeeze — among the Princeton "heavy / hitters" at a Twelfth Night bash: "I insert myself like an ampersand / between

Joyce Carol Oates & Ingemar Johansson" (Ingemar Johansson, sharing his name with a former a Swedish boxing champion, being the heaviest hitter of all). And a new emphasis on the security and pleasing topography of his home contradicts Muldoon's twenty-something attitude, expressed in *Mules* and contemporary reviews, that the tedium of domestic life is what we spend our lives trying to avoid. The poet now seems in his element:

> The Feast of the Epiphany. It's been so mild
> the bell of millet
> strung up for the finches
> is all but dumb: a few inches
>
> of snow, one hard frost,
> might draw the deer out of the forest
> to prune the vines
> from the picket fence
>
> or vault the five-foot chicken-wire cordon
> round our herb-garden.
> In the meantime, my lemon-peel
>
> and bacon-rind mobile
> is losing something of its verve.
> I wait in vain for some small showing forth.

This is one of fourteen sonnets in *The Prince of the Quotidian*. Even many the shorter poems might be called — with only mathematical imprecision — half-sonnets; they often seem like octets with a sestet missing. This prevalence confirms Muldoon's argument that, for him at least, the sonnet is an organic form, the shape and conventions of which naturally lend themselves to his creativity. The 'Epiphany' sonnet could also be printed as seven rhyming couplets. But this would draw attention to what are otherwise very delicate rhymes and half-rhymes, as the poet "wait[s] in vain" for the wildlife to provide a natural epiphany ("epiphany" comes from the Greek *epi* meaning above, after or near, and *phainein*, to show).

At this stage in Muldoon's career one would not expect anything other than strong, technically accomplished poems; and to this degree *The Prince of the Quotidian* never disappoints. The poems are modest successes, but ultimately they lack the scope, ambition and risk-taking that characterize Muldoon's very best work. And the ghost of Lowell is such an overwhelming presence that at one point he even puts in a cameo appearance as a "sprawling, self-invited guest" complete with "amniotic vodka" and "a dash of Old Spice". Only once, in the sonnet which provides the pamphlet's title, does the poet translate the "dreck" of life into an hallucinatory, all-encompassing vision:

> As we zoomed past Loyola and Tulane
> I could think only of my nephew, Dillon,
> born two days ago in Canada.
> 'Let him,' I heard, 'let him be one ignited by the quaint
>
> in this new quotidian: a mound
> of coffee beans in the 'Café du Monde';
> the New Orleans School of Cookery's
> okra-
>
> monious gumbo; a dirigible of Paul Prudhomme
> floating above the Superdome;
> let the Prince of the Quotidian lead an alligator
>
> along the *banquette* of Decatur
> yet let him not, with Alejandro O'Reilly,
> forget the cries of the bittern and the curlew.

Consisting of rhyming couplets, this is written in the same form as the 'Epiphany' sonnet. But its rhymes, its images and its diction are all more adventurous. The "okra- / monious gumbo", for example, has been mentioned as much for the language and the half- (or quarter-) rhyme with "Cookery's" as for what it actually describes: a thick okra soup. The menu for the world café into which the poet's nephew has been born also includes specialities ranging from dirigibles of overweight American chefs to pet alligators. The poet wishes for his nephew not only this cosmopolitan multifariousness, but also a knowledge of natural, non-American wonders which would keep him in touch with his familial origins: unlike Alejandro O'Reilly, a New Orleans hero of Irish descent, he must never forget "the cries of the bittern and the curlew". The quotidian described by Muldoon encompasses the whole world, finding room for the "quaint", the natural and the outlandish. Amidst a volume which emphasises mundanity, the poet at last gives some indication of just how varied, beautiful and downright bizarre quotidian life can be.

* * *

Several times during his writing career, Muldoon's immediate response to completing a major volume has been to undertake a smaller, less ambitious work: as he observes, "having finished any kind of book, you have to start again from scratch. But I've got this particular disease, this compulsion to scribble and what can you do?".[6] This compulsion has produced *The O-O's Party*, written after *Why Brownlee Left*; *The Wishbone*, which appeared within a year of *Quoof*; *Monkeys*, a screenplay for the B.B.C., written after *Meeting the British* and broadcast in 1989; and *The Last Thesaurus*, which despite its delayed publication was in fact completed straight after *Madoc*. *Six Honest Serving Men*, a verse-play commissioned by the McCarter theatre in Princeton and published by Gallery in 1995, belongs to the same category as these works, having been undertaken in the aftermath of *The Annals of Chile*. Set on the border of Armagh and Monaghan, the play records the fissures and recriminations within an I.R.A. cell, after its Chief is killed in what looks like "an inside job" and another three associates mysteriously vanish: one character phlegmatically suggests that the fate of "those three boys" will become clear when a plough "slices the top off one of their heads".

Muldoon has examined the psychology of terrorism before, most notably in 'Anseo', 'Gathering Mushrooms' and 'The More a Man Has'; as if to emphasise the continuity, the names of at least some of the characters will be familiar to readers of Muldoon's earlier work. Joe Ward, the truant in 'Anseo' who becomes an I.R.A. "volunteer", reappears as one of the play's six honest serving men; Clery, Taggart and McAnespie are all mentioned in 'Twice' from *The Annals of Chile*; and McGuffin is drawn from 'Madoc', which had itself taken the name from Hitchcock. These repeated names complement frequent self-allusions in Muldoon's work, as part of the poet's increasing efforts — adapting Yeats's phrase — to hammer his works into unity. They also contribute to the sense that terrorist activities similar to those described in *Six Honest Serving Men* occur in the midst of Muldoon's childhood environment, and no doubt involve old acquaintances. *Six Honest Serving Men* bears resemblances to *Reservoir Dogs* (which apparently Muldoon had not seen): the criminal intimates, the nicknames, the search for the "grass", the violence and torture. But the play is more local and more intimate than a Tarantino film. Ward and Clery were portrayed, in earlier poems, attending the same primary school as Muldoon; and Taggart and McAnespie seemed in 'Twice' to be the poet's neighbours. *Six Honest Serving Men* hints that there would also have been further opportunities for the characters to meet their creator. McGuffin, for example, "dropped out of Queen's after [his] first term", where he would otherwise have been a contemporary of Muldoon. And Clery shares so much in common with Muldoon that it could even be argued his terrorism represents one of the poet's own roads not taken. Clery is mocked by the others for sounding like "some BBC nancy boy", or "the uncrowned *queen* of The Moy"; he often quotes Yeats, and he first appears in the play "*squinting at a book*". McGuffin reveals that it was "'Doctor Timothy'" Clery who introduced him to magic mushrooms; the self-conferred nickname is taken from the drugs guru Timothy O'Leary who had also been the namesake of one of Muldoon's earlier characters — Lieutenant Brendan O'Leary from 'Immram'. If Clery does represent an alternative life, then Muldoon made the right career move: he is finally executed by being drilled through the head with a Black & Decker.

Many of the characters' names have religious connotations in Gaelic: Clery, for example, means "son of a cleric", and McAnespie "son of a bishop" (implying that the I.R.A. terrorists are the illegitimate offspring of the Catholic Church). Despite this obscure etymological link between their surnames, one of the great strengths of *Six Honest Serving Men* is that the characters are differentiated with an impressive economy of means. McAnespie, for example, is portrayed as the fanatical idealist, sacrificing his humanity for the cause. He objects to metaphors derived from soccer on the grounds that he would "as soon have no truck with foreign games"; he accuses Clery of "sacrilege" when the latter alludes to the notorious sexual promiscuity of Kate, the Chief's widow; and it is he who finally "drive[s] home" the "point" into Clery's head with the power-drill. McAnespie and Clery represent the opposing extremes of puritanical fervour and careless cynicism; other characters fall between the two. McGuffin is closest to Clery in his sardonic intellectuality, and apparently "joined up" straight from Queen's with his friend in 1969. McCabe, by contrast, shares McAnespie's brutality, but his idealism takes another form: nicknamed "'Mugabe'" after the Zimbabwean leader, he believes that "'The terrorist of today / is the statesman of tomorrow'". As a "mover and shaker", Taggart straddles both sides: one moment he jokes with Clery about Kate, the next he joins in the interrogation. And Ward is the quiet operator, befriending his colleagues while all the while plotting to achieve his own aims.

Each character is associated with one of the play's three locations: a safe house on the border of Armagh and Monaghan (McAnespie,

McCabe, Taggart, Clery); Kate's house nearby (Kate); and a lookout post where Kate's house is kept under surveillance (Ward and McGuffin). Only two characters, Taggart and Ward, appear in more than one location. These geographical divisions at times bolster, and at times cut across, the complex network of alliances, jealousies and hatreds within the cell. The phrase "six honest serving men" is employed by Muldoon to describe the six surviving members, driven by paranoia as they set about hunting down the "grass" in their midst. Prompted by rumour and personal animosity, each character holds a different theory as to who is guilty of having "The Chief rubbed out": McGuffin suspects Taggart; McAnespie suspects Clery; Clery suspects McCabe and Taggart; Kate suspects Ward. These mutual interrogations and suspicions are ironically related to the play's title, which is taken from Kipling's *Just-So Stories*:

> I keep six honest serving men
>   (They taught me all I knew);
> Their names are What and Why and When
>   And How and Where and Who.

Kipling's association of knowledge with these "six honest serving men" finds no support in Muldoon's play. Kate remembers the Chief's blanket response to Kipling's six honest serving men: "he answered every question / with 'Gilbey'". The Chief would even quote different lines from Kipling back at his interrogators: "'Ask me no questions, so,' / he'd say, 'and I'll tell you no lies'". After his death, the characters cannot even reach a consensus over what questions to ask, and what information is significant. So while, for example, Taggart establishes a lookout post to observe Kate's house — on the grounds that "Whoever it was double-crossed The Chief / will be toodling back for another feel" — McGuffin sees no connection between Kate's adultery and the Chief's death: "Who cares about who's going to hit / her jackpot?". The knowledge derived from repeated or inappropriate questioning can be not just misleading but deadly. When Ward is praised for "hit[ting] / the nail on the head", the cliché evokes the previous scene, where McAnespie penetrates Clery's head with a power drill.

Clery is first suspected of responsibility for the "inside job" because he managed to escape the SAS assault in which the Chief ended up "missing half his head". Mistrustful colleagues ultimately conclude that Clery was actually not in Omagh but Aughnacloy at the time, and has fabricated the whole story about the attack. They remain unpersuaded by Clery's convincing recollection that the first thing he heard when the SAS attacked was the Chief

> screaming, 'Mea culpa, mea culpa ... '
> And I remembered those Sunday mornings
> when we were ... We were on the altar ...
> 'Me a cowboy, me a cowboy,' he'd say,
> 'me a ... '

This is a kind of information which — although perhaps too idiosyncratic to be anything other than authentic — fails to satisfy the interrogators. Clery's compelling, human anecdote is disregarded in favour of dubious intelligence from the faceless sources "Deep Throat" and "Tiger", but the fact that only McAnespie knows the identity of "Tiger" should throw doubt on whether he exists at all. As McAnespie approaches with the Black & Decker, Clery moans "Me a ..." and then "Me a ... Mexican cowboy". This approximates final confession (*mea culpa, mea maxima culpa*); but it also shows Clery's deep-seated allegiance, even in his panic, to the murdered Chief (and to one of the missing terrorists, "Taco" Bell).

Although the cell members are taught nothing reliable by Kipling's six honest serving men, there are apparently more infallible means of gaining information and intelligence to help them towards dependable answers. Muldoon originally intended to call the play *Ambient Starlight*; the phrase comes from a sale item Kate comes across from an in-flight magazine. Kate picks up the magazine in the hope that something in it will "throw some light / on all of this", and (in a sense) she is rewarded when she reads that

> 'The ability to see at night has long eluded mankind. The Nightmaster Second Generation Night Vision Scope changes all that. Our unique hand-held night observation scope magnifies ambient starlight to enhance your natural vision by over twenty thousand times. An admirable tool for turning night into day.'

This night scope literally casts light on the play's murky world, as Muldoon skilfully blends stagecraft and thematic device. McGuffin and Ward, engaged in their surveillance operation, peer through "*a sophisticated night vision scope*" (ironically, Kate suspects she is being watched by MI5). Someone seems to be watching them as well, because later "*A spot suggesting that they are themselves under surveillance through a night vision scope ranges over the sleeping* McGUFFIN, *coming to rest on* WARD". The safe house is also under observation, as a similar "spot" ranges over its occupants. Scrutinizing but never understanding, everyone "throw[s] light" on everyone else (until, that is, it is "lights / out" for those under suspicion); as in 'The More a Man Has', no one has any real idea what is happening. The night scope, ultimately, seems as useless in practical terms as another invention offered by the in-flight magazine: an *"illuminated pepper mill"* which can *"highlight any meal"*. Kate reads aloud the details of several other products which could be adapted for a terrorist campaign: the Digital Voice Changing Telephone, for example, or the Panasonic KX-G5500 Global Positioning System Receiver (GPS). These products are advertised alongside the illuminated pepper mill, a magnetic puzzle globe, and a crossword puzzle solver, as Muldoon implies that the scientific machinery is a futile toy. The characters in *Six Honest Serving Men* merge and confuse wisdom and technology; but the genuine, insoluble conflict between the two is powerfully epitomized by the Black & Decker drilling into a man's skull.

Kate finds that none of the inventions advertised by the in-flight magazines help throw light on "all of this"; the night scope, like the pepper mill, illuminates but never enlightens. She is finally forced to agree that Ward has "hit the nail on the head" after he laconically observes, "These airline magazines are full of shit". This is not the only way of communicating information which is tainted with excremental connotations. When Taggart complains that the Chief "sure as hell did talk through his ass", McAnespie takes him literally, and defends dirty protests as a particularly effective means of spreading the message: "Once you plaster your walls with your own doo / people start to pay attention to you, / he did know that". Similarly, Kate remembers leaving a donation for a local department store: "an extra half-pound of chip- / olatas, so, in which I'd done my job". There are even cruder ways of silencing communication. In a world of misinformation, misunderstanding and mistrust, Kipling's "six honest serving men" can be brutally bypassed: having apparently raised Kate into an icon of Mariolatry, McAnespie accuses Clery of "sacrilege" and warns him that "I'll personally cut off your gonads / and stuff them down your throat". He seems to have learnt from enemy organizations, since one of the UVF's traits, complete with guillotining enjambement, is that "They like to chop / off dicks". Ward tells McGuffin how one victim — presumably the Chief — was found "trussed like a Moy Park chicken with his bollocks / stuffed down his own throat like a bloody plug". Kate seems equally indifferent to such trademarks: she calls MI5 "Cocksuckers", but Taggart imagines how she will revenge herself on the man who "double-crossed The Chief": "when she has his bit between her teeth / hail and farewell". And the dubious inside information which helps convince McAnespie of Clery's guilt comes from "Deep Throat".

This kind of vulgar vitality constitutes the driving force of *Six Honest Serving Men*. Samuel Johnson's definition of "metaphysical" poetry would equally well describe the effects of Muldoon's rhyming and punning: "heterogeneous ideas ... yoked by violence together". So, vandalizing Yeats, Taggart suggests that Parnell loved not so much his "country" as his "*cunt*" — which in turn rhymes with Ceannt, taking the discussion back to the "shopping list" of rebels executed after Easter 1916. Earlier, mention of Parnell's "humdinger", Kitty O'Shea, leads into an impromptu rendition of the U.S. national anthem: "'O shay, can you shee'". In Muldoon's poetry, similar-sounding words are an aid to analogic progression, as they are shown to possess some deeper, inscrutable relationship. The ingenious formal structure of *Six Honest Serving Men* reveals many of these secret associations. The play could be interpreted as encapsulating techniques from the sonnet sequence of 'The More a Man Has', the corona of '7, Middagh Street', the exploded sestinas of 'Yarrow' in *The Annals of Chile*, and the recurring leitmotifs of *Shining Brow*. Scattered through *Six Honest Serving Men* is a sonnet of sonnets, or double corona: that is, the last line of each sonnet becomes the first of the succeeding one, the fourteenth sonnet concludes with the first line of the opening sonnet, and the fifteenth sonnet consists entirely of the fourteen repeated lines. Although Muldoon does not repeat each line verbatim, the rhymes and many of the earlier words are consistent. This would itself be an extraordinary achievement, suggesting a poet of breathtaking resources. All the more remarkable, however, is the fact that this formal ingenuity remains so unobtrusive. In performance even the sharpest audience would only be aware that certain words and phrases kept recurring, in the way of leitmotifs; and the formal structure never impairs the demotic flow of the terrorists' speech. The most careful reader might not notice that some of the sonnet-scenes are sonnets at all. The fifteenth sonnet, for example, includes the following exchange:

> McCABE You sure?
> McANESPIE   Sure.
> CLERY   You're talking through your ass if you think I'd shop you.

McANESPIE   We have a list
     we happened to get past the SAS.
   McCABE   From our own 'Deep Throat'.
McANESPIE   Tie him by his wrists ....

It is easy to miss the fact that these four lines form a rhyming quatrain; Muldoon crams the sonnet with a radical diction and subject-matter to which, outside his own poetry, the form is unaccustomed. The first broken line is derived from "though he sure as hell does talk through his ass", and "The Chief sure as hell did talk through his ass". The second has more adventurous and comic variants: "was incredible. That's some shopping list" and 'In-credi-ble. We heard Chopin and Liszt". This is one of many examples in *Six Honest Serving Men* where Muldoon employs near-duplications in alternatively orthodox, inventive and outrageous ways. The line "and hand me over that Black & Decker" appears earlier as "No more rockets launched from double-deckers" and "Dessie Gillespie? That's Desmond Decker". As in *Shining Brow*, the characters unwittingly repeat each other; but each repetition can suggest subtle shifts of emphasis and nuances of personality, as well as uncovering surprising similarities.

Where Muldoon once employed sources as templates for his longer poems — the 'Immram Mael Duin' or the Trickster cycle of the Winnebago Indians — he now seems increasingly to manipulate established forms. Just as technically awesome as Muldoon's sonnet of sonnets is the double sestina disseminated through the text of *Six Honest Serving Men*. Each of the six cell-members contributes one twelve-line stanza (although McGuffin's, unaccountably, has thirteen lines) in the form of a monologue; and the envoi, in the final scene of the play, consists of a six-line exchange between Kate and Ward. Kate also has two long monologues which encompass the sestina's repeated words. But these formal structures in no way prevent the increasing fragmentation of understanding and consensus. As the play develops, any putative interpretation of events seems more and more arbitrary. Characters repeat each other's words and each other's lines as if going over the same ground; but they reach hopelessly conflicting conclusions. The audience is also confined to making guesses on the basis of inadequate information. It is only possible to hypothesize about the fates of the three missing associates (two of whom will turn up in the forthcoming *Vera of Las Vegas*, only to cast more darkness on the events of *Six Honest Serving Men*), or about what happens after Taggart brandishes an automatic pistol at McGuffin and Ward; two pistol shots are heard during the next scene, but it is Ward, and not Taggart, who re-emerges from the lookout post.

Several of the sestina's end-words develop the impact of leitmotif through constant repetition; but even these fail to provide any reliable thread through the growing confusion. "Green", for example, is the traditional nationalist colour, and it occurs in the well-known sentimental ballad Kate plays over and again on her gramophone, 'I'll Take You Home Again, Kathleen': "And when the fields are fresh and green, / I'll take you to your home again". But green is also the colour of more than one kind of "grass". In what serves as the play's final revelation, Kate quotes the nursery rhyme 'Ding dong bell':

> KATE   Ding dong *bell*,
>   the cat is in the well ...
> WARD 'When you come home, put up your feet and have a
>   rest ...'
> KATE Who put her in?
> WARD   McCabe worked for Securicor ...
> KATE (*Angrily*) McCabe was in-fucking-terned ...
> WARD   What's
>   this 'jojoba'?
> KATE Who put him in?
> WARD   'Jojoba'.
> KATE (*Correcting his pronunciation*) *Jojoba* ... Little Johnny
>   Green.
>
> KATE *turns away from* WARD. *Fade out.*

This envoi appears less a dénouement than a further intricate knotting of the mystery. "Jojoba" is a diluted wax derived from the desert plant *Simmondsia chinensis*; Kate's pronunciation perhaps re-establishes the presence of Ward's first name in the word. But the passage seems to mock the audience expectation that matters will be clarified: in a play where information is at best irrelevant, and often deceptive or just false, the penultimate disclosure concerns nothing more pertinent than the correct pronunciation of a massage oil which is the plant substitute for ambergris. Kate's closing announcement that "Little Johnny Green" put "the cat in the well" seems equally unhelpful. Earlier in the play Ward "*pulls on a baseball cap which bears the legend* 'Stutz Bearcat'", to which Kate alludes in one of her monologues as she runs systematically through Kipling's six honest serving men: "what use has Ward for Paraquat? / Why does his hat say 'Stutz Bearcat'?" Why indeed. The "bearcat" may sound like one of the odder hybrids in Muldoon's work, but in its hyphenated form it can mean either a panda or an aggressive person. Ward is clearly not the "cat" in the well; nor is it established that he is the "Little Johnny Green", who sounds no more specific than a republican version of Joe Soap. The whodunnit is insoluble, and in a way, insignificant. The major resolution of *Six Honest Serving Men* is signalled by that final stage direction: "*Fade out*". Muldoon's extended parable ends, fittingly, in the dark, having managed not to throw light on the guilty, but to illuminate the characters' narrow world in all its brutality, its mayhem, and its ignorance.

Notes

1. 'Paul Muldoon', interviewed by John Haffenden, *Viewpoints* (London: Faber, 1981), 137.
2. 'Lunch with Paul Muldoon', interviewed by Kevin Smith, *Rhinoceros* 4, 1991, 76.
3. Heaney, S. 'The Mixed Marriage', *Preoccupations: Selected Prose 1968-1978* (London: Faber, 1980), 211.
4. Interviewed by Kevin Smith, 80, 90. Other examples from the same interview: "I'm more excited — insofar as I can get excited about anything — by the prospect of writing another poem" (83); 'Not that I think of myself as a humorous writer — as far as I can think of myself at all" (84); "I don't pretend to be a thinker or an expert in any of these matters" (85); "I'm very bad at any kind of thinking at all — in fact I think I'm probably ... stupid" (85); "I put a lot of time and energy into it — not that that necessarily means anything" (90); "I've no natural facility for writing anything at all" (92).
5. Interviewed by Kevin Smith, 91.

A Deep-Seated Hurt: *The Annals of Chile*

Seamus Heaney has described reading Muldoon's poetry as akin to being faced with two informants, one who always tells the truth and one who always lies; "the problem is to formulate the question which will elicit an answer from either one that can be reliably decoded".[1] This aptly conveys the untrustworthiness of Muldoon's first person voice, which lures the reader with the promise of autobiographical confidences, but ultimately evades, misleads and obscures. Nothing can be instantly accepted or dismissed in Muldoon's work: poems about a living father are written *in memoriam;* or an "eldest sister" called May turns out to be a younger sister called Maureen. Muldoon's reputation for mischief-making grants him considerable freedoms, which allow even what Edna Longley has called his "one-night stanzas" to seem anything but confessional in tone.[2] On those few occasions when the poetry does convey purely autobiographical material, Muldoon finds haven in obliquity (*The Wishbone*) or mundanity (*The Prince of the Quotidian*); and there is more than enough ellipsis and legerdemain in these pamphlets to support his comment that "we mustn't take anything at face value, not even the man who is presenting things at face value".[3] The one poem prior to *The Annals of Chile* which contradicts these generalizations is 'The Soap-Pig', Muldoon's elegy for his friend and colleague Michael Heffernan: "Many others have autobiographical elements in them, but ['The Soap-Pig'] is so brutally naked".[4] Such personal loss does not as easily allow for mischief. So it is no coincidence that *The Annals of Chile*, Muldoon's most elegiac collection to date, is also his most candidly autobiographical.

The Annals of Chile is dedicated to the memory of Muldoon's mother, Brigid Regan. However, part one of the volume is dominated by 'Incantata', a 360-line poem binding the elegiac and autobiographical strains in a plangent lament for Mary Powers, who died of cancer in 1992. Written over five days, 'Incantata' seems the closest Muldoon has ever come to fulfilling Wordsworth's concept of poetry as the spontaneous overflow of powerful feelings. The poem is an intense effusion which mourns the poet's loss while both celebrating and commemorating his relationship with Mary Powers; it constitutes an extraordinary technical success, conveying an apparently relentless rhythmic and emotional momentum. The poem is written in what Muldoon has called an eight-line "stadium stanza" (*aabbcddc*), invented by Cowley for elegiac purpose in his

'On the Death of Mr William Harvey', and adopted by Yeats for 'In Memory of Major Robert Gregory'. But Muldoon conducts more variations within this stanzaic pattern than Cowley — or than Yeats, who introduces only local changes to a heavily iambic pentameter. Muldoon's lines vary from four to seventeen syllables, and there is really no constant underlying rhythm. Rhyme is the central organizing device; so much so that 'Incantata' occasionally lapses into awkwardness as lines make rhythmic sacrifices in order to reach their rhyme-word. At one point, for example, the poet remembers walking with Mary, who must have known "that cancer had already made such a breach / that you would almost surely perish". And earlier, needing a rhyme with "rums", Muldoon's persona recalls how he was "deaf and blind / to the fact that not only was I all at sea, but in the doldrums": by linking the clichés Muldoon revitalizes the nautical significance of "the doldrums", but at the expense of writing a flat-footed, turgidly monosyllabic line.

'Incantata' has a higher prevalence of technical blemishes than readers of Muldoon's mature work are accustomed to expect. This does not, however, invalidate the poem's considerable achievement — no more, at least, than Yeats's elegy is disqualified by such lines as "They were my close companions many a year, / A portion of my mind and life, as it were". 'Incantata' is a new kind of poem for Muldoon — less polished, more openly emotional — where occasional lapses are an inevitable product of spontaneous overflow, and perhaps even a guarantee of authenticity: the poetry, almost, does not matter. Technically, 'Incantata' can still stand comparison with Yeats. Muldoon's greater experimentation with the form allows shifts in pace and tone which exceed anything in the Gregory elegy:

> I saw you again tonight, in your jump-suit, thin as a rake,
> your hand moving in such a deliberate arc
> as you ground a lithographic stone
> that your hand and the stone blurred to one
> and your face blurred into the face of your mother, Betty
>   Wahl,
> who took your failing, ink-stained hand
> in her failing, ink-stained hand
> and together you ground down that stone by sheer force of
>   will.

The rhythm of the stanza is "deliberate": conjunctions insist on continuity, and the full repetition of the "failing, ink-stained hand" refuses abbreviation in favour of exactness. That final line is itself ground out by sheer force of will: remarkably, seven of its last nine syllables could be stressed, embodying the extent of the physical, rhythmical and emotional effort. Later in the poem, by contrast, alliterative mania takes over as Muldoon gabbles of "the early-ripening jardonelle, the tumorous jardon, the jargon / of jays, the jars / of tomato relish and the jars / of Victoria plums". These considerable variations in the stanzaic form of 'Incantata' would alone single out the poem as one of Muldoon's most ambitious works.

Muldoon's technical range in 'Incantata' may be extensive, but so is his subject matter. His praise of Byron for forging a poetic style which ranges "from Aristotle to hitting the sack to hitting a bottle of sack"[5] signifies Muldoon's own ambition to find an all-inclusive voice. Everything should become matter for poetry: as 'Incantata' admiringly notes, André Derain even made art out of "nothing more than a turn / in the road". Muldoon makes art in 'Incantata' out of anything from the necessary ingredients for a "passable plum baba" to the plays of Beckett, from Vivaldi to "a little fol-de-rol-de-rolly" from getting drunk, to Thomism, to sex, to bombs on the line, to art criticism, to a debate on free will, while incorporating everything from Van "'His real name's Ivan'" Morrison to Rouen Cathedral along the way. These disparate elements are all united by their association with the relationship between Muldoon and Mary Powers; and together they constitute incontrovertible evidence that Muldoon, perennial spoofer of false piety, resists turning 'Incantata' into a po-faced dirge. The poem presents "a ground bass of sadness, yes, but also a sennet of hautboys", integrating commemoration and celebration. So Muldoon can still delight in memories

> of the priest of the parish
> who came enquiring about our 'status', of the hedge-clippers
> I somehow had to hand, of him running like the clappers
> up Landseer Street, of my subsequent self-reproach.

Few other contemporary elegists are capable of juxtaposing such low comedy with the more orthodox emotions of an anguished lament. Enforced by the rhyme "clippers / clappers", the scene is pure slapstick; Muldoon's mention of the hedge-clippers "I somehow had to hand" is wickedly *faux-naïf* and his "subsequent self-reproach" seems not quite so profound as to prevent this evident relishing of the incident.

Combining heartbreak and humour, 'Incantata' has an accessibility which promises to open up Muldoon's work to new audiences. Sean

Dunne, reviewing *The Annals of Chile* in the *Irish Times*, speaks for those sceptics who travesty Muldoon's poetry by arguing that it only satisfies "those for whom the complicated and allusive are preferable to the clear and the felt"; but even Dunne, continuing his Heaneyish tone, admits that in 'Incantata' Muldoon "moves among experiences that have the tang of the real". As Ian Duhig suggests in *Fortnight*, "if any poem of Muldoon's deserves to be quoted whole for a sceptical audience, it is this elegy". Not that 'Incantata' is without allusion and complexity. Its central image, for example, has its genesis in an earlier poem, 'Mary Farl Powers *Pink Spotted Torso*' from *Quoof*, which presents a woman (presumably either Powers or one of her artistic creations) carving a "hieroglyph" into a potato; this action seems to have become for Muldoon a personal mnemonic, because in 'Incantata' it is while cutting "from a spud the Inca / glyph for a mouth" that the poet first thinks of Mary. He tries to make sense of the incessant, almost meaningless keens which are vicariously emitted from it:

> the '*quaquaqua*'
> of that potato-mouth; that mouth as prim
> and proper as it's full of self-opprobrium,
> with its '*quaquaqua*', with its 'Quoiquoiquoiquoi-
>   quoiquoiquoiq'.

The potato-mouth is, on one level, an "all-too-cumbersome" substitute for the poet's own mouth. The potato-mouth may be an unlikely dramatic mask, but it allows Muldoon to speak, for much of the poem, "unencumbered" by the burden of direct eulogy. The initial "'*quaquaqua*'" is an abridged form of Lucky's "quaquaquaqua" in his famous babble from act one of *Waiting for Godot*; it seems to translate into "'Quoiquoiquoiquoiquoiquoiquoiq'", what the thunder says in *Finnegans Wake*, as well as Muldoon's jokey effort to return to a supposed French original.

References to characters from the works of "His Nibs Sam Bethicket" are scattered throughout 'Incantata': Watt and Knott, Hamm and Clov, Nagg and Nell, Krapp, Belacqua, Lucky and Pozzo are all mentioned and identified with, while Vladimir and Estragon even accompany the poet for "a couple of jars". 'Incantata' inhabits a Beckettian world, and often speaks out of a shared perspective. Muldoon's speaker "crouches" in Lucky's "Acacacac- / ademy of Anthropopopometry", examining the human condition, the evidence for the existence of God and of free will, and the inevitability of death, in a style which sometimes seems almost as frenetic as Lucky's. Mary Powers' indebtedness is explicit: her "*Summa / Theologiae*" is "tempered" by Beckett among others; and the poet employs one of Beckett's most characteristic Biblical borrowings when he imagines bodying out Mary's "disembodied *vox / clamantis in deserto*". Whether 'Incantata' consistently endorses Beckett's cosmology is more doubtful. Often the poem circles round a void of despair and nihilism (this is not to suggest that Beckett's cosmology can be reduced merely to these elements). But ultimately Muldoon's delight in the craziness of human experience — acknowledging its horrors and banalities as well as its kaleidoscopic variety — produces a life-affirming, even joyous work: 'Incantata' duplicates Mary's belief that all creation "sing[s] out in a great oratorio". Beckett is not the only artistic presence. Muldoon's allusion to one of Mary's favourite paintings, Derain's *The Turning Road, L'Estaque*, defends art as more than laughter in the dark:

> I thought again of how art may be made, as it was by André Derain,
> of nothing more than a turn
> in the road where a swallow dips into the mire
> or plucks a strand of bloody wool from a strand of barbed wire
> in the aftermath of Chickamauga or Culloden
> and builds from pain, from misery, from a deep-seated hurt,
> a monument to the human heart
> that shines like a golden dome among roofs rain-glazed and leaden.

That last line remembers the related domes of 'Kubla Khan' and 'Madoc', even if its inversion makes the line more leaden than golden-domed. The reader is unused to expect anything so grandiose from Muldoon as a "monument to the human heart". Nevertheless, the stanza still offers a summary of his artistic procedures. The barbed wire may seem anachronistic in relation to Chickamauga or Culloden, but it does imply that the swallow, building its nest in the aftermath of terrible battles, finds a twentieth-century parallel in Muldoon's artistic enterprise: a "deep-seated hurt", whether caused by contemporary Ulster or by private grief, so often underlies the surface spectacle of Muldoon's work. Having earlier claimed to have seen Mary's death-mask in the swallow's nest, Muldoon reveals an integral part not just of his elegiac intent but of his *ars poetica*. Edwin Cheney asserts in *Shining Brow* that "For everything that's built / something is destroyed"; more generously, 'Incantata' suggests that for everything destroyed, something — a "monument", a nest, a golden dome, a poem or some other work of art — must be built.

Reflecting the preoccupations of Mary Powers, there are numerous references to visual art in 'Incantata'. Besides Derain, the poem alludes to Pissarro, Seurat, Rembrandt, to Braque's "great painting *The Shower of Rain*", and, apparently drawing on the same private reference as *The Wishbone's* 'Bears', to Manet's *Le dejeuner sur l'herbe*. The lovers' respective artistic disciplines are combined when Muldoon's speaker thinks of Mary "lying there in your long barrow / colder and dumber than a fish by Francisco de Herrera"; this does not specify which of the two artists of the same name is intended, but the piscine image also originates in Yeats's desire from 'All Things can tempt Me' to become "Colder and dumber and deafer than a fish". Even after death, Mary can be preserved in different artforms: Derain unknowingly paints her death-mask; a "nocturne, maybe, by John Field" rises between her breasts; and 'Incantata' is a "monument" to her life with the poet. Mary Powers and Muldoon are themselves the strongest artistic presences in 'Incantata'. Muldoon details not only Mary's enthusiasms and her aesthetic, but alludes directly to several of her works: the "pink / spotted torso"; the "tidal-wave of army-worms" in 'Emblements'; and "the Christ [she] drew for a Christmas card as a pupa / in swaddling clothes". Muldoon's work is also conspicuous: the subject of 'The Frog' appears in the guise of a "fizzy, lemon or sherbet-green *Ranus ranus* / plonked down in Trinity like a little Naugahyde pouffe"; mention of "how mordantly hydrochloric acid must have scored and scarred" remembers the excruciating fate of Wright's chef, Carleton; the "sow dropping dead from some mysterious virus" is perhaps the same sow which, 'The Soap-Pig' reports, "dropped dead from a chill in 1966"; and "the horse's hock suddenly erupting in those boils and buboes" recalls "the black pustule / or blood-blistereen" which is the first sign of the onset of Bucephalus's syphilis in 'Madoc'. These allusions are not self-congratulatory. While Muldoon ranks Powers among the "truly great", she detects in him

> a tendency to put
> on too much artificiality, both as man and poet,
> which is why you called me 'Polyester' or 'Polyurethane'.

Even this seems to go over old poetic ground; in 'Capercaillies' "St Joan" (perhaps the poet's wife, Jean) also toys with Muldoon's name, asking him "'Paul? Was it you put the *pol* in polygamy?'" But in 'Incantata' Muldoon's supposedly synthetic character and work contrast poignantly with Powers's naturalness, as evidenced by anything from her trust in homoeopathic medicine to her "fervent eschewal of stockings and socks".

It may be that Muldoon's autobiographical honesty in 'Incantata' is a belated effort, in Mary's honour, to rectify his "artificiality". Mary is addressed directly as "you" throughout 'Incantata' — conforming to John Stuart Mill's theory that poetry should be "overheard" — as Muldoon emphasises her continuing proximity even after death. At times *The Wishbone* and *The Prince of the Quotidian* present inscrutably private references, so that what is overheard by the eavesdropper remains annoyingly impenetrable, a dialect less of tribe than family or lovers. Shibboleths are important devices throughout Muldoon's poetry: in 'Quoof' the reader, as much as the "lovely heads", must enter the poet's personal world; inevitably, those who refuse or who cannot are debarred. However, 'Incantata' is more inclusive. Many of the poem's references have private connotations applying to Muldoon's relationship with Mary Powers; but even though the particular significance of these references is never explained, 'Incantata' does convey a shared intimacy which incorporates the reader. So the potato-mouth's "'*quaquaqua*'" is all that's left

> Of that poplar-flanked stretch of road between Leiden
> and The Hague, of the road between Rathmullen and Ramelton,
> where we looked so long and hard
> for some trace of Spinoza or Amelia Earhart,
> both of them going down with their engines on fire.

Such passages make no concessions, but neither do they erect barriers: while many of the *Wishbone* poems, with their cramped style and recondite narratives, deliberately repel understanding, 'Incantata' ignores the reader altogether. Muldoon never divulges why the "poplar-flanked stretch of road" is important, nor why the remnants of Spinoza or Amelia Earhart should be found between Rathmullen and Ramelton. But for all their obscurity, these references grant the reader access to a recognizably private world which the poet once shared with Mary.

As in 'The Soap-Pig', the first person voice of 'Incantata' is more directly identifiable with Muldoon than is usually the case; but by addressing Mary, the poem is able to assume in its reader a private knowledge which only she could possess. Despite the autobiographical elements, Muldoon still manages to continue the process remembered in the poem of creating "false trails and reversed horseshoe tracks" and dragging aniseed "across each other's scents". There is very little revelation: the acknowledgement that "when we met, my idea of 'R and R' / was to get smashed, almost every night, on sickly-sweet Demarara / rum and Coke" offers no new insight or scandal after an earlier admission in 'The Soap-Pig' that many an Arts Club night would end "with me throwing up / at the basin". 'Incantata' is never indiscreet. While 'Emily' from *The Wishbone*, for example, recalls how "I called you / by another's name: / Emily", 'Incantata' employs direct address with greater logic and greater potency: when the poet remembers "let[ting] slip a name — her name — off my tongue", he does not need to elaborate, because Mary will already know the name of this old rival. Similarly, Mary's response to this hint of infidelity is to "deliver the sting / in [her] own tail, to let slip [her] own little secret"; Muldoon does not bother spelling out to Mary, merely for the reader's benefit, the nature of her own "little secret". Nor does he name the friend who once "ended up lying ... in a ditch" with Mary, "somewhere on the border of Leitrim, perhaps, or Roscommon". If 'Incantata' is ever confessional, it presents itself as unintentionally so; readers are given the opportunity to eavesdrop, but the poem steadfastly maintains its shared world with Mary, without once offering to outsiders any kind of gloss or gratuitous detail which she herself would not require.

It would be naive, of course, to argue that Muldoon is genuinely oblivious of, or indifferent to, his wider readership in 'Incantata', despite the poem's pretence. The problematic issue of audience is even acknowledged within the text, as the poet is forced to retract his attractive notion of Mary's continuing presence after death:

> I wanted the mouth in this potato-cut
> to be heard far beyond the leaden, rain-glazed roofs of Quito,
> to be heard all the way from the southern hemisphere
> to Clontarf or Clondalkin, to wherever your sweet-severe
> spirit might still find a toe-hold
> in this world: it struck me then how you would be aghast
> at the thought of my thinking you were some kind of ghost
> who might still roam the earth in search of some earthly
>   delight.

'Incantata' can be heard by others far beyond the southern hemisphere, but this is portrayed as irrelevant or merely accidental: the one intended recipient is Mary. Yet the conditional "you would be aghast" admits that the poem addresses an absence, that the idea of such an afterlife is preposterous: according to her own theological beliefs, Mary is now unable to be aghast at anything. Her cosmology does allow for some sense of a larger order, a sense that everything, including her own death, is preordained; nevertheless, there is no God controlling events, "nothing over / and above the sky itself". The demented gabbling from Lucky's "Acacacac- / ademy of Anthropopopometry", and the potato-mouth's obliteratingly repetitive "Quoiquoiquoiquoiquoiquoiquoiq" which is "all that's left" of the relationship, seem in these circumstances not only heartbroken laments but also signals of near despair in what is apparently an empty, nihilistic universe.

The fundamental paradox of 'Incantata', however, is that by listing the diverse elements of the relationship which have been reduced to the potato-mouth's note of anguish, Muldoon surreptitiously affirms and even exalts them. The poem's turning point occurs in the twenty-fourth stanza, which inaugurates a long inventory recording those shared pleasures, tragedies, and preoccupations of which the potato-mouth's ululation is "all that's left":

> That's all that's left of the voice of Enrico Caruso
> from all that's left of an opera-house somewhere in Matto Grosso,
> all that's left of the hogweed and horehound and cuckoo-pint,
> of the eighteen soldiers dead at Warrenpoint.

As each stanza extends the list, the tag "that's all that's left" is dropped altogether, and the only reminder that these various items are being reduced rather than eulogized is the tiny word "of", which introduces every new article: "of Vivaldi's *Four Seasons*, of Frankie Valli's". This tenuous, residual connection with the potato-mouth is soon overwhelmed by the volume and sheer brio of what could be considered Muldoon's poetic equivalent of a catalogue aria. No detail is too insignificant to be noted down and celebrated, from the "many moons of glasses on a tray" to Mary's "avoidance of canned goods" on account of the "exceeeeeeeeeeeeeeeedingly high risk of ptomaine". 'Incantata' does not attempt a chronology of the relationship between Muldoon and Powers, and nor does it offer psychological insights into motives and actions. More effectively, what it does convey are the private shibboleths, the quirks and shared familiarities, which go together to form a convincingly intimate commemorative portrait.

All but the last three stanzas of 'Incantata' are end-stopped. This provides necessary pauses for what would otherwise become an unwieldy list during the second half of the poem, and keeps some sort of check on a seemingly incessant rhythmical impetus. This impetus takes over completely, however, towards the conclusion of 'Incantata'; the poem's last sentence consists of twenty-four lines, with no pause stronger than a comma. Having built up this powerful finale, Muldoon reports Mary's belief that we cannot "deviate" from a preordained fate, no more

> than that this *Incantata*
> might have you look up from your plate of copper or zinc
> on which you've etched the row upon row
> of army-worms, than that you might reach out, arrah,
> and take in your ink-stained hands my own hands stained
>   with ink.

Mary's belief in the inescapability of a preordained destiny is paralleled by an undeviating rhythmical trajectory which moves persistently towards this final resolution. But 'Incantata' tacitly demurs from Mary's argument. Just as Muldoon exalts the various aspects of his relationship with Powers despite their supposedly having shrunk to nothing more than the potato-mouth's "'*quaquaqua*'", so now he attains what the poem considers unattainable. 'Incantata' finally does manage to reach the intended audience: Mary. Its emotive conclusion grants a moment of communion with the dead, imaginatively achieved even while acknowledged as impossible.

The Annals of Chile corresponds in some measure to the customary two-part division of Muldoon's volumes, where a series of miniatures leads to a long concluding poem: part two of *The Annals of Chile* consists of the 140-page 'Yarrow'. But that a poem the length of 'Incantata' should be found in the volume's first section confirms the shift of emphasis in Muldoon's canon. As *The Prince of the Quotidian* testifies, the lyrics are gradually beginning to seem like "Muldoodles", compared with the "Mulboon" of the fully orchestrated work into which the poet has channelled most of his creative energies; one of the short poems in *The Annals of Chile*, 'The Sonogram', is even reproduced from *The Prince of the Quotidian*. It would be wrong to conclude, however, that the poems surrounding 'Incantata' are just fillers; as should be expected by now from Muldoon's organizational procedures, they establish themes and motifs which are integral to the longer poems. The South American locations in 'Brazil', for example, relate to 'Incantata', which had been heard far beyond Quito in Ecuador. Remembering that in 'Immrama' from *Why Brownlee Left* the father settles in Brazil —

which is also Hy Brasil, the land of youth — 'Brazil' opens with some geographical confusion:

> When my mother snapped open her flimsy parasol
> it was Brazil: if not Brazil,
>
> then Uruguay.
> One nipple darkening her smock.
>
> My shame-faced *Tantum Ergo*
> struggling through thurified smoke.

The combination of Oedipal desire, childhood guilt, exoticism and strict religious observance in 'Brazil' prepares for a fuller treatment of the same elements in 'Yarrow'. Yet although these lines were much quoted by reviewers, their significance was missed. As Craig Raine has observed, what is described, in a "shame-faced" circuitous manner, is a memory of the poet's mother preparing to breast-feed one of his younger siblings — thus the otherwise curious mention of "*One* nipple darkening her smock" (my italics). This childhood introduction to sexuality and sexual desire is stressed in the poem's third section, situated in an imaginary Uruguay or Ecuador, "somewhere on or near the equator // given how water / plunged headlong into water". Muldoon has described 'Brazil' as a poem about "a world in which there are no notions of clockwise or anti-clockwise; everything is either straight up or, more accurately, straight down".[6] This refers not only to water disappearing down the plug-hole, but to the moral context imposed on sexuality. Recalling how his mother left *What a Boy Should Know* under his pillow, Muldoon's speaker revitalizes the cliché "holy show" to suggest the inextricable fusion of religion and sexuality:

> now *vagina* and *vas*
>
> *deferens* made a holy show
> of themselves. 'There is inherent vice
>
> in everything,' as O'Higgins
> would proclaim: it was O'Higgins who duly
>
> had the terms 'widdershins'
> and 'deasil' expunged from the annals of Chile.

Bernardo O'Higgins, a man of Irish descent, was the liberator of

Chile. He expunges the words "widdershins" and "deasil" — respectively, an English word for anti-clockwise and an Irish word for clockwise — to create a language and a society without moral ambiguity; Muldoon, in response, reinstates them for his own *Annals of Chile*. Both words have undesirable connotations for censorious regimes: "widdershins", or, more commonly, withershins, can mean not only going against the sun, but moving in a direction opposed to the usual; and "deasil", as 'Yarrow' points out, has "regrettable overtones / of sun worship" because the Celts considered it an act of religious worship to follow the apparent course of the sun. It is the belief that there is "inherent vice in everything", even in these arcane and archaic words, which associates O'Higgins with the poet's mother. 'Brazil' is a poem about how childhood innocence, and adult knowledge, are permanently tainted by these imposed moral or religious notions.

Circling — whether in a clockwise or an anti-clockwise direction — is reasserted elsewhere in part one of *The Annals of Chile*. 'Twice', for example, describes Muldoon's protagonist and two friends cutting "a sod / of water" from a barrel after a particularly cold night. When he later "squinn[ies]" through the ice, he is reminded of a schoolboy incident involving 'Lefty' Clery,

> grinning from both ends of the school photograph,
> having jooked behind the three-deep rest of us to meet the
>   Kodak's
> leisurely pan; 'Two places at once, was it, or one place twice?'

The circular ice duplicates, for a moment, the "leisurely pan" of the camera. Other poems in *The Annals of Chile* also come full circle. 'Oscar', for example, ends at the grave of Muldoon's parents, as the poet suggests that though she preceded him by a decade, his mother's skeleton will have "managed to worm / its way back on top of the old man's, / and she once again has him under her thumb"; there is something gruesomely appropriate about the verb "to worm", as the relationship's customary hierarchy is re-established in the grave. The extended villanelle 'Milkweed and Monarch', a poem about the interdependence of the poet's parents, is also situated at Collegelands graveyard:

> He looked about. Cow's-parsley in a samovar.
> He'd mistaken his mother's name, 'Regan', for 'Anger':
> as he knelt by the grave of his mother and father
> he could barely tell one from the other.

In its last two lines this coda follows villanelle conventions by repeating the poem's first and third lines; there would be nothing formally remarkable in this, except that the line "as he knelt by the grave of his mother and father" occurs only twice in the poem, as Muldoon emphasises that his meditation begins and ends at the same desolate spot. The poet's confusion over "tell[ing] one from the other" relates to mistaking his mother's name: "Regan" is the formally correct end-word, the villanelle's *b* rhyme, but it has been displaced by an emotive response. The confusion also concerns the poet's ability to distinguish between his parents; like the monarch butterfly and milkweed flower, theirs is seen to be an inextricable, symbiotic relationship. After the death of the poet's father, their circle is complete again.

These smaller circles are also an integral part of what 'Yarrow' calls "the great wheel" of *The Annals of Chile*. So 'Oscar' describes the poet having "taken off, over the towns of Keady / and Aughnacloy and Caledon"; in 'Yarrow', "across the drumlins of Aughnacloy and Caledon and Keady / I myself flap like a little green heron". And while one of the many confusions in 'Milkweed and Monarch' is between Portland, Maine and Portland, Oregon, so in 'Yarrow' the mysterious S— "must have gone off to Portland, Oregon, / with Yogi Bear and Boo-Boo // rather than Portland, like, Maine". 'Yarrow' even refers to Muldoon's difficulties in "get[ting] to grips" with the trickiest passage of his compelling translation, 'Cesar Vallejo: *Testimony*': "that phrase in Vallejo having to do with the 'ache' / in his forearms". As these examples suggest, the lyrics in *The Annals of Chile* constitute not just a prelude or overture to the larger work, but at times they seem to consist of leitmotifs or bits of exploded sestina scattered outside the radius of the grand scheme of 'Yarrow'. 'Incantata', written after 'Yarrow', even employs the same end-words. The great wheel extends beyond the volume; as *Shining Brow* had already begun to indicate, Muldoon's ambition is now such that he seems to have determined to turn his whole poetic output into a "great wheel". 'Incantata' typifies *The Annals of Chile*'s frequent allusions to Muldoon's earlier work, which are just as common among the shorter lyrics. The volume opens with a translation from Ovid's *Metamorphoses*, book VI, lines 313-381; the translation is, by Muldoon's standards, a pedestrian effort which has presumably been collected because it refers back to a much more economical and spirited version of the same passage in 'The More a Man Has' (beginning, "In Ovid's conspicuously tongue-in-cheek / account of an eyeball / to eyeball / between the goddess Leto / and a shower of Lycian reed-cutters"). And when the poet's mother in 'Brazil' finally manages to pronounce "her triumphant '*Champi-ÑON*", Muldoon does not need to labour the significance of mushrooms in his poetry or his family background. Similarly 'Oscar' describes the poet's dog lying "between us like an ancient quoof": Muldoon's reader, as well as his wife, should be familiar enough with the shibboleth to make any explanations extraneous. So confident is Muldoon that his readers have become initiates that even poems from separate volumes begin to explain each other. The third poem in *The Prince of the Quotidian*, for example, contains a parenthetical reference to the fact that "(At Exit 9, the man in the toll-booth / almost lost an arm // to Oscar MacOscar, as we call the hound ...)". Muldoon does not bother to complete the sentence, presuming that no one will miss the obvious reference to 'Oscar': "as we call the hound / who's wangled himself / into our bed".

'Oscar' proves that although Muldoon has begun to prefer a broader canvas, he can still produce subtle miniatures. The poem's second section conveys, with almost haiku-like economy, one of the chief concerns of *The Annals of Chile*

> I'm suddenly mesmerized
> by what I saw only today: a pair of high heels
> abandoned on the road to Amherst.

This is another of the disappearing acts so common in Muldoon's poetry. The "high heels" are in one sense equivalent to Brownlee's unbroken rig, and Muldoon even employs the same word to describe their fate: "abandoned". What triggers this mesmerizing flashback to the high heels is the poet's dog, Oscar, which wakes him by "whin[ing] at something on the roof"; and the memory takes the poet off imaginatively, over the towns of Keady, Aughnacloy and Caledon, to his parents' grave. These three sections of 'Oscar', although at first seeming quite disparate, are therefore linked by the fact that, like 'Incantata' with its direct address to Mary, each breaks down distinctions between presence and absence. The high heels are a potent symbol for *The Annals of Chile*, a volume which yearns for and at times senses the continuing proximity of an elusive woman, whether she be Mary or the poet's mother.

Yet this mournful theme is at least partly offset by a sequence of three poems celebrating the gestation and birth of Muldoon's first child, Dorothy. The first of these, 'The Sonogram', focuses on a time when she was "just a little bit more than a twinkle in the eye".[7] That is to say, the sonogram can make out "not only a hand / but a thumb":

> on the road to Spiddal, a woman hitching a ride;
> a gladiator in his net, passing judgement on the crowd.

Dorothy possesses a precocious knowledge of her destination: Spiddal, a town in Galway, is thought to be a corruption of "hospital" (or in Gaelic, *ospideal*). The possibility that Muldoon intends some connection between the high heels "on the road to Amherst" and the hitchhiking woman "on the road to Spiddal", despite the ocean separating them, is reinforced by a further allusion: in 'Incantata' Mary is described getting herself up "as a retiarius", "armed with net and trident"; the fact that Dorothy is also portrayed as a *retiarius*, caught up in her own net, suggests that Muldoon deliberately encourages parallels and blurs distinctions between the various female characters in *The Annals of Chile*.

The sonnet 'Footling' adds new metaphors to an already considerable list describing the developing baby: first she is "an old-time Channel swimmer", swathed in fat and Saran-Wrap; but after she gets "cold feet" — "footling" is the technical term for a breach position where the foot is down — she turns in on herself, "the phantom 'a' in Cesarian". 'The Birth' records the result of this reluctance, as the "windlass-women ply their shears / and gralloch-grub / for a footling foot". The verb "gralloch" derives from the Gaelic for intestines, and means to disembowel (normally, a deer). The poem therefore seems to echo 'Not for nothing would I versify' from *The Prince of the Quotidian* (which also appeared in an early draft of *The Annals of Chile* under the title 'The Martyrdom of St. Erasmus'); in 'Not for nothing' St Erasmus is portrayed having his viscera "cranked out by a windlass". This allusion, coupled with the word "gralloch", reveals a sublimated horror and violence in 'The Birth', which might otherwise pass unnoticed. The poem is more superficially a celebration of life and language, as Dorothy is hauled "into the inestimable / realm"

> of apple-blossoms and chanterelles and damsons and
>   eel-spears
> and foxes and the general hubbub
> of inkies and jennets and Kickapoos with their lemniscs
> or peekaboo-quiffs of Russian sable
>
> and tallow-unctuous vernix, into the realm of the widgeon —
> the 'whew' or 'yellow-poll', not the 'zuizin'.

Muldoon has performed this alphabetizing trick before, in *The*

O-O's Party, New Year's Eve, where he exchanges Chaucer's parliament for a party of fowls. The catalogue aria of 'The Birth' (the volume's second) also ends in the realm of the avian, with only the American zuizin excluded. Muldoon grants his daughter almost the whole world, with all its wonders and glories and endless variety. Yet the horrors of the Caesarean are still not forgotten. Having given Dorothy "a quick rub-a-dub" and whisked her off to the nursery, the "windlass-women" "check their staple-guns for staples", as they set about closing the Caesarean's incision.

It is difficult to think of a major poet in English, certainly since Keats, who has seemed such an avid reader of the dictionary as Muldoon; it could even be argued that the dictionary is the biggest influence on his more recent poetry. Muldoon rescues neglected words which the language cannot afford to lose — "widdershins", "gralloch" — or revitalizes words in the same way as he revitalizes cliché, by releasing their etymologies. His children's book *The Last Thesaurus*, ending as it does with a "Colossal Glossary", is further evidence of Muldoon's lexicographical enthusiasms. From *Quoof* onwards, his poetry has also gradually begun to employ more neologisms and nonce-words. 'The Birth' brings all these linguistic elements together. And 'Cows', the final poem of part one of *The Annals of Chile*, itself switches into lexicographical mode as it parenthetically relays information concerning the word "boreen":

> (a diminutive form of the Gaelic *bóthar*, 'a road',
> from *bó*, 'a cow', and *thar*
> meaning, in this case, something like 'athwart',
>
> 'boreen' has entered English 'through the air'
> despite the protestations of the O.E.D.).

A passage like this would have no place in Muldoon's early work; it typifies a middle-aged spread — not so much flabbiness as a fuller, more relaxed style — in his recent poetry. The extract takes obvious pleasure in its lexicographical detailings. So much so, that 'Cows' also employs other words to which the *O.E.D.* might object: "oscaraboscarabinary", "emphysemantiphon", "metaphysicattle" and "hi-firing" are all, apparently, invented words; and "cwm" and "corrie" have origins similar to "boreen", having entered the English language from the Welsh and Gaelic respectively. The definitions of some of Muldoon's compounds are self-evident. "Emphysemantiphon", for example, clearly consists of emphysema and antiphon, so that "an emphysemantiphon / of cows" is what Muldoon calls the "smoker's cough" of cattle responding to noises from their "kith and kine". But Muldoon's definition of "oscaraboscarabinary" — "a twin, entwined, a tree, a Tuareg; / a double dung-beetle; a plain / and simple hi-firing party; and off-the-back-of-a-lorry drogue" — only succeeds in adding to the obscurity. What 'Cows' actually records, in its bizarre, neologistic language, is an incident on a dark night, "part-jet, part-jasper or -jade", in smuggling territory near the Irish border; a cattle truck is as likely to be laden with microwaves or hi-fis as with cows. Although the poem never mentions that the truck may be carrying an altogether more deadly hardware, the sudden shift of tone in its final section would suggest that such a possibility is certainly implicit:

> Enough of Colette and Céline, Céline and Paul Celan:
> enough of whether Nabokov
> taught at Wellesley or Wesleyan.
>
> Now let us talk of slaughter and the slain,
> the helicopter gun-ship, the mighty Kalashnikov:
> let's rest for a while in a place where a cow has lain.

This is an enigmatic concluding passage: 'Cows' never does provide the promised talk of "slaughter and the slain", but nor does it discuss Colette, Céline, Celan and Nabokov. It would be tempting to suggest that Muldoon is presenting a distinction between art and life, as he proposes to abandon finicky literary disputes in favour of the brutal realities of the Ulster troubles; in fact, as 'Cows' and other work attests, there can be no such clear-cut distinction. Everything is tainted by associations of violence — the cow's form as much as the cattle-truck.

'Cows' precedes part two of *The Annals of Chile*, which consists entirely of 'Yarrow'. 'Yarrow' also avoids "the helicopter gun-ship, the mighty Kalashnikov", though it does mention Nabokov. John Redmond has pointed out in conversation that there is another subtle way in which it seems to carry on from 'Cows'. 'Yarrow' opens, "Little by little it dawned on us that the row / of kale would shortly be overwhelmed"; Muldoon was possibly conscious that the word "kale" immediately follows "Kalashnikov" in many dictionaries (though not, as it happens, the *O.E.D.*). 'Yarrow' also contains a number of neologisms and unusual compounds, which nevertheless can be easily interpreted: "expiapiaratory", "knobkerrieknout", "lillibullabies". Another compound, "the bittern's bibulous *Orinochone O*", combines the South American Orinoco River with the Gaelic lamentation "ochone". And when an aeroplane overshoots the runway, the poet again hears "Oglalagalagool's / cackackle-Kiowas / as blood gushed from every orifice"; "Oglalagalagool" plays on the fused identities of Gallogly and the Oglala Sioux in 'The More a Man Has', while "cackackle-Kiowas" combines cack, cackling, and an Apache tribe, the Kiowa.

Predictably, such linguistic strategies did not help endear 'Yarrow' to every critic. Jamie McKendrick in *The Independent* (London) argued that the best poems "are all in the first part of the book"; and Sean Dunne complained that "We are watching a clever poet at practised play rather than being absorbed by the power of his poems". This could hardly be more wrong. 'Yarrow' is as emotionally charged as anything Muldoon has ever written; it is a frantic and at times painful elegy for the poet's mother which can barely bring itself to register the loss. *The Prince of the Quotidian* had ended with the "horse-head" ordering Muldoon to

                         atone
for everything you've said and done

against your mother: meet excess of love
with excess of love; begin on the Feast of Saint Brigid.

It is intriguing to wonder whether 'Yarrow' was itself begun on Brigid's Feast-day; but the poem is undoubtedly Muldoon's most generous response to an "excess of love" which seems to have taken the form of snobbery, over-protection and moralistic strictures. 'Yarrow' reads like a reluctant but overwhelming love poem. Its endless allusions to adventure stories, its intricate formal patterning, and its time-shifts and channel-hops, constitute desperate swervings away from the source of grief; but the poem still homes in agonizingly on Brigid's death-bed and the poet's subsequent desolation. This desolation is so intense, and so entwined with negative emotions, that it can apparently only now be confronted, from a distance of twenty years.

The title of 'Yarrow' immediately connects the poem with the other long elegy in *The Annals of Chile*, 'Incantata'. Mary relies on "all the idle weeds" to cure her cancer, and the poet imagines the legendary Lugh searching "through his vast herbarium / for the leaf that had it within it, Mary, to anoint and anneal". Yarrow is itself renowned for medicinal properties, and its botanical name, *achillea millefolium*, is derived from the fact that Achilles is said to have used it at the siege of Troy to stanch blood. The poem's opening also

A Deep-Seated Hurt: *The Annals of Chile*

associates yarrow with time:

> Little by little it dawned on us that the row
> of kale would shortly be overwhelmed by these pink
> and cream blooms, that all of us
>
> would be overwhelmed, that even if my da
> were to lose an arm
> or a leg to the fly-wheel
>
> of a combine and be laid out on a tarp
> in a pool of blood and oil
> and my ma were to make one of her increasingly rare
>
> appeals to some higher power, some *Deo*
> this or that, all would be swept away by the stream
> that fanned across the land.

Embodied in this passage is a Heraclitean philosophy: everything flows and nothing stays. Human endeavour, as represented by the row of kale, will be swept away; but so, inevitably, will human suffering. Yarrow therefore symbolizes both loss and comfort; it simultaneously overwhelms and heals. There is a further reason why yarrow seems a fitting emblem for Muldoon's elegy: "with its bedraggled, feathery leaf / and pink (less red / than mauve) or off-white flower, its tight little knot // of a head, / it's like something keeping a secret / from itself, something on the tip of its own tongue". The poem's persona keeps his grief and his true subject a secret from himself, unspoken but constantly "on the tip of [his] own tongue".

However, the implicit attitude in the opening passage that time is linear and encroaching is not maintained by the quick-cuts, cross-fades and chronological confusions of 'Yarrow', which together even surpass the labyrinthine narratives of 'The More a Man Has' and 'Madoc'. Again yarrow is the poem's perfect emblem: rooted in the home ground of the family farm yet splitting into the thousand leaves signalled by its botanical name (and by its alternative name, milfoil), yarrow is a suggestive symbol for the workings of memory and imagination. Suitably, it is the scent of a sprig of yarrow which, not long into the poem, takes the poet "all the way back" from a den in Newfoundland to his childhood world. The poem's form is appropriately thousand-leaved as well. Muldoon described 'Yarrow'— before completion — as a "very complex poem involving nine or ten intercut exploded sestinas", which "uses repetition in a way that wouldn't have occurred to me before *Shining Brow*".[8] Actually, when considering the form of 'Yarrow' it is more helpful to consider each page — that is, incidentally, each sentence — as a unit, to which a letter might be designated in the same way as rhyme-schemes are described; there are twelve units of end-words which recur throughout the poem. So for example the opening passage contains the following end-words: "row", "pink", "us", "da", "arm", "wheel", "tarp", "oil", "rare", *"Deo"*, "stream", "land". Nine pages later, these end-words are reproduced together as "eland" (in place of "land"), "bobolink" ("pink"), "Arrow" ("row"), "Dada" ("da"), "video" (*"Deo"*), "peel" ("wheel"), "metacarp-" ("tarp"), "talus" ("us"), "rare" ("rare"), "foil" ("oil"), "seams" ("stream") and "farm" ("arm"). This same unit of end-words, in varying orders and with varying modulations, occurs on a further fifteen occasions. Each page of 'Yarrow' fits one of the twelve units, but Muldoon's patterning is not random: ignoring the envoi, it is apparent that the same end-words are employed by the opening and the concluding page, the second and the penultimate, and so on, with the result that the second half of the poem is a mirror image of the first half. Effectively, 'Yarrow' consists of a series of concentric circles, matching the smaller circles from part one of *The Annals of Chile*. This is the dominant, but not the only, formal pattern; several end-words occur in more than one unit, cutting across the poem's structure. On three occasions 'Yarrow' acknowledges its irregularity, by explaining how a "conventional sestina" or "tornada" or "envoy" would proceed. And the extent of Muldoon's tampering with the form can be gauged just by tracing the first end-word, "row", through various manifestations: "Pharaohs", *"Arrow"*, "sorrow", "Row", "sparrow", "Cicero", "arrow", "arrow", "marrow", "barrow", "cruzeiro", "Pizarro", "Navarro", "Arrow", "marrow", "arrow", *"Zero"*, *"Sendero"*, *"Arrow"*, "Navarro", "arrow", "Assaroe", "Zorro", "crow", "arrow", "yarrow", and aided by a wonderfully arbitrary enjambement, "the Cathedral of Ero- / tic Misery".

Each end-word passes through similarly unexpected modifications, as Muldoon's concentric sestinas gradually give up their intricate networks of sound, of mutuality and of association. Often thematic preoccupations are also uncovered by focusing on a single end-word. The prevalence of the word "arrow", for example, reasserts the linearity of time's arrow, and also stresses the importance of an allusion to Psalm 91:

> He shall defend thee under his wings, and thou shalt be safe

> under his feathers: his faithfulness and truth shall be thy
> shield and buckler.
> Thou shalt not be afraid for any terror by night: nor for the
> arrow that flieth by day;
> For the pestilence that walketh in darkness: nor for the
> sickness that destroyeth in the noon-day.

This passage is first specifically alluded to when the poet remembers the Profumo affair (which he had also tackled in 'Profumo' from *Meeting the British*). 'Yarrow' describes one of the women involved in the scandal, Christine Keeler, as having an "end" "sharp / as a two-edged sword, as the arrow / that flieth by day". An unconnected allusion occurs later in the poem, when Lear enters "with a rare // and radiant maiden in his arms / who might at any moment fret and fream, / 'I am the arrow that flieth by day. I am the arrow'"; Cordelia, it seems, is both destroyer and destroyed. The psalm is more integral to 'Yarrow' even than these explicit references suggest: a "shield" mentioned in the poem may seem to have more to do with a child's Arthurian fantasies, but it is also awarded Biblical significance; and the poem's extensive avian imagery relates not only to a "fearsome fowl of ill" perched on Armagh Cathedral, but to the Christian God who "shall defend thee under his wings". Following his mother's death the poet feels "a wing-beat" "past [his] head". This may be the "fearsome fowl", or the traditional image of the soul taking flight at the point of death. But by evoking Psalms it also suggests a divine presence.

Muldoon's imagination is liberated by the elaborate form of 'Yarrow', which like the double corona and double sestina of *Six Honest Serving Men*, has replaced literary sources as the poem's template or scaffolding; the mythical method in recent volumes has been superseded by a formal method. No matter how complex or seemingly arbitrary, Muldoon's chosen form is always integral to his subject: as Louis Sullivan would say, form and function are one. The scattered sestinas of 'Yarrow', for example, correspond to the poem's "intercut, exploded" time-schemes and locations. Events from 1963 — the Profumo affair, the death of Plath, the "loiter[ing] with intent" of a "great bird" on the west spire of Armagh Cathedral — are confused with memories of Brigid's death in 1974, and with the poet's present-day channel-surfing from his "den" in St John's, Newfoundland:

> I zap the remote control: that same poor elk or eland
> dragged down by a bobolink;

>   a Spanish *Lear*; the umpteenth *Broken Arrow*;
>
>   a boxing-match; Robert Hughes dismantling Dada;
>   a Michael Jackson video ...

King Lear, the bobolink, boxing and Dada feature later in 'Yarrow', as does the assemblage of curios decorating the den's walls: the arm of the "pugilist-poet" Arthur Cravan (which turns out in fact to be a prize carp or bream), a plaster of Paris cow's skull, and "a stuffed ortolan, or Carolina crake". When the poet wonders if he is himself "laid out on a da- / venport in this 'supremely Joycean object, a nautilus / of memory jammed next to memory'", 'Yarrow' self-referentially smuggles in a description of its own procedures; but as memories follow each other, without regard for chronology or for nice distinctions between fact and fiction, they are coloured by the poet's immediate surroundings in his Newfoundland den.

Muldoon's imagination switches channels as rapidly as his remote control. One moment he cracks a good joke about Michael Jackson's "moon-suit", the next he indulges in some (rather dodgy) close reading of Plath's 'Edge', or becomes consumed in memories of childhood Arthurian adventures. 'Yarrow' is a profound meditation on time: as an arrow, as Heraclitean flux, as loss, as devourer ("*tempus rerum edax*"), as the Big Bang and the expanding circles emitted from it. The poem's own temporal duration is also meticulously recorded. Not far into 'Yarrow' the reader is told that "It's 1:43 / by the clock / on the V.C.R.". Over a hundred pages later, there is a final time-check:

>   It's 1:49 and the video's
>   now so wildly out of synch
>   there's no telling *Some Experiences of an Irish R.M.*
>
>   from *The Shaggy D.A.*

This is another self-referential description, as Muldoon's narrative reminiscences are by this stage themselves "wildly out of synch". But in the six minutes that have elapsed between the two passages, Muldoon has managed to cram in an hallucinatory portrait of the artist as a young man, flying by the nets of mundane reality, of his mother's moral and religious doctrines, and of the self-destructive lifestyle and political obsessions of the mysterious S—. Those six minutes of objective time seem finicky and irrelevant by comparison with the soarings of the imagination; nevertheless, they are a stubborn reminder — grimly appropriate for an elegy such as 'Yarrow' — that in one inescapable sense time is constant and linear, relentlessly devouring the short span of life.

Partly to offset the temporal and narrative confusions of 'Yarrow', Muldoon employs a organizing technique clearly learnt from *Shining Brow*. Several phrases are repeated to provide a necessary sense of structure, most of which have to do with time or movement: "All would be swept away", "Would that I might", "Again and again", "That was the year", "Little did I know", "Even now", "The bridge. The barn", "All I remember", "As we neared". The extent of Muldoon's juxtaposition of childhood home and immediate circumstances is comically exhibited during one of these repetitions, when his first landscape becomes merged with the meal he happens to be eating: "The bridge. The barn. The all-too-familiar terrain" modulates into "The bridge. The barn. The all-too-familiar seal-flipper terrine". The all-too-familiar terrain of the Muldoon family farm is the starting-point for 'Yarrow', and the location to which, despite the poem's quest motif and its frequent refuge in adventure stories, it always attempts to return. 'Yarrow' is, ultimately, a moving elegy not just for the poet's mother but for this first home. Enjoying the vestigial scent of yarrow, the adult poet wishes that it would take him back to this landscape; but later, just as he is about to "touch down" by the pebble-dashed wall, it "hits [him]" that the house has changed hands. *The Annals of Chile* seems to have been profoundly affected by the poignancy of returning to a home which is no longer home; traces of the poet's emotional bewilderment seem evident in 'Milkweed and Monarch' and 'Oscar', but are most deeply engrained in 'Yarrow'. When the poem reports that "a mushroom-mogul has since built a hacienda" on the land, the implications of a high-powered business enterprise, financial riches, and an exotic lifestyle contrast sharply with the comparatively simple rural existence of Muldoon's parents.

Before being lost to the adult poet, the family home provides a perfect backdrop and environment for the child's fantasy world in 'Yarrow'. The barn, for example, serves as the site where the Pharoahs buried Tutankhamen, where Aladdin discovered the magic lamp and ring, where Morgiana poured boiling oil on the forty thieves, where "Cicero smooth-talked the senators", and where "I myself was caught up in the rush / of peers and paladins who ventured out with Charlemagne". The neighbouring farmer's cattle cross-fade into a Western's "stampeding herd". And the "rusted blade of a griffawn // embedded in a whitewashed wall" substitutes as the sword in the stone; as the child tugs at it, he braces himself against "the plunge into Owl Creek" (and by doing so, introduces a story by Ambrose Bierce which also plays on the disparity between imaginary and real time). The child has a happily eclectic approach to his fantasies: Popeye can exist alongside Lady Guinevere, Peyton Farquhar alongside Davy Crockett. An exhaustive delight in adventure stories is reflected by the sources for the characters assimilated into this world: Scott, Rider Haggard, Browning's 'How they brought the good news from Ghent to Aix', Arthurian legend, the myths of the Wild West, Robert Louis Stevenson (the latter seeming Muldoon's particular favourite, especially considering his pivotal importance in 'The More a Man Has'). These fantasies co-exist with a quotidian reality and responsibility: the exasperated mother asks what she did to deserve a child who takes off in a U-boat when the "spuds needed sprayed". They also provide some refuge from the mother's endless sententiousness:

> 'For your body is a temple,' my ma had said to Morholt,
> 'the temple of the Holy Ghost':
> even now I see Morholt raise the visor of his pail
>
> as he mulled this over;
> the memory of an elk, or eland, struggling up a slope
> must have been what darkened his dark mien.

This is an instance where the poem's narrative procedures become "wildly out of synch", as "Morholt" has a memory of something he has not yet seen. The elk or eland struggling up a slope is presumably the same "poor elk or eland / dragged down by a bobolink" on a television channel in Newfoundland. Morholt is, of course, the poet as a child, acting out another Arthurian legend; such fantasies in 'Yarrow' are powerful enough to resist the demands of the real world and even at times to subsume them. The division of self inherent in the child's rôle-playing allows him to elude his mother's morality, freely slipping into personae and worlds to which such codes no longer apply.

The mother in 'Yarrow' spouts a constant supply of moral axioms: "but to the girdle to the gods inherit"; "For Satan finds some mischief still for idle hands"; "May your word be as good as or better than your bond"; "*seachain droch-chómhluadar*" (mind bad company). Bernardo O'Higgins's proclamation in 'Brazil' that "There is inherent vice / in everything" finds an ally in her attitudes, as she pronounces that every woman is "at heart a rake / and the purest heart [is] itself marred by some base alloy". According to her theology, a single "lapse" is enough to cast a body "into the outer dark". Unlike Stephen in Joyce's *Portrait*, the child does not need to wrestle with his conscience before rejecting this stern morality; in fact, he never seems to engage with it at all, and treats it as an irrelevance. But in 'Yarrow' as in *Portrait*, the first "lapse" is caused by sexual desire; more specifically, by what Muldoon punningly calls "a slip // of a girl" ("lapse" coming from *lapsus*, meaning a slip or stumble). As the child grows older, his fantasy world is updated but not abandoned. It incorporates detailed hidden allusions to the likes of *Henry IV*, and it exhibits greater awareness of Irish history and mythology. It also becomes overtly sexualized, mixing innocence and experience as *Quoof* had done. A heroin-addicted lover, "S—", now accompanies the poet during his continuing adventures with the likes of Allan Quatermain, Nemo, Livesey and Squire Trelawney. S— seems the opposite of the poet's mother:

> To find a pugilist-poet who'd tap his own prostate gland
> for the piss-and-vinegar ink
> in which he'd dash off a couple of 'sparrow-
>
> songs', then jump headfirst into her fine how-d'-ye-do
> heedless of whether she'd used a deo-
> dorant, that was S—'s ideal:
>
> after a twelve-hour day at Skadden, Arps
> she wanted me to play Catullus
> to her, like, Clodia ...

Between them, S— and the poet "outparamour the Turk". She dons a "ski-hood or -mask" and begs him to "like, rim / her"; later she develops a "fondness for the crop". A representative character for a poem which seamlessly blends fact and fiction, S— merges these worlds. Even her enigmatic name could be read either as denying her full humanity, or keeping her real-life identity a secret. She acts as a kind of diseased Cathleen ni Houlihan, like Anorexia from *Quoof*'s 'Aisling'; but she also assimilates elements of Sylvia Plath, whose suicide haunts 'Yarrow' ("and remember one who did herself in *utcunque placuerit Deo*"), and especially Maud Gonne. At one point she even cross-fades into the poet's mother, emphasising an erotic desire which remains latent in 'Brazil'. Since S— is a projection, it is fitting that the poet observes how her "face in the freeze-frame / was not unlike Maud Gonne's" after a projector goes "totally out of whack".

S— is nevertheless the most physical of projections; the poet reports back from their sexual skirmishes that her "*arrière-/goût*" is of "sweat and patchouli oil", or later "patchouli oil and urine". And as S— declines into drug-addiction and develops sores "not unlike those of herp-/es or chlamydia", he notes from under her "cheese-cloth skirt" that what he had "taken for a nutmeg-clove // tasted now of monk's-hood, or aconite". Before such adventures start to leave a bad taste, they combine with a growing interest in hallucinogens and a temporary attraction to S—'s fanatical politics, to lure the poet from his mother's domain:

> as I crossed the bridge, I was so intent
> on Freedom's green slip and Freedom's green sprout
>
> her '*Ná bac leis an craoibhín aoibhinn*'
> and 'Stay clear of those louts and layabouts'
> were quite lost on me; I promptly stepped on the gas.

The poet soon undertakes a psychedelic sea-voyage with S— and a crew consisting chiefly of characters from different adventure stories; the *Hispaniola*, the *Golden Hind*, the *Pequod*, the *Marie Celeste* and the *Fighting Téméraire* are some of the ships boarded, while temporal chaos is further ensured by their encountering Athenian galleys, Carthaginian hydrofoils, and a crew of legionnaires who had been set adrift in the year 211 A.D. As the journey with S— progresses, it quickly becomes evident that she represents not escape but merely a different form of entrapment; in fact she is no less sententious than the poet's mother, although her moralizing exhibits a more enthusiastically political sensibility. Comparisons with Maud Gonne seem apt for a woman who decrees that "a poet who wants to last" must dirty his hands with wars and armed struggles. But her sexual predilections remain more appealing to the poet than her politics or her taste in poetry. While S— respectfully quotes Yeats — "'The women that I picked spoke sweet and low / and yet they all gave tongue, gave tongue right royally'" — Muldoon's persona adopts a familiarly hooligan attitude to "*Il Duce* of Drumcliff", claiming that these lines mean that Diana Vernon and Maud Gonne "gave good head", and that the far-off, most secret, and inviolate rose is "a cunt". S— becomes rapidly disillusioned with the poet's dismissive refusal of any kind of political engagement:

> 'What have *you* done for the cause?
> You're just another Sir Pertinax

> MacSycophant,
> brown-nosing some Brit who's sitting on your face
> and thinking it's, like, really cool.'
>
> She brandished a bottle of Evian;
> "Thing is, *a Phóil* your head's so far up your own fat butt
> you've pretty much disappeared.'

'Yarrow' is a guilt-ridden poem, struggling to allay a deep-seated hurt and atone for a difficult relationship between the poet and his mother. This seems to have encouraged an increasing self-interrogation and even self-flagellation in Muldoon's work. S— joins a growing band of prosecutors in his recent poetry: the horse-head from *The Prince of the Quotidian*, Mary in 'Incantata', the poet's mother in 'Yarrow'. But ultimately the poet flies by the nets of commitment to S—'s "cause", as he also flies by the self-destructive fate which she addictively embraces: "that must have been the year S— wrote 'Helter-skelter' / in her own blood on the wall; she'd hidden a razor in her scrubs".

The voyage in 'Yarrow' is a weird *immram* through isolated islands of memory. It is not, however, the poem's only quest. Running concurrently, and at times even becoming confused with the sea-journey, is a sporadic effort to track down and destroy the "ominous bird of yore" perched on the west oriel of Armagh Cathedral (as a "great bird" apparently did in the winter of 1962-3). This "fowl" — possibly a stork or a grebe, probably a heron — is, like yarrow, a multi-faceted symbol. It represents, variously, the God of Psalm 91, the soul of the poet's mother, and even the poet himself:

> Like a little green heron, or 'fly-up-the-creek',
> I flap above Carrickmore and Pomeroy
> with volume one of Burton's translation of *The Lusiads*.

He hears a cry go up in Irish, "'*S'é tuar oilc // an t-éan sin, agus leabhar in a chroibhín*'" (that bird, with a book in its fist, is a sign of evil). As a symbol the heron is therefore reminiscent of the techniques of *Shining Brow*, in that it draws together apparently disparate elements (including good and evil) and suggests a philosophy of mutuality: Muldoon's later works adapt an Anaxagorian principle of universal mixture, where everything resembles or contains a portion of everything else. The poet never does manage to shoot the heron with his hogweed blow-gun, having been "diverted from [his] quest" by his nautical adventures; this delay is fatal to a Cardinal, "who'd taken a turn — surprise, surprise — / the very day and hour he looked upon that fearsome fowl of ill". From this point onwards, the dominant imagery is avian. In bizarre guises, the bird reinforces the underlying sense of mutuality, as it is traced "flap[ping]" through the rest of the poem: an American bomber; a bobolink who is "some goddess of battle", cross-fading disconcertingly into a sexual temptress and then the poet's mother; a "maudlin towhee"; a "chewink" crying "'*Fadó, fadó*'" (long, long ago); S— uttering "a lonesome tu-whit tu-whoo"; the poet as a heron, about to touch down at his childhood home; a British bomber; a "scald crow"; an "old crate" overshooting the runway. The avian imagery culminates in a mournful envoi, where a rail, a bittern, a corncrake, a nightjar, a quail, and a gowk join the chorus of lament.

Switching from bird to bomber and back again, the heron is both a portent of evil and its agent, leaving a trail of destruction along an increasingly unpredictable flight-path. As the bird seems gradually to turn towards the deathbed of the poet's mother, the quick-cuts grow ever more frenetic in their attempted delays and evasions. Whether literary or televisual, all the poet's previous distractions, as he channel-hopped in his den in Newfoundland, now focus on death. The bobolink feeds on a corpse. Plath is imagined "turn[ing] on the oven" and renewing her vows "to the moon-goddess". And the final, agonizing scene of *King Lear* become all-pervasive, infiltrating even a Michael Jackson video after the singer has been "excoriate[d]" by his "friends", the Sioux: "all that's left of him is his top note; / 'Why should a dog, a horse, a rat have life'". In turn *King Lear* cross-fades into the death-throes of the poet's mother:

> The bridge. The barn. Again and again I stand aghast
> as I contemplate what never
> again will be mine:
>
> 'Look on her. Look, her lips.
> Listen to her *râle*
> where ovarian cancer takes her in its strangle-hold.'

The passage doubles up repeated phrases — "The bridge. The barn", "Again and again" — but now such phrases neither order nor deaden the grief. The bridge and barn become material proof, refuting the unbelievability of the poet's loss. An inaccuracy in this passage is later rectified: "'Ovarian,' did I write? Uterine". The cancer is murderous but horribly intimate, as Muldoon returns to one of his commonest themes: the frailty of the body. The body is self-destructive, in a sense giving birth ("Uterine") to the very disease which kills it.

The thirty-six line envoi of 'Yarrow' is one of the greatest passages Muldoon has written. In terms of its formal complexity alone, the passage is an astonishing technical feat. Not only does it run through the end-words of the exploded sestinas, but remarkably, Muldoon manages to unloose from his scheme a powerful *terza rima*:

> In a conventional tornada, the strains of her '*Che sera, sera*'
> or 'The Harp That Once' would transport me back
> to a bath resplendent with yarrow
>
> (it's really a sink set on breeze- or cinder-blocks):
> then I might be delivered
> from the rail's monotonous 'alack, alack';
>
> in a conventional envoy, her voice would be ever
> soft, gentle and low
> and the chrism of milfoil might over-
>
> flow
> as the great wheel
> came full circle; here a bittern's bibulous '*Orinochone O*' ...

In a way, this does indeed come "full circle", duplicating an earlier desire; towards the beginning of 'Yarrow' the poet hopes, "Would that I might as readily follow / this nosegay of yarrow" back to his childhood home. 'Yarrow' sets about achieving exactly this feat of memory, but it ends with an irreversible loss. Although circling may be integral to the structure of 'Yarrow' and to *The Annals of Chile* as a whole, the "great wheel" of 'Yarrow' does not, in this envoi, manage to send the poet back once more to an idyllic childhood protected from mortality; there is no deliverance, this time, from "the rail's monotonous 'alack, alack'". While 'Incantata' created its final effects by achieving what it simultaneously declared to be impossible, 'Yarrow', a much greater poem, ends in partial defeat.

Those six crucial minutes which the V.C.R. recorded as having elapsed now seem to suggest that the workings of memory and the imagination can only offer the most temporary salve: the poet must admit that even so many years later, "there's no more relief, no more respite / than when I scurried, click, down McParland's lane / with my arms crossed, click, under my armpits". Those clicks are presumably either from the second hand of a clock, or the "great cog" which 'Yarrow' mentions in its concluding stanzas:

> though it slips, the great cog,
> there's something about the quail's 'Wet-my-foot'
> and the sink full of hart's-tongue, borage and common
>   kedlock
>
> that I've either forgotten or disavowed;
> it has to do with a trireme, laden with ravensara,
> that was lost with all hands between Ireland and Montevideo.

That last line alone contains at least five of the sestinas' end-words: "lost" (last), "all", "hands", "Ireland" (land) and "Montevideo" (deo or video). But why a trireme would be sailing between Ireland and Montevideo with a cargo of Madagascan nutmeg remains an enigma; as does its relevance to the "quail's 'Wet-my-foot'" and the sink full of "hart's-tongue, borage and common kedlock". As would be expected, Muldoon's key is as obscure as the mystery it might solve. The only clues are from motifs which run throughout *The Annals of Chile*. Most obvious is the Ireland-South America axis, fundamental to the volume. The sunken "trireme" seems to be generally associated with the time-slips and anachronisms of other sea-voyages in 'Yarrow'; but more specifically with the "yawl" carrying the poet-pugilist Arthur Cravan, which sinks "like a stone", and with the *Girona* from the ill-fated Spanish Armada, sunk off the coast of Ireland. The phrase "lost with all hands" not only echoes "those who have died by their own hands", but again remembers Cravan's demise: "There's not even an arm, not an arm left of Arthur Cravan". Yet these piecemeal allusions and half-echoes do not add up to a full description of whatever the poet has "either forgotten or disavowed"; 'Yarrow' may be, among other things, a tribute to the salvaging powers of memory, but it ends with a reference to something apparently too painful to be retrieved or even acknowledged. Despite the poem's emotional courage, despite the obliquities, evasions and displacements, it seems that even after twenty years there are elements of the deep-seated hurt still too distressing to be brought to the surface.

It is impossible to do full justice to the complexities of 'Yarrow' in such a short space; for example the significance of a whole network of leitmotifs — a carbon-slip, a ring, a salamander brooch recovered from the *Girona* — has hardly been touched on. 'Yarrow' must surely stand alongside 'The More a Man Has' as Muldoon's masterpiece to date. Marginally less exasperating than entertaining,

'Yarrow' challenges our fundamental assumptions of how poetry should be read. That such radically innovative work can already be appreciated, however imperfectly, is sure evidence of Muldoon's poetic genius. As Wordsworth claimed every great and original writer must, Muldoon has himself "created the taste by which he is to be relished".

Notes

1. Heaney, S. *Place and Displacement: Recent Poetry of Northern Ireland* (Grasmere: Trustees of Dove Cottage, 1985), 15.
2. Longley, E. 'Poetic Forms and Social Malformations', *The Living Stream: Literature & Revisionism in Ireland* (Newcastle-upon-Tyne: Bloodaxe, 1994), 225.
3. 'Paul Muldoon', interviewed by John Haffenden, *Viewpoints* (London: Faber, 1981), 135.
4. 'Lunch with Paul Muldoon ...', interviewed by Kevin Smith, *Rhinoceros* 4, 1991, 85.
5. Muldoon, P. 'Introduction', *The Essential Byron* (New York: Ecco, 1989), 5.
6. Introducing 'The Sonogram', *Muldoon in America*, B.B.C. Radio 3, 1994.
7. *ibid.*
8. 'An Interview with Paul Muldoon', interviewed by Lynn Keller, *Contemporary Literature* 35 (1), Spring 1994, 9.

Bibliography

The following bibliography makes no claims to inclusiveness. The priority has been to list Muldoon's major poetry collections and pamphlets, his important prose writings, and his most helpful interviews. Book reprints are not recorded. Many uncollected poems are listed; while most poets orphan only those poems with which they are dissatisfied, Muldoon has sometimes excluded accomplished work because it does not fit the themes of his current volume. Reviews and essays are also cited.

The bibliography is intended to encourage rather than preclude a more thorough account of publications by and about Muldoon; nevertheless, I hope it will prove sufficiently detailed for all but the most hardy professionals. Many thanks again to Paul Muldoon; and also to the Publicity Department at Faber & Faber, without whose help the bibliography would have been even more patchy.

By Paul Muldoon

Poetry Volumes

New Weather (London: Faber, 1973).
Mules (London: Faber; Winston-Salem: Wake Forest University Press, 1977).
Why Brownlee Left (London: Faber; Winston-Salem: Wake Forest University Press, 1980).
Quoof (London: Faber; Winston-Salem: Wake Forest University Press, 1983).
Mules and Early Poems (Winston-Salem: Wake Forest University Press, 1985).
Selected Poems 1968-1983 (London: Faber, 1986).
Meeting the British (London: Faber; Winston-Salem: Wake Forest University Press, 1987).
Selected Poems 1968-1986 (New York: Ecco Press, 1987).
Madoc — A Mystery (London: Faber; New York: Farrar, Straus & Giroux, 1990).
The Annals of Chile (London: Faber; New York: Farrar, Straus & Giroux, 1994).
New Selected Poems 1968-1993 (London: Faber, 1996).

Important Pamphlets and Selections

Knowing My Place (Belfast: Ulsterman Publications, 1971).
Poetry Introduction 2 (London: Faber, 1972). [Includes fourteen poems by Muldoon.]
Spirit of Dawn (Belfast: Ulsterman Publications, 1975).

Names and Addresses (Belfast: Ulsterman Publications, 1978).
The Wishbone (Dublin: Gallery Press, 1984).
The Prince of the Quotidian (Dublin: Gallery Press; Winston-Salem: Wake Forest University Press, 1994).

Libretto

Shining Brow (London: Faber, 1993).

Play

Six Honest Serving Men (Dublin: Gallery Press, 1995).

Screenplay

Monkeys (B.B.C., 1989).

Children's Books

The O-O's Party, New Year's Eve (Dublin: Gallery Press, 1980).
The Last Thesaurus (London: Faber, 1995).

Translation

The Astrakhan Cloak: Poems in Irish by Nuala Ní Dhomhnaill with Translations into English by Paul Muldoon (Dublin: Gallery Press, 1992).

Editor

The Scrake of Dawn: Poems by Young People from Northern Ireland (Belfast: Blackstaff Press, 1979).
The Faber Book of Contemporary Irish Poetry (London: Faber, 1986).
The Essential Byron (New York: Ecco Press, 1989).

Articles and Reviews

'Closely Observed Raine's', review of *The Onion, Memory* by Craig Raine, *Honest Ulsterman* 61, Jan/Feb 1979, 61-67.
'A Book of Evasions', review of *Visitors Book*, *London Review of Books*, 20 March 1980, 10-11.
'Paul Muldoon writes ...', *Poetry Book Society Bulletin* 106, Autumn 1980, 1.
'Ordinary People', review of *Close Relatives* by Vicki Feaver, *Times Literary Supplement*, 1 May 1981, 496.
'Paul Muldoon writes ...', *Poetry Book Soicety Bulletin* 118, Autumn 1983, 1.

'Sweaney Peregraine', review of *Station Island* and *Sweeney Astray* by Seamus Heaney and *Rich* by Craig Raine, *London Review of Books*, 1 November 1984, 20-22.
'A Tight Wee Place in Armagh', *Fortnight* (Belfast), July/August 1984, 19 & 23.
'The Irish at the Odeon', review of *Cinema and Ireland* by Kevin Rockett, Luke Gibbons and John Hill, *Times Literary Supplement*, 25 March 1988, 325-326.
'Western Ways', review of *Dances with Wolves*, *Times Literary Supplement*, 8 February 1991, 17.
'Canon and Colcannon', review of *The Rattle of the North* ed. Patricia Craig, *Times Literary Supplement*, 2 October 1992, 22.
'Big Hair', review of *The Last of the Mohicans*, *Times Literary Supplement*, 6 November 1992, 17.
'Paul Muldoon writes ...', *Poetry Book Society Bulletin* 162, Autumn 1994, 1-2.
'Barbie, but no bimbo', review of *Pocahontas*, *Times Literary Supplement*, 13 October 1995, 21.

Interviews, Profiles and Recordings

'Paul Muldoon', interviewed by John Haffenden, *Viewpoints* (London: Faber, 1981), 130-142.
Ted Hughes and Paul Muldoon (London: Faber Poetry Cassette, 1982).
'A Conversation with Paul Muldoon', interviewed by Michael Donaghy, *Chicago Review* 35 (1), Autumn 1985, 76-85.
'Reclaiming Poetry', interviewed and profiled by Alan Jenkins, *Sunday Times*, 14 December 1986.
'An Interview with Paul Muldoon', interviewed by Clair Wills, Nick Jenkins and John Lanchester, *Oxford Poetry* III (1), Winter 1986/7, 14-20.
'Q & A: Paul Muldoon', interviewed by Kevin Barry, *Irish Literary Supplement* 6 (2), Fall 1987, 36-37.
'Way down upon the old Susquehanna', interviewed and profiled by Blake Morrison, *The Independent on Sunday*, 28 October 1990, 37.
'Lunch with Paul Muldoon ...', interviewed by Kevin Smith, *Rhinoceros* 4, 1991, 75-94.
Muldoon in America, interviewed by Christopher Cook, with readings by Paul Muldoon, B.B.C. Radio 3, 1994.
'An Interview with Paul Muldoon', interviewed by Lynn Keller, *Contemporary Literature*, 35 (1), Spring 1994, 1-29.
'Interview with Paul Muldoon', interviewed by John Redmond, *Thumbscrew* 4, Spring 1996, 2-18.

Uncollected Poems

'January', *Honest Ulsterman* 13, May 1969, 35.
'Taking the Rust', *Honest Ulsterman* 20, December 1969, 5.

'Hawk', *Honest Ulsterman* 21, Jan/Feb 1970, p. 6.
'The Man without a Name', *Honest Ulsterman* 22, Mar/April 1970, 14.
'The Kiss', *Aquarius* 4, 1971, 55.
'The Pink Tandem', *Honest Ulsterman* 28, May/June 1971, 16.
'Faces', *Honest Ulsterman* 30, Sept/Oct 1971, 11.
'The Music Lesson', *Honest Ulsterman* 32, Jan/Feb 1972, 5.
'A Flock of Robins', *Honest Ulsterman* 34, Jun-Aug 1972, 7.
'The Glass Boat', *Honest Ulsterman* 35, Sept/Oct 1972, 15.
'The Lap Dog', *Honest Ulsterman* 38, March-May 1973, 11.
'Uncle Pat', *Honest Ulsterman* 53, Nov/Dec 1976, 49.
'Under Saturn', *Times Literary Supplement*, 27 February 1981, 219.
'The High Chair', *Times Literary Supplement*, 19 March 1982, 316.
'Fugue', *Times Literary Supplement*, 26 March 1982, 320.
'The Brownlows', *London Review of Books*, 1 December 1983, 8.
'Tibet', *Times Literary Supplement*, 10 February 1984, 137.
'Toxophilus', *Times Literary Supplement*, 10 February 1984, 137.
'Caprice des Dieux', *Times Literary Supplement*, 11 May 1984, 516.
'Other Women', *Honest Ulsterman* 75, May 1984, 11.
'As for the Quince', *Times Literary Supplement*, 5 July 1985, 742.
'The Sentence', translation of Marin Sorescu's 'Condamnare', *Irish Review* 1, 1986, 79.
'Sweet Road', translation of Marin Sorescu's 'Drum Dulce', *Irish Review* 1, 1986, 79.
'The Teardrop', translation of Marin Sorescu's 'Lacrima', *Irish Review* 1, 1986, 79.
'Seascape', translation of Marin Sorescu's 'Peisaj Mare', *Irish Review* 1, 1986, 80.
'Oblique', translation of Marin Sorescu's 'Unghi', *Irish Review* 1, 1986, 80.

'Precautions', translation of Marin Sorescu's 'Precautie', *Irish Review* 1, 1986, 80.
'Home', *Soho Square*, ed. Fonseca, I., 1988, 15-16.
'Poplars', *First and Always: Poems for Great Ormond Street Hospital*, ed. Sail, L. (London: Faber, 1988), 43-44.
'A Tennyson Triptych', *Times Literary Supplement*, 2 October 1992, 9.
'From *Wow and Flutter*', *Harvard Review* 8, Spring 1995, 23-26.
'Triad', *Times Literary Supplement*, 19 May 1995, 13.
'Three Deer, Mount Rose, August 1995', *Times Literary Supplement*, 25 August 1995, 23.
'A Telegram for Seamus Heaney', *The Observer (Review)*, 8 October 1995.
'The Throwback', *Poetry*, October/November 1995, 75.
'My Dark Master', translation of Nuala Ní Dhomnaill's 'Mo Mháistir Dorcha', *Poetry*, October/November 1995, 76-79.

About Paul Muldoon

Bibliography

Reviews of *New Weather*

Allen, M. 'New Weather, by Paul Muldoon', *Honest Ulsterman* 38, March-May 1973, 51-55.
Anon. 'Vaguely Nouvelle', *Times Literary Supplement*, 20 April 1973, 442.
Conover, R. '*New Weather*, by Paul Muldoon', *Eire-Ireland* X (2), Summer 1975, 127-133.
Dunn, D. 'The Speckled Hill, the Plover's Shore', *Encounter* XLI (6), December 1973, 70-76.
Maclean, A. 'Highland Guide', *The Listener*, 16 August 1973, 223-4.

Reviews of *Mules*

Allen, M. 'Horse-People and Others', *Honest Ulsterman* 56, May-Sept 1977, 136-141.
Barrow, C. W. '*Mules*, by Paul Muldoon', *Eire-Ireland* XIII (2), 1978, 149-151.
Dunn, D. 'Young Fools, Old Fools', *Encounter* XLIX (4), October 1977, 89-94.
Heaney, S. 'The Mixed Marriage: Paul Muldoon', *Preoccupations: Selected Prose, 1968-1978* (London: Faber, 1980), 211-213.
Lucy, S. 'Uncertainties of Living', *The Tablet*, 24/31 December 1977.
Scupham, P. 'Learning from the Landscape', *Times Literary Supplement*, 1 July 1977, 801.
Stevenson, A. 'Snaffling and Curbing', *The Listener*, 13 October 1977, 486-7.

Reviews of *Why Brownlee Left*

Annwn, D. 'Why Brownlee Left', *Anglo-Welsh Review*, 1981, 74-7.
Carson, C. 'Past Imperfect, Future Conditional', *Honest Ulsterman* 67, 83-86.
Dodsworth, M. 'Why Brownlee Left', *The Guardian*, 6 November 1980.
Hamilton, I. 'Origins of the poetic species', *Sunday Times*, 28 September 1980.
Hollinghurst, A. 'Telling Tales', *Encounter* LVI (2&3), February/March 1981, 80-85.
Jenkins, A. 'The art of gentleness', *Times Literary Supplement*, 14 November 1980, 1287.
Mahon, D. 'Long Goodbye', *London Review of Books*, 20 November 1980, 6.
Motion, A. 'Some New Strain', *New Statesman*, 26 September 1980, 21-22.
Porter, P. 'In the spirit of Browning', *The Observer*, 19 October 1980.
Pybus, R. 'Matters of Ireland: Recent Irish Poetry', *Stand* 22 (3), 1981, 72-78.

Reviews of *Quoof*

Allen, M. 'Muldoon's Magic Mushrooms', *Honest Ulsterman* 75, May 1984, 61-68.
Corcoran, N. 'The Shy Trickster', *Times Literary Supplement*, 28 October 1983, 1180.
Dodsworth, M. 'Lightly on the Raw', *The Guardian*, 17 November 1983.
Dunne, S. 'Gentlemen Prefer the Muse', *Poetry Ireland Review* 9, Winter 1983-4, 19-22.
Kerrigan, J. 'The New Narrative', *London Review of Books*, 16-29 February 1984, 22-3.
Longley, E. 'Edna Longley on Paul Muldoon's *Quoof*', *Fortnight* 200, 31.
Mahon, D. 'Quaat?', *New Statesman*, 11 November 1983.
Mathews, A. C. 'Coiner of Words', *Irish Times*, 24 March 1984.
Mole, J. 'The Reflecting Glass', *Encounter* LXII (3), March 1984, 46-52.
O'Donoghue, B. 'Magic Mushrooms', *Poetry Review* 73 (4), January 1984, 53-55.
Porter, P. 'Redskins in Belfast', *The Observer*, 16 October 1983.
Reid, C. 'The brave talent of Ted Hughes', *Sunday Times*, 23 October 1983.
Stokes, G. 'Bloody Beautiful', *Village Voice Literary Supplement*, March 1984, 15.
Tracy, R. 'Infatuation with Native Americans', *Irish Literary Supplement*, Spring 1984, 31.

Reviews of *The Faber Book of Contemporary Irish Poetry*

Bold, A. 'Traditions at War', *The Scotsman*, 14 June 1986.
Craig, P. 'Green Martyrs', *London Review of Books*, 24 July 1986, 17-18.
Dunn, D. 'Manoeuvres', *Irish Review* 1, 1986, 84-90.
Hofmann, M. 'The recent generations at their song', *Times Literary Supplement*, 30 May 1986, 585-6. Also reviews *The Wishbone*.
Jenkins, A. 'More than just a touch of the Irish', *Sunday Times*, 8 June 1986.
Kelly, C. 'Blood Music', *Poetry Ireland Review* 21, Autumn 1987, 39-47.
MacRéamoinn, S. 'An Irish way with words', *The Tablet*, 2 August 1986.
Mahon, D. 'The Sheep and Goats', *Irish Times*, 7 June 1986.
O'Brien, C. C. 'Micks and Prods', *The Observer*, 8 June 1986, 25.
O'Neill, J. 'An inclusive view of Ireland', *The Spectator*, 5 July 1986.
Ormsby, F. 'Personal Gestures', *Times Educational Supplement*, 11 July 1986.

Reviews of *Meeting the British*

Allen, M. 'Realism meets Phantasmagoria', *Honest Ulsterman* 83, 96-97.
Bedient, C. 'The Crabbed Genius of Belfast', *Parnassus* 16 (1), 195-216.
Carey, J. 'The stain of words', *Sunday Times*, 21 June 1987, 56.
Corcoran, N. 'Flâneur along the Shopfronts', *Poetry Review* 77 (3), 1987, 44-46.
Eagleton, T. 'Fishmonger's Window', *The Observer*, 3 May 1987, 25.

Ford, M. 'Out of the Blue', *London Review of Books*, 10 December 1987, 20-21.
Imlah, M. 'Abandoned Origins', *Times Literary Supplement*, 4 September 1987, 946.
Lucas, J. 'Escape Artist', *New Statesman*, 22 August 1987.
O'Driscoll, C. *'Meeting the British* by Paul Muldoon', *Cyphers* 30, Spring 1989, 51-55.
Scammell, W. 'Mid-air Street?', *Irish Review* 3, 1988, 144-146.
Sealy, D. 'The Wider World', *Poetry Ireland Review* 22, Spring 1988, 47-50.
Wilson, W. 'The Adventuresome Muldoon', *Irish Literary Supplement* 6 (2), Fall 1987, 37-38.

Reviews of *Madoc — A Mystery*

Allen, M. 'Locked in a Putterbuss Stalemate', *Honest Ulsterman* 92, 73-77.
Banville, J. 'Slouching Toward Bethlehem', *New York Review of Books*, 30 May 1991, 37-39.
Carnell, S. 'Te Deums', *London Magazine* 31 (1-2), Feb-March 1991, 112-115.
Dawe, G. 'Paul Muldoon, *Madoc*', *Linen Hall Review*, April 1991, 21.
Dunn, D. 'Slippery Verse', *Glasgow Herald*, 10 November 1990.
Finch, P. 'Paul Muldoon: *Madoc — A Mystery*', *Poetry Wales* 27 (1), June 1991, 64-65.
Goodby, J. 'Elephantiasis and Essentialism', *Irish Review* 10, Spring 1991, 132-137.
Hofmann, M. 'Muldoon — A Mystery', *London Review of Books*, 20 December 1990, 18-19.
Longley, E. 'Way down upon the Susquehanna', *Irish Times*, 3 November 1990.
McDiarmid, L. 'From Signifump to Kierkegaard', *New York Times*, 28 July 1991.
Mackinnon, L. 'A dream diffused in words', *Times Literary Supplement*, 12 October 1990, 1105.
Maguire, S. 'Play Pen', *The Listener*, 1 November 1990.
O'Brien, P. 'A Poem of Disturbing Originality', *Irish Literary Supplement* 10 (2), Fall 1991, 29-30.
Patten, E. 'Clever, Comic, Liberating', *Fortnight* 291, 26-27.
Redmond, J. *Irish University Review* 21 (1), Spring/Summer 1991, 96-97.

Reviews of *Shining Brow*

Driver, P. 'Upstaging', *London Review of Books*, 19 August 1993, 22-23.
Kendall, T. 'The Poetry of Architecture', *Oxford Poetry*, VII (2), 1993, 17-19.
Mayer, G. 'Shining Brow', *Ambit* 133, 1993, 65-66.
Oestreich, J. 'Frank Lloyd Wright Joins Opera's Pantheon', *New York Times*, 28 April 1993.
Sirr, P. 'Opera Houses', *Irish Times*, 27 February 1993.

Reviews of *The Annals of Chile*

Brennan, R. 'Flexible Enemy', *Irish Independent*, 21 January 1995.
Calder, A. 'Could the real Ireland please stand up?', *Scotland on Sunday*, 16 October 1994.
Cramer, S. '*The Annals of Chile*', *Harvard Review* 8, Spring 1995, 144-5.
Dallat, C. 'Describing the Circle: Tom Paulin and Paul Muldoon', *Southfields* 1, 1995, 63-71.
Duhig, I. 'Annals mirabilis', *Fortnight*, September 1994.
Dunne, S. 'A poet's box of puzzles', *Irish Times*, 20 August 1994.
Foden, G. 'A lore unto himself', *The Guardian*, 25 October 1994.
Ford, M. 'Little Do We Know', *London Review of Books*, 12 January 1995, 19.
Haughton, H. 'Lord of the Red Herrings', *The Independent on Sunday*, 9 October 1994.
Heaney, S. 'Filling the cup above the brim', *Sunday Independent* (Dublin), 25 September 1994.
Kendall, T. 'A Deep-Seated Hurt', *London Magazine* 34 (7&8), 1994, 89-93.
McKendrick, J. 'Peekaboo quiffs and eel-spears', *The Independent*, 24 September 1994.
Ní Chuilleanáin, E. '*New Selected Poems 1957-1994*, Ted Hughes; *The Annals of Chile*, Paul Muldoon', *Poetry Ireland Review* 46, Summer 1995, 67-72.
Norfolk, L. 'The abundant braes of Yarrow', *Times Literary Supplement*, 32-33.
Padel, R. 'Sing out in a great oratorio', *The Times*, 15 September 1994.
Redmond, J. 'Indicting the Exquisite', *Thumbscrew* 1, Winter 1994-5, 72-81.
Roberts, M. 'Strongtease', *New Statesman*, 30 September 1994.
Thorpe, A. 'Primal Energies and Meddling Gods', *The Observer*, 22 January 1995.
Thwaite, A. 'Too many games to play?', *Sunday Telegraph*, 13 November 1994.

Essays and Articles

Allison, J. 'Questioning Yeats: Paul Muldoon's "7, Middagh Street"', *Learning the Trade: Essays on W.B. Yeats and Contemporary Poetry*, ed. Fleming, D. (Connecticut: Locust Hill, 1993), 3-20.
Brown, R. 'Bog Poems and Book Poems: Doubleness, Self-Translation and Pun in Seamus Heaney and Paul Muldoon', *The Chosen Ground: Essays on the Contemporary Poetry of Northern Ireland*, ed. Corcoran, N. (Bridgend: Seren, 1992), 153-167.
Buchanan, B. 'Paul Muldoon: "Who's to know what's knowable?"', *Contemporary Irish Poetry*, ed. Andrews, E. (London: MacMillan, 1992), 310-327.

Burris, S. 'Some Versions of Ireland: The Poetry of Tom Paulin and Paul Muldoon', *Kenyon Review* VII (4), Fall 1985, 129-135.

Burt, S. 'Paul Muldoon's Binocular Vision', *Harvard Review* 7, Fall 1994, 95-107.

Clifton, H. 'Available Air: Irish Contemporary Poetry', *Krino* 7, 1989, 20-30.

Corcoran, N. 'In Ireland or Someplace: A Second Generation from Northern Ireland', *English Poetry Since 1940* (London: Longman, 1993), 205-220.

Frazier, A. 'Juniper, Otherwise Known: Poems by Paulin and Muldoon', *Eire-Ireland* XIX (1), Spring 1984, 123-133.

Gauthier, D. '*Meeting the British* de Paul Muldoon: Brèves rencontres, libres parcours', *Etudes Irlandaises* 15 (1), June 1990, 97-110.

Goodby, J. '"Armageddon, Armagh-geddon": Language and Crisis in the Poetry of Paul Muldoon', *Anglo-Irish and Irish Literature: Aspects of Language and Culture*, eds. Bramsback, B. and Croghan, M. (Uppsala: Uppsala University Press, 1988), vol. 2, 229-236.

____ '"The Narrow Road to the Deep North": Paul Muldoon, the Sonnet, and the Politics of Poetic Form', *Swansea Review* 14, 26-35.

____ 'Hermeneutic Hermeticism: Paul Muldoon and the Northern Irish Poetic', *In Black and Gold: Contiguous Traditions in Post-War British and Irish Poetry*, ed. Barfoot, C. (Amsterdam: Rodopi, 1994), 137-168.

Haberer, A. 'Les Emigrés de l'intérieur: Seamus Heaney, Derek Mahon, Paul Muldoon et Tom Paulin, poètes d'Ulster', *Etudes Anglaises* 38 (2), 1985, 193-207.

Heaney, S. *Place and Displacement: Recent Poetry of Northern Ireland* (Grasmere: Trustees of Dove Cottage, 1984).

____ 'The Pre-Natal Mountain: Vision and Irony in Recent Irish Poetry', *The Place of Writing* (Atlanta: Scholar's Press, 1989), 36-53.

Hobsbaum, P. 'Paul Muldoon', *Contemporary Poets*, 3rd edition, ed. Vinson J. (London and Chicago: St. James Press), 600-601.

Jenkins, A. *Paul Muldoon* (London: Book Trust in conjunction with the British Council, 1988).

Johnson, D. 'Toward "A Broader & More Comprehensive Irish Identity"', *Irish Poetry after Joyce* (Notre Dame: University of Notre Dame Press, 1985), 247-272.

____ 'Poetic Discoveries & Inventions of America', *Colby Quarterly* (Waterville, ME) XXVIII (4), December 1992, 202-214.

Kendall, T. 'Paul Muldoon and the Art of Allusion', *Verse* 11 (1), Spring 1994, 78-83.

____ '"Parallel to the Parallel Realm": Paul Muldoon's *Madoc — A Mystery*', *Irish University Review* 25 (2), Autumn/Winter 1995, 232-241.

Kerrigan, J. 'Ulster Ovids', *The Chosen Ground: Essays on the Contemporary Poetry of Northern Ireland*, ed. Corcoran, N. (Bridgend: Seren, 1992), 235-269.

Kirkland, R. 'Paul Muldoon's "Immram" and "Immrama": Writing for a

Sense of Displacement', *Essays in Poetics* 17 (1), 1992, 35-43.

Longley, E. 'Poetry and Politics in Northern Ireland', *Poetry in the Wars* (Newcastle-upon-Tyne: Bloodaxe, 1986), 185-210.

―――― '"Varieties of Parable": Louis MacNeice and Paul Muldoon', *Poetry in the Wars* (Newcastle-upon-Tyne: Bloodaxe, 1986), 211-243.

―――― '"A Barbarous Nook": The Writer and Belfast', *The Living Stream: Literature & Revisionism in Ireland* (Newcastle-upon-Tyne: Bloodaxe, 1994), 86-108.

―――― '"When Did You Last See Your Father?": Perceptions of the Past in Northern Irish Writing', *The Living Stream: Literature & Revisionism in Ireland* (Newcastle-upon-Tyne: Bloodaxe, 1994), 150-172.

―――― 'Poetic Forms and Social Malformations', *The Living Stream: Literature & Revisionism in Ireland* (Newcastle-upon-Tyne: Bloodaxe, 1994), 196-226.

―――― 'No More Poems About Paintings?', *The Living Stream: Literature & Revisionism in Ireland* (Newcastle-upon-Tyne: Bloodaxe, 1994), 227-251.

―――― 'The Room Where MacNeice Wrote "Snow"', *The Living Stream: Literature & Revisionism in Ireland* (Newcastle-upon-Tyne: Bloodaxe, 1994), 252-270.

Marken, R. 'Paul Muldoon's "Juggling a Red-Hot Half-Brick in an Old Sock": Poets in Ireland Renovate the English Language Sonnet', *Eire-Ireland* XXIV (1), Spring 1989, 79-91.

Matthias, J. 'Not for Sale in the U.S.A.', *Another Chicago Magazine* 26, Fall 1993, 196-205.

McCracken, K. 'A Northern Perspective: Dual Vision in the Poetry of Paul Muldoon', *Canadian Journal of Irish Studies* 16 (2), December 1990, 92-103.

McCurry, J. '"S'Crap": Colonialism Indicted in the Poetry of Paul Muldoon', *Eire-Ireland* XXVII (3), Fall 1992, 92-109.

O'Brien, G. 'Paul Muldoon', *Critical Survey of Poetry*, ed. Magill, F., 2401-2407.

O'Donoghue, B. '"The Half-Said Thing to them is Dearest": Paul Muldoon', *Poetry in Contemporary Irish Literature*, ed. Kenneally, M. (Gerrards Cross: Colin Smythe, 1995), 400-418.

O'Neill, C. 'Paul Muldoon's *Madoc — A Mystery* and the Romantic Poets', *The Wordsworth Circle* 24 (1), Winter 1993, 54-6.

Racz, I. 'Mask Lyrics in the Poetry of Paul Muldoon and Derek Mahon', *A Small Nation's Contribution to the World*, ed. Morse, D. *et al* (Gerrards Cross: Colin Smythe, 1993), 107-118.

Stabler, J. '"Alive in the Midst of Questions": A Survey of the Poetry of Paul Muldoon', *Verse* 8 (2), Summer 1991, 52-61.

Stanfield, P. 'Another Side of Paul Muldoon', *North Dakota Quarterly* 57 (1), Winter 1993, 129-143.

Wills, C. *Language, History and Sex in the Poetry of Paul Muldoon and Medbh McGuckian* (Oxford: unpublished D. Phil thesis, 1989).

―――― 'The Lie of the Land: Language, Imperialism and Trade in Paul Muldoon's *Meeting the British*', *The Chosen Ground: Essays on the*

      Contemporary Poetry of Northern Ireland, ed. Corcoran, N. (Bridgend: Seren, 1992), 121-149.
―― 'Paul Muldoon: Dubious Origins', *Improprieties: Politics and Sexuality in Northern Ireland* (Oxford: Oxford University Press, 1993), 194-235.

Wilson, W. 'Paul Muldoon and the Poetics of Sexual Difference', *Contemporary Literature* 28 (3), Fall 1987, 317-331.
―― 'The Grotesqueries of Paul Muldoon, "Immram" to *Madoc*', *Eire-Ireland* 28 (4), Winter 1993, 115-132.
―― 'Yeats, Muldoon, and Heroic History', *Learning the Trade: Essays on W.B. Yeats and Contemporary Poetry*, ed. Fleming D. (Connecticut: Locust Hill, 1993), 21-38.

Index

Adcock, Fleur 18
Alcott, Louisa May 194
Allegro, John 103; *The Sacred Mushroom and the Cross* 99, 103-04
Allen, Michael 16
Amundsen, Roald 188
Anaximenes 158
Aristotle 21, 211
Armitage, Simon 18
Auden, W.H. 126, 127, 176; 'In Memory of W.B. Yeats' 125; 'The Public v. the Late Mr Willam Butler Yeats' 124; appears in '7 Middagh Street' 123-26, 127, 128, 129, 130, 132, 135
Austin, H.W. 127
Ayer, A.J. 158

Banville, John 157
Baudelaire, Charles 49
Beckett, Samuel 194, 211, 212-13; *Play* 123; *Waiting for Godot* 212
Bernstein, Leonard 177, 179; *A Quiet Place* 177, 179
Berryman, John: *The Dream Songs* 110
Bierce, Ambrose 232
Birn, David 177
Bishop, Elizabeth 109; 'The Moose' 116
Blake, William 49
Blemmings, James 10
Boland, Eavan 20
Boswell, James 171
Brant, Joseph (appears in 'Madoc') 169, 171
Braques, Georges 214
Breton, André 126
Britten, Benjamin 179; appears in '7 Middagh Street' 123, 130
Brooke, Rupert 106; *The Poems of Rupert Brooke* 13
Brown, Richard 82
Browning, Robert: 'How they brought the good news from Ghent to Aix' 232
Brownjohn, Alan 25
Buchan, John 125
Burnett, George (as a character in 'Madoc') 169, 170
Burr, Aaron (as a character in 'Madoc') 166
Byron, Lord 21, 86, 108, 137, 157, 162; *Don Juan* 86, 157; *The Vision of Judgement* 157; as a character in 'Madoc' 158

Camus, Albert 106
Canalejos 188
Carey, John 20, 110, 123, 125
Carleton, Julian 214; appears in *Shining Brow* 187, 188, 189
Carpenter, Humphrey 126; *W.H. Auden: A Biography* 125, 126
Carroll, Lewis 109, 112
Carson, Ciaran 16, 113, 114, 147
Catlin, George 162, 129; *North American Indians* 168
Celan, Paul 225
Céline, Louis-Ferdinand 225
Chandler, Raymond 55, 81, 86-87, 114, 123, 125; *Farewell My Lovely* 86
Chaucer, Geoffrey 153, 224
Chekhov, Anton 193; *Three Sisters* 193
Cheney, Edwin (appears in *Shining Brow*) 183, 184, 185, 213
Cheney, Mamah 176; appears in *Shining Brow* 177, 180, 181, 182, 183, 184, 185, 186, 189, 190
Cinnamond, Alexander (appears in 'Madoc'): 164, 165, 170-71
Clarke, Austin 20
Clarke, William (as a character in 'Madoc') 162, 166
Coleridge, S.T. 17, 154, 155, 180; 'Kubla Khan' 159, 160, 213; appears in 'Madoc' 149, 155, 157, 158, 159, 163, 164, 165, 166, 167, 168, 169, 170, 171, 172, 185
Colette, Sidonie Gabriele 225
Conover, Roger, 28
Conway, Anne Marie (PM's first wife) 17
Corcoran, Neil 92, 140
Cowley, Abraham 209, 210; 'On the Death of Mr William Harvey' 210
Craig, Patricia 82

Index

Cravan, Arthur 230, 238
Cu Chulain and the Birds of Appetite (tr. Standish O'Grady) 77-78, 106

da Ponte, Lorenzo 181
Dada 230
Dali, Salvador 126, 132, 192; appears in '7 Middagh Street' 123, 126, 127, 130, 131
Dante 109, 180, 186; *The Divine Comedy* 186
Davitt, Michael 101
de Herrera, Francisco 214
de Lorrean, John 21
Deane, Seamus 193, 194
Derain, André 211, 214; *The Turning Road, L'Éstaque* 213
Descartes, René 54
Devlin, Denis 20
Dickens, Charles 180
Donaghy, Michael 25
Donne, John 29, 180; 'Good Friday, 1613. Riding Westward' 29
Douglas, Barry 196
Driver, Paul 22, 175, 179
Duhig, Ian 18, 212
Dunn, Douglas 18
Dunne, Séan 212, 226
Duns Scotus 132
Durcan, Paul 20
Durrell, Lawrence 61-62
Duval, Jeanne 49

Eagleton, Terry 125, 167
Earhardt, Amelia 215
Elgar, Edward: *Enigma Variations* 130
Eliot, T.S. 14, 27, 82; *Four Quartets* 108; *The Waste Land* 110
Empson, William 32
Euclid 81
Evans, John (appears in 'Madoc') 170
Evans, Mary (appears in 'Madoc') 169, 170
Ewart, Gavin 18, 64

Faber Book of Modern Verse 14
Faber Poetry Introduction 2 15, 25, 26, 27, 29, 30
Fallon, Peter 19, 192
Faulkner, William 37
Favell (appears in 'Madoc') 168

Fell, Barry: *America, B.C.* 161
Field, John 214
Foden, Giles 23
Foley, Jack 150
Ford, John 13
Forster, E.M. 143
Fricker, Sara (appears in 'Madoc') 162, 164, 166, 169, 170
Friel, Brian 34, 193, 194; *Translations* 34
Frost, Robert 14, 17, 27-28, 29, 35, 36, 50, 55, 84, 109, 116, 141, 158; 'For Once, Then, Something' 113; 'Home Burial' 123; 'The Most of It' 26, 28; 'The Mountain' 55; 'The Road Not Taken' 17, 65, 69, 159; 'Tree at My Window' 28-29

Gay, John 64
Gerald of Wales (Giraldus Cambrensis) 93, 94, 149
Gibbons, Stella: *Cold Comfort Farm* 60
Gilbert, William 179
Gill, Brendan 182; *Many Masks* 182
Ginsberg, Allen 123
Goethe, Johann 180, 181, 187, 189, 190; 'Hymn to Nature' 189
Golding, William 29; *Free Fall* 29; *The Inheritors* 29, 41
Gonne, Maud 233-34
Gowrie, Grey 157
Griffiths, Paul 177

Haffenden, John 160
Hagen, Daron 22, 23, 176, 177-79, 184
Hammond, David 90
Haggard, Rider 232
Hardy, Thomas 37
Hawking, Stephen 149
Hawthorne, Nathaniel 109, 112; *The Scarlet Letter* 112
Heaney, Seamus 14-15, 16, 18, 20, 25, 26, 28, 32, 47-48, 50, 90-91, 97, 109, 112, 140-41, 153, 167, 180, 181, 192, 193, 194, 195, 209; 'Away from it All' 132; 'The Badgers' 140-41; 'Broagh' 111; *Death of a Naturalist* 14; *The Government of*

the Tongue 90-91; *The Haw Lantern* 20, 44; 'The Interesting Case of Nero, Chekhov's Cognac and a Knocker' 90; 'A Kite for Michael and Christopher' 180; 'Lough Neagh Sequence' 153; *North* 47-48, 80, 113; 'Punishment' 112-13; *Station Island* 140; 'Widgeon' 140; *Wintering Out* 140
Heffernan, Michael 135-37, 138, 195, 209
Hemmingway, Ernest 131, 137
Henry, O. 142
Heraclites, 227, 228, 230
Hewitt, John 180, 181
Hicks, Jerry 14
Higgins, F.R. 19
Hitchcock, Alfred 160
Hobsbaum, Philip 14, 15
Homer, 180
Hofmann, Michael 121, 153, 157
The Honest Ulsterman 15
Hopper, Edward 109
Hovey, Richard 180
Howe, Julia Ward 179, 185
Hughes, Howard 87
Hughes, Ted 18, 104, 109
Hutchinson, Sara 154
Huxley, Aldous 53, 100, 109; *Brave New World* 100; *The Doors of Perception* 53, 95, 100; *Heaven and Hell* 100

Imlah, Mick 20, 129
Immram Mael Duin (tr. Whitley Stokes) 40, 73, 82, 83-87, 126, 158, 206

Jackson, Michael 230, 236
Jefferson, Thomas (appears in 'Madoc') 158, 159, 161
Jenkins, Alan 18, 64
John of the Cross 186
Johnson, Dillon 18, 156
Johnson, Roland 177
Johnson, Samuel 205
Jonson, Ben 58, 130
Joyce, James 37, 130, 194, 230; *Finnegans Wake* 212; *Portrait of the Artist as a Young Man* 233; *Ulysses* 82

Kallman, Chester (appears in '7 Middagh Street') 123, 127

Kavanagh, P.J. 20, 28, 59, 128
Keats, John 180, 224
Keeler, Christine 229
Kennedy, John F. 141
Kennelly, Brendan 25
Kerrigan, John 92, 102, 110, 127
Kinsella, Thomas 20
Kipling, Rudyard 64, 145, 202, 203, 204, 207; *Just-So Stories* 202
Korelitz, Jean Hanff (PM's second wife) 19, 20, 119-20, 214

Lake, Veronica 55
Larkin, Philip 74
Lawrence, D.H. 29; 'Lizard' 29; *Sons and Lovers* 9, 10
Lee, Gypsy Rose (appears in '7 Middagh Street') 123, 126, 128
Leone, Sergio 13
Lévi-Strauss, Claude: 'Pythagoras in America' 152
Lewis, Merriwether (as a character in 'Madoc') 162, 166
Longley, Edna 16, 25, 38, 55, 66, 70, 101, 110, 113, 123, 143, 166-67, 209
Longley, Michael 14, 15, 16, 20, 27, 32, 140, 180, 181, 194; 'In Mayo' 180; *No Continuing City* 14
Lowell, Robert 121, 192, 198
Lucas, John 123
Lucy, Séan 44, 60

The Mabinogion 146
MacKinnon, Lachlan 22
MacLean, Alisdair 18, 25
MacNeice, Louis 19-20, 30-31, 38, 47, 70, 81, 126, 128; 'Homage to Cliches' 31; 'Snow' 70; *Varieties of Parables* 79; appears in '7 Middagh Street' 123, 124-25; 127, 128, 129, 130, 131
Mahon, Derek 14, 18, 20, 32, 64, 69, 128, 193, 194; 'Courtyards in Delft' 193; *Night-Crossing* 14
Manet, Edouard: *Le Dejeuner sur l'herbe* 121, 124
Marken, Ronald 144
Marquez, Gabriel Garcia: *One Hundred Years of Solitude* 50

Index

Masefield, John: 'Cargoes' 106, 126, 147, 162
McCarter, John 14
McCool, Dinny 11
McCullers, Carson (appears in '7 Middagh Street') 123, 128, 130
McCurry, Jacqueline 48
McDiarmid, Lucy 21, 153
McFadden, Roy 92
McGuckian, Medbh 16, 20, 192, 194
McKearney, Kevin 194
McKendrick, Jamie 226
Mill, John Stuart 215
Miller, Karl 15
Milosz, Czeslaw 132-33, 193; *Native Realm* 132
Milton, John 70
Monroe, Marilyn 141
Montague, John 20, 194
Monteith, Charles 15
Morrison, Blake 12
Morrison, Van 211
Motion, Andrew 18, 64, 78
Muldoon, Brigid (mother) 9, 10, 11, 13, 17, 137, 209, 219, 220, 221, 222, 226, 229
Muldoon, Dorothy (daughter) 22, 192, 222, 223, 224
Muldoon, Joseph (brother) 9, 137
Muldoon, Maureen (sister) 9, 10, 75, 137
Muldoon, Patrick (father) 9-10, 11, 12, 18, 19, 65, 119, 134, 137, 138-39, 154, 221
Muldoon, Paul 'Aisling' 95-96, 104, 105, 113, 233; '[Anaximenes]' ('Madoc') 158; *The Annals of Chile* 18, 23, 120, 139, 147, 155, 175, 192, 195, 200, 205, 209-39; '[Anselm]' ('Madoc') 165; 'Anseo' 74-75, 76, 80, 85, 200; 'Armageddon, Armageddon' 11, 45, 49, 54, 59, 61, 62, 64, 75; 'Asra' ('Madoc') 154; *The Astrakhan Cloak* (with Nuala Ní Dhomhnaill) 22, 156; 'At Martha's Deli' 52, 66; 'The Avenue' 70-71; '[Bacon]' ('Madoc') 158; 'Bang' 45, 54; 'The Bearded Woman, by Ribera' 49, 57, 106; 'Bears' 103, 120, 121, 214; 'The Bears' 121; 'Beaver' 103, 105; 'Bechbretha' 144, 146; 'Behold the Lamb' 15, 39, 103; 'Belfast' 36; '[Berkeley]' ('Madoc') 158; 'Big Foot' 103; 'The Big House' 45, 54, 57; 'The Birth' 23, 223, 224; 'The Bishop' 67-68, 73; 'Blemish' 49, 50, 52, 66; 'Blewits' 97, 100, 105; 'Blowing Eggs' 27, 30; 'Boon' 58, 79; 'The Boundary Commission' 79-80; 'Bran' 65, 78; 'Brazil' 218-19, 220, 222, 232, 233; 'The Briefcase' 153-54; 'Brock' 94, 103, 139-41; '[Burnet]' ('Madoc') 158; 'Capercaillies' 103, 155-56, 161, 214; 'Cass and Me' 45, 49; 'Cauliflowers' 154-55; 'The Centaurs' 45, 47, 48-49, 50, 54; 'Cesar Vallejo: *Testimony*' 221; 'Cheesecake' 52, 57; 'Cherish the Ladies' 101; 'Chinook' 103, 134; 'Cider' 44, 67; '[Clarke]' ('Madoc') 158; 'Clonfeacle' 34, 36, 38, 97; 'Come into My Parlour' 73, 76, 77; 'The Coney 103, 138-39; 'The Country Club' 55, 56; 'Cows' 224-25; 'Cows' (*The Annals of Chile*) 103; 'Crossing the Line' 146; 'Cuba' (aka 'Cuba, 1962') 75-76, 80, 85; 'Cuckoo Corn' 38; 'The Cure for Warts' 40, 41; 'Dancers at the Moy' 37-38, 54; 'The Destroying Angel' 104, 105; 'The Ducking School' 52; 'Duffy's Circus' 45, 53-54, 57, 58, 77, 98; 'Early Warning' 80; 'Easter Island' 27; 'Edward Kienholz: *The State Hospital*' 110; 'The Electric Orchard' 39, 47; 'Elizabeth' 30, 38; 'Emblements' 214; 'Emily' 122, 216; 'Epiphany' 199; *The Essential Byron* (ed) 21; *The Faber Book of Contemporary Irish Verse* (ed) 19, 21, 47, 119; 'February' (aka 'Derryscallop') 31, 34-36, 38, 41, 97; 'The Field Hospital' 13, 31-32, 33, 35, 44; 'Footling' 23, 223; 'The Fox' 19, 103, 134-35, 138, 139; 'The Frog' 49, 93-94, 95, 96, 103, 105, 214; '*from* Last Poems' 94, 107, 119; 'Gathering Mushrooms' 92-93, 98, 99-100, 101, 106, 196, 200; 'The Geogra-

phy Lesson' 73; 'The Girl in the Poolroom' 106; 'Glanders' 105-06; 'Gold 14, 141; 'Gone' 142; 'Good Friday: 1971. Driving Westward' 29-30, 36, 47; 'Grief' 73, 76; '[Hamilton]' ('Madoc') 158; 'The Hands' 97; '[Hartley]' ('Madoc') 158; 'Hedgehog' 32-33, 38, 103; 'History' 70, 73; 'Holy Thursday' 71; 'How to Play Championship Tennis' 45, 52; 'I Remember Sir Alfred' 80-81; 'Identities' 33, 38; 'Immram' 29, 40, 55, 64-66, 67, 71, 73, 81, 82, 83-85, 86-88, 103, 109, 114, 123, 125, 129, 138, 158, 160, 161, 201; 'Immrama' 65-67, 218; 'Incantata' 18-19, 23, 195, 209-18, 221, 222, 223, 226, 235, 237; 'The Indians on Alcatraz' 26-27, 41; 'The Inheritors' 29; 'Ireland' 78-79; 'Kate Whiskey' 27; 'Keen' 45, 54; 'The Key' ('Madoc') 149-51, 153, 161, 181; 'Kissing and Telling' 106; 'The Kissing Seat' 34; *Knowing My Place* 25, 27, 34, 36; 'Largesse' 45, 51, 62; 'The Lass of Aughrim' 121, 131; *The Last Thesaurus* 22, 200, 224; 'Leaving an Island' 27; 'Leda and the Swan' 50, 52; '[Lewis]' ('Madoc') 158; 'Lives of the Saints' 40, 81; 'Lunch with Pancho Villa' 44-45, 55, 114; 'Ma' 13, 106; 'Macha' 37, 38; *Madoc — A Mystery* 16, 17, 21-22, 38, 98, 149-174, 175, 200; 'Madoc' 132, 149-72, 182, 183, 185, 186, 200, 213, 214, 227; 'Making the Move' 64-65, 71-72, 86, 87, 152; 'The Marriage of Strongbow and Aoife' 121-22, 143-44, 146; 'Mary Farl Powers: *Pink Spotted Torso*' 19, 110, 212; *Meeting the British* 14, 19, 20, 21, 73, 94, 103, 106, 119-148, 149, 152, 167, 170, 200, 229; 'Meeting the British' 145-46; 'The Merman' 46-47, 49, 50, 52, 53, 79, 98, 131; 'Milkweed and Monarch' 220, 221,231; 'Mink' 103; 'The Mirror' 101; 'The Mist-Net' 138; 'The Mixed Marriage' 9-10, 50, 106, 145; *Monkeys* 21, 200; '[Moore]' ('Madoc') 158; 'The More a Man Has the More a Man Wants' 13, 29, 92, 96-97, 99, 103, 105, 106, 108-11, 113, 114, 115, 116, 123, 125, 127, 129, 158, 160, 161, 162, 200, 204, 221, 226-27, 232, 238; *Mules* 9, 10, 18, 19, 25, 35, 44-63, 64, 65, 66, 67, 73, 76, 77, 78, 86, 98, 104, 128, 130, 145, 198; 'Mules' 45, 49, 50-51, 103, 131; 'Mustard Seed Mission' 62; 'My Grandfather's Wake' 4, 103, 139, 140; *Names and Addresses* 75; 'Ned Skinner' 10, 11, 45, 58-59; *New Weather* 13, 15, 18, 25-42, 44, 45, 46, 47, 49, 53, 54, 60, 61, 145, 149; '[Newman]' ('Madog') 158; 'Not for nothing would I versify' (aka 'The Martyrdom of St. Erasmus') 223; 'October 1950' 65, 73-74, 77, 81; 'The One Desire' 77; 'Ontario' 134; *The O-O's Party, New Year's Eve* 22, 200, 224; 'Oscar' 103, 220, 221, 222, 231; 'Our Lady of Ardboe' 56; 'The Ox' 103, 121-22, 142, 195; '[Paine]' ('Madoc') 158; 'Palm Sunday' 70, 71; 'Pandas' 103; 'The Panther' 103, 153; 'Paris' 56, 62; '[Parmenides]' ('Madoc') 159; 'Party Piece' 27; 'Paul Klee: *They're Biting*' 142-43, 147; 'Poem for Lawrence' 29; *The Prince of the Quotidian* 22, 99, 147, 192-99, 209, 218, 222, 223, 226, 235; 'The Princess and the Pea' 70, 72, 73; 'Profumo' 106, 147, 152, 162, 229; 'Promises, Promises' 163; '[Putnam]' ('Madoc') 158; '[Pythagoras]' ('Madoc') 152; *Quoof* 10, 18, 46, 48, 49, 65, 90-118, 119, 121, 122, 140, 195, 200, 212, 224, 233; 'Quoof' 102-03, 107, 215; 'The Radio Horse' 33, 103; '[Reid]' ('Madoc') 158; 'The Right Arm' 10, 97, 98; 'Rodgers at Longhall' 36; 'The Rucksack' 44; '[Russell]' ('Madoc') 158; '7 Middagh Street' 73, 123-30, 149, 186, 187, 197, 205; 'The Salmon of Knowledge' 103, 104; 'Seanchas' 32; *Selected*

Poems 20, 21, 129, 147; '[Seneca]' ('Madoc') 166; *Shining Brow* 22, 42, 167, 175-91, 205, 206, 213, 221, 228, 231, 235; 'The Sightseers' 97, 107-08; *Six Honest Serving Men* 23, 171, 199-208, 229; 'Skeffington's Daughter' 27, 31; 'Sky Woman' 106; 'The Soap Pig' 12, 13537, 138, 142, 143, 147, 195, 209, 214, 215-16; 'Something Else' 132, 133-34, 140, 144, 147; 'Something of a Departure' 71, 72, 106; 'The Sonogram' 23, 218, 222-23; *Spirit of Dawn* 86; 'Spirit of Dawn' 87; 'Sushi' 131, 132, 142, 195; 'Tea' 151-53; '[Thales]' ('Madoc') 157; 'Thinking of the Goldfish' 27, 30, 32, 33, 39, 103; 'Thrush' 15, 39, 103; 'A Tight Wee Place in Armagh' 10; 'The Toe-Tag' 131, 135; 'Trance' 4, 100, 101; 'A Trifle' 91-92, 105, 107; 'Truce' 79; 'Twice' 200, 220; 'Unborn' 15; 'Under Saturn' 128; 'The Unicorn Defends Himself' 104, 106; 'Vampire' 32; 'Vaquero' 45, 54; 'Vespers' 30, 34; 'The Waking Father' 27; 'The Weepies' 76; 'Whim' 64, 65, 73, 77, 106; '[Whitehead]' ('Madoc') 160; *Why Brownlee Left* 16, 17, 18, 40, 55, 61, 64-88, 92, 101, 105, 142, 152, 159, 163, 200, 218; 'Why Brownlee Left' 68-69; 'Wind and Tree' 26, 28-29, 33; *The Wishbone* 119, 120-22, 130, 143, 154, 197, 200, 209, 214, 215, 216; 'The Wishbone' 19, 137, 142, 147; 'Yarrow' 19, 23, 139, 155, 175, 195, 205, 218, 219-21, 225-39; 'The Year of the Sloes, for Ishi' 17, 32, 40-42, 64, 109, 129, 145, 149; 'Yggdrasill' 94, 97
Murphy, Richard 20

Nabokov, Vladimir 225
National Enquirer 32, 154
Ní Dhomhnaill, Nuala 20, 22, 156, 194; 'The Lay of Loughadoon' 156

O'Boyle, Sean 13, 14

O'Donoghue, Bernard 69
O'Higgins, Bernardo 219-20, 232
O'Leary, Timothy 81, 82, 201
O'Reilly, Alejandro 199
O'Shea, Kitty 205
The Odyssey 82, 83
Oisin 61-62
Ormsby, Frank 16
Ovid 109; *Metamorphoses* 221

Padel, Ruth 23
Parnell, Charles Stewart 205
Patterson, Don 18
Paulin, Tom 20, 111
Picasso, Pablo 109; *Guernica* 110
Pissarro, Camille 214
Plath, Sylvia 27, 229, 233, 236; 'Edge' 230
Plato 130, 136
Pliny 103
Plunkett, Joseph Mary 74
Pollock, Jackson 109
Porter, Peter 18, 25, 49, 64, 80, 92
Pound, Ezra: *The Cantos* 110
Powell, Enoch (character in 'Bechbretha') 144
Powers, J.F. 121
Powers, Mary Farl 18-19, 119, 120, 121, 136, 142, 143, 209-10, 211, 212-18, 222, 226, 235
Praed, Winthrop 64
Proust, Marcel 106

Quinn, Gerard 14, 141

Radin, Paul: *The Trickster: A Study in American Indian Mythology* 109
Raine, Craig 131, 219
Raleigh, Walter 152, 163
Rasmussen, Knud: *The Netsilik Eskimos* 105
Red Jacket (character in 'Madoc') 162, 165
Redmond, John 225
Rees, Merlin (character in 'Becbretha') 144
Rembrandt van Rijn 214
Rimbaud, Arthur 119
Rodgers, W.R. 36
Roethke, Theodore 121
Roosevelt, Theodore 145

Index

Rousseau, Jean-Jacques 171

Scammell, William 123, 147
Scott, Walter 232
Scotus Eriugena 16, 131, 132
Scupham, Peter 18, 44, 51
Seneca (appears in 'Madoc') 155, 158
Seurat, Georges 214
Seymour, Dermot 38
Shakespeare, Williams 108, 19, 180; *Henry IV* 233; *King Lear* 236; *Macbeth* 38; *The Tempest* 83
Simmonds, James 20
Sirr, Peter 22, 184
Southey, Edith (character in 'Madoc') 164
Southey, Robert 17, 162; appears in 'Madoc' 149, 157, 159, 160, 163, 164, 165, 166, 167, 168, 169, 171, 172, 183-84, 185
Soutine, Chaim: *Hare on a Green Shutter* 141
Spinoza, Baruch 215
Stafford, Ella 55
Stein, Gertrude 109
Sterne, Lawrence 74, 194; *Tristram Shandy* 65, 74
Stevenson, Anne 18
Stevenson, R.L. 109, 125, 232; *Dr Jekyll and Mr Hyde* 116; *Treasure Island* 110, 116
Straus, Richard, 179
Sunday Times (reviews in) 20
Sullivan, Louis 167, 176, 177, 179; appears in *Shining Brow* 180, 181, 183, 184, 185, 186, 187, 188, 189, 190, 229
Sweeney 109, 110
Swift, Jonathan 60, 99, 194; *Gulliver's Travels* 60

Tarantino, Quentin: *Reservoir Dogs* 200
Tennyson, Alfred 32, 180; 'The Lady of Shalott' 32; 'The Voyage of Maeldune' 83
Thales of Miletus 149
Thomas Aquinas 16
Tobler 181
Toklas, Alice B. 112

U2 22, 192, 194

Vaughan, Henry 155
Vernon, Diana 234
Vivaldi, Antonio 211

Wadsworth, Stephen 177
Wagner, Richard 175
Walcott, Derek 194
Waugh, Evelyn 120-21
Wills, Clair 96, 102, 141, 167
Wilson, William 106, 123
Wilson, Woodrow 188
Wordsworth, William 209, 239
Wright, Frank Lloyd 22, 167, 175, 176, 177, 182, 214; appears in *Shining Brow* 180, 181, 182, 183, 184, 184, 185, 186, 187, 188, 189, 190
Wyeth, Andrew: *Christina's Dream* 139

Yeats, W.B. 19, 23, 37, 49, 50, 109, 123-24, 128, 129, 132, 181, 194, 200, 201, 205, 210, 214, 234; 'All Things can tempt Me' 214; 'A Coat' 128; 'In Memory of Eva Gore-Booth and Con Marciewicz' 128; 'In memory of Major Robert Gregory' 210; 'Man and the Echo' 128; 'Tom at Cruachan' 50